THE UNVEILING
OF TIMBUCTOO

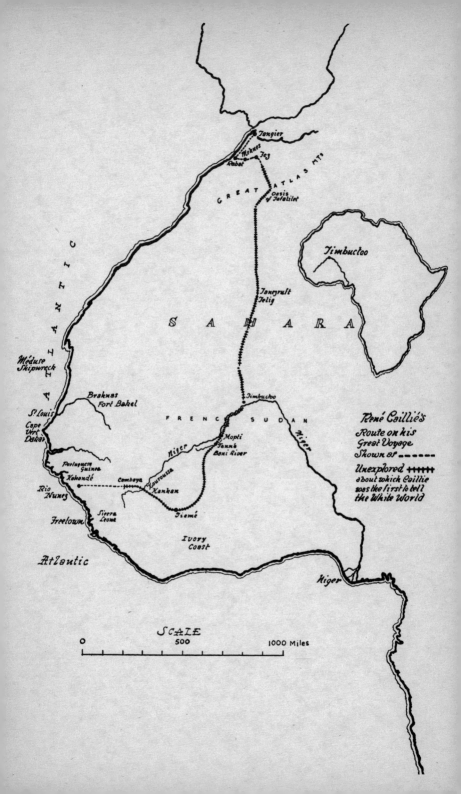

Tangier

Meknes

Rabat

Fes

GREAT ATLAS MTS

Oasis
of Tafilelt

Timbuctoo

Taneyrult
Telig

S A H A R A

ATLANTIC

Méduse
Shipwreck

Braknas
Fort Bakel

Timbuctoo

St Louis

Cape
Vert
Dakar

F R E N C H   S U D A N

Niger

Niger

Mopti

Portuguese
Guinea

Kahandé

Cambaya

Tunné
Bani River

Rio
Nunez

Kouroussa

Kankan

René Caillié's
Route on his
Great Voyage
Shown as ------

Unexplored ++++++
about which Caillie
was the first to tell
the White World

Sierra
Leone

Freetown

Tiemé

Atlantic

Ivory
Coast

Niger

SCALE

0   500   1000 Miles

THE UNVEILING OF TIMBUCTOO

The Astounding Adventures of Caillié

Galbraith Welch

Carroll & Graf Publishers, Inc.
New York

Published originally by William Morrow & Company.

First Carroll & Graf edition 1991

Carroll & Graf Publishers, Inc.
260 Fifth Avenue
New York, NY 10001

Library of Congress Cataloging-in-Publication Data

Welch, Galbraith.
    The unveiling of Timbuctoo : the astounding adventures of Caillié
/ by Galbraith Welch.—1st Carroll & Graf ed.
        p.   cm.
    Originally published: New York : W. Morrow, 1939.
    ISBN 0-88184-790-9 : $11.95
    1. Africa, French-speaking West—Description and travel.
2. Caillié, René, 1799–1838—Journeys—Africa, French-speaking West.
3. Welch, Galbraith—Journeys—Africa, French-speaking West.
4. Tombouctou (Mali)—Description.   I. Title.
DT527.W45   1991
916.6′09175410423—dc20   91-27055
                                                               CIP

Manufactured in the United States of America

To

JAMES FRANCIS DWYER

*My companion on eight African journeys
and my choice for the
ninth*

The New York Times
Book Review
(February 1939)

This review of *The Unveiling of Timbuctoo* is here reprinted in its entirety because it offers a fair, indeed exuberant, appraisal of the book. It also functions as an intelligent introduction for the contemporary reader.

The Astounding Story Of Timbuctoo

A Portrait of Caillié, the Frenchman Who Also Saw the Heart of Darkness

THE UNVEILING OF TIMBUCTOO: The Astounding Adventures of Caillié. By Galbraith Welch. With illustrations and map. 351 pp. New York: William Morrow & Co. $3.50

By KATHERINE WOODS

The road to Timbuctoo at the beginning of the nineteenth century was as alluring, as fabulous, as was ever the road to Cathay or Samarkand. It was a road of indescribable peril to a forbidden, fanatical city, and although many tales were told of uncounted wealth behind walls that rose to golden roofs by the sands of the Sahara, no one knew what tales were true, because no white man had ever seen Timbuctoo. Even the great Mungo Park had not approached it. But it was a name of enchantment in England and France. "Not only white travelers and adventurers but European governments believed that who first reached Timbuctoo would have all Africa in his pocket." And in a flat little village in Poitou an unhappy child, lonely, delicate, poverty-stricken, heard the tales of Timbuctoo and fell in love with the name. It was a love to which he remained indomitably faithful: at 16 he set out on his pilgrimage and at 28 he attained his goal.

René Caillié was a French peasant boy, a village cobbler's apprentice, who, alone and almost destitute, penetrated the forbidden secrets of the heart of Africa. He was the first white man to tear the veil of mystery from Timbuctoo. He saw more of Africa than any other white man who had ever lived to tell it. He was one of the greatest explorers of modern times, and one of the strangest and least known. A century after his death his story is now fully told for the first time in English: by a worthy narrator, and at a singularly apt moment in history. As the attention of the world fastens with heavy anxiety upon the French African empire—France Beyond-the-Sea, as the French, not without reason, call it—we may read this astonishing story of an important incident in that empire's establishment. It is from first to last the astonishing story of one man and his all but incredible achievement. It is also a story which begins and ends in paradox.

For where experienced and richly equipped explorers had failed—and where nearly all of them had died in their failure—this unsupported, insignificant, practically penniless youth succeeded, not in spite of his poverty and obscurity but in large part because of it. And although his astounding exploit did have an important influence on French colonial development, no group of white men entered Timbuctoo, after his perilous visit, for more than sixty-five years. René Caillié made his way into Timbuctoo and out of it again in the only way in which such a feat could be accomplished. He took back to his country the much-desired facts about the secret city of the desert and he won the prize offered by the Paris Geographical Society to "the man who should clear up the Timbuctoo mystery." But until a French military force under Joffre occupied Timbuctoo only twenty years before the Battle of the Marne, only two white men had followed in Caillié's footsteps; between Caillié and the first of the two there was a gap of a quarter of a century. It was not Timbuctoo which proved important to French expansion in Africa, though Timbuctoo seemed "the strangest city in the world." It was Caillié's report of his whole amazing journey. His Niger story was a revelation to the white world and his enthusiasm was the original cornerstone on which his country based its African colonial ambitions, its occupation of French Sudan and the lands south and north. Caillié's victory over Timbuctoo was spectacular. His Niger story was inspiring. Timbuctoo may have been a disappointment, the Niger was a "call to conquest."

Boy and man, René Caillié was and continued to be a creature of one idea; and the eleven years between his first departure for Africa and his final successful expedition made in fact a harsh and helpful novitiate. He had little education, no training, not even good physical health; but he had, and used, a peasant's shrewdness and common sense, the wisdom of tact, observation, adaptability and a spirit of simple neighborliness for which "democratic" seems to be the best word; and from his first appalling experience with an ill-fated colonial expedition to Senegal he had the preparation of hard and hardening living and the teaching of other men's mistakes. It was on his third trip to Africa that he at last set out toward Timbuctoo; he had already studied the Africans, accustomed himself to African existence and, as a member of Gray's exploring party, he had seen the folly of the white men's large, rich caravans. Their very wealth, he saw, must doom such expeditions to failure: overburdened, overmanned, overbearing, they were fair lure for plunder, fair object for fear and hate. And whether or not he saw any justification for the African Moslem's loathing of the Christian, he knew that a Christian had small chance of getting out of Timbuctoo alive, even if he ever got there in the first place. So he thought out his wild plan and made his thorough preparations. He would go into forbidden Africa as a Moslem; poor, defenseless, a lonely pilgrim with just a few trade goods to pay his way.

First—a venture as perilous as any—he must live with the desert Moors and learn the Moslem faith and custom. Then he must have a little money: just a little, for his bag of trinkets and a tiny nest-egg. The French were eager to learn about Timbuctoo; would the French in Senegal help him? Well, maybe; well, after all, no. Then the English in Sierra Leone: would the English help him? No. The English, however, would give him a well-paid job in Freetown, and he was slow in learning that this would keep him immobilized while the English Major Laing made his way to the forbidden city. When Caillié did realize his complete lack of support, he made up his mind to work at his job and save his money. When he had laid by the almost ludicrously small sum of 2,000 francs, he started at last to Timbuctoo.

The date of his departure was April 19, 1827. The place was Kakandé, where, forty-two years later, a monument to his achievement was put up at the suggestion of the great French soldier and administrator, Faidherbe, the "creator of French West Africa." In just a year he was to reach the goal of his pilgrimage which was only the middle of his journey and the heart of his peril. Laing had got to Timbuctoo before him; and Laing had been savagely murdered on the way out. Caillié spent two weeks in that strange city, a parasite of trade in the desert, and its sophisticated merchant-force never pierced through his disguise. Then he went on to further perils and explorations, as the first white man to traverse the Western Sahara. That terrible crossing took eighty-one days. At the end of it he staggered ragged, dirty, half-starved, into the house of the French consul at Tangier with his epoch-making announcement, "I am a Frenchman; I have been to Timbuctoo." But his situation then was as menacing as it had been at any time: Tangier was one of the most fanatical of Moslem cities. Caillié was kept in hiding then until he could be smuggled aboard a French ship in a new disguise.

Every step in the whole singleminded and singly achieved adventure had been a defiance of death in one way or another; and the ways of death had been many and various. It was not surprising that his story was doubted when he reached home. The French by careful examination satisfied themselves of its truth but the English, whose brave Major Laing had so recently been killed, could not believe that this untrained peasant had succeeded where he had failed. Now, as Galbraith Welch says, nobody even remembers that there was any controversy about Caillié's report; all lingering doubts were removed by the German explorer Barth, who reached Timbuctoo under English sponsorship in 1853. And yet, the author adds, the feat was so extraordinary, the man who accomplished it was so unusual and unexpected a personality, that the aura of the incredible may well hang still over the whole truth and straightforward tale.

As it comes at last to the English-speaking public, the tale is blest in its telling. Galbraith Welch, an American resident in France, is a member of the Société de Géographie of Paris who not only has followed in Caillié's still difficult footsteps but has made several other African journeys, and who not only has documented her book but has immersed herself in the facts and conditions which form its historical, geographical, personal and sociological background. The events of the biography were not difficult to come by: René Caillié wrote the story of his exploit, and his compatriots had written books about him. What was less easy to achieve was the story's ripe flavor, its pungent and colorful scene, the very sense of Caillié's Africa. The author has not obtruded herself into her narrative; she has identified herself with it. With the ease and richness of complete absorption, with vividness and clarity, she has written one of the most amazing and exciting of all true adventure stories, and one of the best.

THE UNVEILING
OF TIMBUCTOO

BOOK I

THREE YEARS AGO I made a pilgrimage in Africa. I crossed the Sahara to Timbuctoo. I rode on the Niger and went to the Guinea Coast—a long, hard journey. The motive of my pilgrimage was to see mile by mile the way over which a lone explorer struggled more than a century ago, to see a certain little clay house in Timbuctoo where he slept in triumph.

In this little clay house a hero hid himself away in native disguise for a fortnight in the spring of 1828. Had his disguise been suspected he would have been killed. He was René Caillié, the first white man who ever invaded forbidden, fabulous Timbuctoo and got safely back to tell Europe what he had seen.

Today this house bears a plaque placed there by France. It reads:

Souvenir Colonial Français
à
René Caillié
1799–1838
Il habita cette maison
en avril mai 1828 lors de son
voyage de Guinée au Maroc
19 avril 1827–7 Septembre 1828

Three other old native houses are preserved at Timbuctoo, those which sheltered the only three other whites who managed to see the place until its military occupation by the French at the very end of the nineteenth century. These three other whites were the Scot, Laing, who reached the fanatical savage capital twenty months before Caillié, only to be murdered, and two much later travellers, Barth, a German (1853), and Lenz, an Austrian (1880).

Before Caillié's house at the Caillié centenary celebration in 1928 passed a review of honour, a splendid, colourful procession—Saharan soldiers, black troops of the French Sudan, the Governor of the colony, dapper officers in gala uniforms of starched white, breasts fatigued by rows of glorious medals.

It was tropic Africa on parade, a unique, splashing, reverent circus. Dazzling sunshine. Clouds of churned sand. Meharistes on their lean angry camels, black troops with tribal carvings on their simple faces and the magnificent bodies of young animals, the *nouba*—the native military band—trumpets and drums playing a few simple bars over and over with solemn, savage intensity. The black populace, leaping and pushing, crazed at the fine show. Rhythmic clapping of black palms; sheen of negroes' teeth and eyeballs; bare fine breasts of negresses; naked poddy piccaninnies strapped to their mothers' backs; pretty girls squealing delighted *you-yous*; the sober stare of the "Ancients", the old men of local consequence, portly and wrapped in fine silky robes of Sudanese bright light blue; the glitter of quaint, gay head-dresses, gold balls twinkling, coral and coloured beads ashine. Everybody, whether they understood it or not, honouring the memory of the white hero who lived in the little clay house just a century ago.

René Caillié's story has never been fully told in English. What he did was extraordinary. What he was, even more so. Caillié was probably the oddest adventurer in all history. And Caillié's journey was probably the hardest piece of exploration ever performed.

This briefly is what Caillié did. Inspired by a determination to discover mysterious Timbuctoo he plunged into

Africa from a point on the Guinea coast called Kakandé, at the mouth of the Rio Nunez, and disappeared. It was on April 19, 1827. He was in native disguise and pretended to be a Mohammedan. All that he possessed was a little trade outfit worth less than 2,000 francs. He had no geographical instruments, no scientific knowledge. He was a small man physically, and had almost no education. He had no backing. He had received no aid of any sort.

Nothing was heard of him until on September 7, 1828, near death, he staggered into the house of the French consul at Tangier and whispered: "I have been to Timbuctoo!"

During his whole journey he had not spoken to a white man. No one had penetrated his disguise. He had crossed mountains, brush, forest and swamp, had lain near death for half a year in a savage hut, had ridden the Niger in a huge native canoe, had wormed his way into secret, hostile Timbuctoo and remained there fifteen days (April 20, to May 4, 1828), had dragged himself across the terrible Sahara in midsummer, and made his way with infinite danger through fanatical Morocco to the Atlantic coast.

The distance he had covered was, at the lowest estimate, 3,150 miles, and throughout the whole of that distance he was always going forward over new ground. His own daily record total 2,849¼ miles, but toward the end his eagerness and impatience to reach home caused him to underestimate the distance.

Alone and quite without help he had accomplished by far the longest single one way journey ever safely made across Africa. Mungo Park had not been able to push a quarter the distance into Africa on the only journey he lived to finish, nor indeed was his second, fatal journey nearly so extended as Caillié's. Neither on his first journey nor on the second which killed him, did Clapperton go so far into Africa; nor did the murdered Laing. The exploration of Africa in those days was hard beyond our comprehension, and so hazardous that it was almost suicide. We have only to read the list of the brave men of all nations who tried and died.

There was something almost miraculous about Caillié. His experience seems more like a triumphant series of adventures in a book for boys than the life story of a real man. It is easy to understand how some people misjudged him and thought him a fake, and why a fantastic legend has grown up around him. Caillié's exploit *is* unbelievable, and the more we find out about Africa, the more incredible it seems.

But all of Caillié's claims were true. The Paris Geographical Society, doyen of the Geographical Societies of the world, studied his notes and records, examined him personally, tested and re-tested his story, and finally gave him the prize of 10,000 francs which they had offered to the first European who should penetrate the mysteries of Timbuctoo and bring home an account of what he had seen.

Those days when René Caillié was young were days of opportunity. A great adventurer could buy himself a thrill which is no longer for sale. Caillié had the chance at an exciting exploit which the bravest could not perform today. Caillié had the chance to make geography.

Much of the world was then dark and mysterious. Africa was a giant question mark. Upon maps nearly the whole interior of the continent was marked "Unexplored Regions". Africa was challenge and promise!

From childhood René longed to see Africa, not knowing what Africa meant. He fell in love with a name, with a mystery. He heard of Timbuctoo the forbidden, and was tortured by intolerable curiosity.

With a determination that was almost a sort of madness he clung to his boyish dream and gave his youth to preparation for his great journey—minor explorations, the study of another creed, the laborious earning of money for his outfit.

Then at twenty-seven he shot into Africa. Soon he was in quite unexplored country. To his odd nature this was ecstasy. Curiosity made him invincible. The knowledge that he was seeing alone wide stretches on which the eyes of a white man had never before rested thrilled him and gave him unearthly strength. He pushed forward tirelessly, lured by the longing to see and feel and taste new things. Death perched on his shoulder; starvation, burning heat, thirst, sickness tortured him. But there was a surprise in every mile.

He watched the gigantic savage panorama. Like the mad king alone in the centre of a theatre while a great spectacle is shown for his sole delight, Caillié looked at this vivid, outsize world, enormous yet grotesque. A thousand miles of unbroken sand; a river vast as an ocean; trees like castles aflame; comic, deadly animals; men stranger than wild beasts; the flash of queer birds that were brilliant as the glass of a cathedral window; big flowers like fallen stars. A day-long procession of lovely and hideous marvels, all seen in a loneliness so absolute that it had the tang and potency of a strange drug. His ego was intoxicated. Nothing could stop him.

Caillié paid his way in pain. He paid in flesh and blood and teeth. But he was thoroughly contented with his bargain. For he saw more of Africa than any other white man who had ever lived.

2

AFRICA WAS A land of fables and irresistible allure, thrilled and horrified by whispers of awful cruelties. It catered to lust with tales of women possessed of charms such as the white world never knew.

Recapture for an instant the colossal curiosity, the charming ignorance, the ready credulity about what was inside the mystery continent. Recall the jumble of romantic fancies and thrilling rumours: grotesque tales passed down from classic times; sensuous, colourful stories told by Arab travellers with Oriental hyperbole; wild, half-understood babblings of savages to coastal traders; boastful and horrible reminiscences and inventions of sailors.

Every man who was lucky enough to get home trom these tropic shores was full of fantastic yarns. Africa has always been the liar's paradise! The taverns of Europe's ports seethed with sailors' yarns, and from the taverns the stories spread.

Gold—easy gold—was the favourite theme. Men listened with glittering eyes and passed on tales of tropic wealth, of a load of gold to be had in exchange for a load of common salt, of the "Hills of Gold" of inner Africa. From these hills the natives took what they desired and proceeded to the coast, where—poor, ignorant creatures that they were—they gave up their nuggets and precious grains and gold-dust for trumpery trash. Why, the poor fools would actually buy bilge water, thinking it a charm for toothache!

Gold that blinded your eyes: massive gold ornaments on black bodies, great gold bracelets that weighed men's arms to cracking point, thrones and stools of solid gold for royal negro thighs to rest upon, negro wenches shuffling along with gold anklets that crippled their fine black legs, beautiful slave-boys in golden chains, gold breastplates dappled with blood. The listening taverns trembled with lust and greed.

And they quivered in horror at stories of ghastly cruelty —some of them true. Bowdich, for instance, reported the following scene which he witnessed when he visited the interior of the Gold Coast in 1817:

"An inhuman spectacle was paraded before us. . . . It was a man whom they were tormenting previous to sacrifice; his hands were pinioned behind him, a knife was passed through his cheeks, to which his lips were noosed like the figure 8, one ear was cut off and carried before him, the other hung to his head by a small bit of skin, there were several gashes in his back, and a knife was thrust under each shoulder-blade; he was led with a cord passed through his nose by men disfigured with immense caps of shaggy black skins."

Stories of all sorts startled the taverns. It was indeed a weird land. Nightmare animal novelties—crocodiles, elephants, hippopotami, serpents "so large and strong they could devour bulls", and other serpents "whose bite caused a man's skin to peel away from all over his body", monkeys which were really men under some strange bewitchment, and other monkeys who lusted after negro women and cohabited with them. Nauseating insects—spiders big as kittens, scorpions like two-pound lobsters, feathery centipedes with death in every twinkling leg, ants that fell on men in armies and ate them up, dainty flying creatures which settled on travellers in clouds at night, singing caressingly and stinging and stinging until after many nights men went mad with sleeplessness and died. Humans as monstrous as the animals—cannibals, pygmies, natives with faces slashed and carved like so much wood, with teeth filed in fancy points, and with great pieces of wood let into their tortured lips.

The ground itself was strange. There was a desert unimaginably vast, waterless travel for months over burning sand. The climate was so hot that "the water in men's bodies turned to blood", so hot that "unless men ate salt their blood would putrefy"—and salt so rare that it was worth its weight in gold!

There were hideous illnesses: a mysterious, unnatural horror that made men sleep their lives away, shocking ulcers and skin diseases; leprosy; swift fevers—a man grew rich in a day, fell ill and died on the morrow, hands full of gold.

It was taunting and enticing! What grand things a man might do if he was strong enough, what feats he might perform, what wonders he might see. He might see Prester John, the mythical Christian King whose capital, some said, was "to the east of Timbuctoo". What fun and glory to present oneself at the court of this potentate and give him his first news about the Christian world outside! Or a man might have the chance to play that game of night trading with shy negroes—a most romantic and profitable sport. Leave one's trinkets on the great river's bank and find next morning a high heap of gold on the same spot. Or a man might see that great black King of the Desert whose dogs wore golden collars and who tied his horse to a golden hitching-post—that would be a sight to see! And those ants as large as cats who were trained to collect gold for their masters . . . but tavern listeners agreed that they'd collect their own gold unaided. Easy work picking up gold!

And Timbuctoo! Every head came forward as the sailors whispered the old legends over which men had smacked their lips for centuries, legends of wealth and legends of love—of women quite nude and so lovely that men fainted before them, women who were full of kind impulses toward travellers. . . . Timbuctoo, what a place! No one had seen it, everyone wanted to!

Timbuctoo was regarded as the bull's eye of Africa. Secret and forbidden, geographically almost unattainable, queerly named, and the subject of endless glamorous gossip, it had taken on enormous prestige. Not only white travellers and adventurers but European governments believed that who first reached Timbuctoo would have all Africa in his pocket.

But the centuries passed and no one succeeded, though the corpses of many brave men marked the way—usually at points pitifully near the starting point on the coast. Mungo Park's name stands out. On his first journey he got nowhere near Timbuctoo. When he left on his second he was instructed to push into the closed city and report on it, but this he dared not venture to attempt, and he rode by its port on the hostile Niger to his death.

Apart from the symbolic value which attached to Timbuctoo in the old days—a value which we now cannot understand—there was a very real and tangible reason for the desire to open up the city to the white world. Timbuctoo was regarded as the centre of the African gold trade—a place prodigiously rich. People said soberly that its merchants handled gold nonchalantly with shovels like grocers weighing out sugar, that the palace had a golden roof, that a lump of gold could be bought for 400 cowries—cowries being shell tokens of minute value, so easily come by that ships going to Africa spaded them into the hold for ballast.

Timbuctoo was said to be in a marvellously fortunate situation for trade. It was at the junction of the Sahara and the great Nile of the Negroes, the Niger, mysterious river discovered by Mungo Park whose source and outlet were still unknown. The city was the port of the Sahara, the place "where the camel and the canoe meet". Through Timbuctoo the North and South mingled their trade. To it negroes came in their canoes, bringing with them the gold which was supposed to lie beneath the ground over whole sections of Africa, just waiting to be scratched out. To it came plodding Moorish caravans from the Mediterranean bearing trinkets and other caravans bearing salt from the desert mines. Meeting at Timbuctoo, the gullible negroes eagerly exchanged their gold for the Moors' goods and salt. And then the Moors, tired and demoralized after their cruel journey over the terrible sands and in horror of the return journey before them, frittered this gold away. They spent gorgeously for nights of joy, banquets and song. They offered extravagant gifts to the complaisant and lovely girls of the city, who, because of their habit of slipping about the streets of Timbuctoo with never a stitch of clothes to hide their beauty, seemed especially lovely to Mohammedan eyes used to the veiled and swaddled female. Thus gold piled up in Timbuctoo and the city on the desert's fringe had become rich beyond imagining: such was the belief of the white world.

These colourful panegyrics were all of Arab origin, let it be understood. Notably there was the report of Leo Africanus, whose name sounds white, but who was really a Moor of cosmopolitan experience, for he was born in Spain, turned Christian in Rome where he was named after the Pope, and travelled widely in Africa and Asia. His account of the golden sceptres and plates used by the King of Timbuctoo, "some whereof weighed 1,300 pounds", made rich reading; and "it is perhaps not too much to say that in the whole annals of literature there is not another passage which has conduced more materially to the progress of geography". No doubt the progress of geography was also furthered by the writings of another Arab chronicler, Ibn Batuta, who went to Timbuctoo in the fourteenth century and complained piously of the slackness of local morals and manners, telling how even in the sacred month of Ramadan the city was full of open sinning, with slaves both male and female walking about the streets without clothing, and the Sultan's daughters appearing before their royal father and even parading the streets naked. Another Arab enthusiast merely made the quiet claim : "this is the greatest city which God has created".

But of this grand city where gold and love were free there was no authentic account from any white explorer or reliable traveller. Fake travellers had of course pretended to have been there. Most prominent of these was one Adams (alias Benj. Rose), an American who created a certain commotion when Caillié was a boy by his claim to have been shipwrecked on the coast and taken to Timbuctoo [1] And there were a few honourable men of white race who found themselves by accident in Timbuctoo but whose unrecorded visits made the white world no wiser—for example, Imbert the French captive taken there by his Moorish master in the seventeenth century. There were vague rumours, too, of the journey of "the two Portuguese" in the time of Henry the Navigator: this mythical pair in any event would have kept anything they saw a secret, geographical knowledge being then regarded by Portugal as national treasure not to be given away.

There was never a place more difficult to approach geographically. The traveller, whatever route he attempted, would find the natives particularly hostile, for Timbuctoo was precious, not only a rich city but a black trade monopoly and a symbol of black empire. Worst barrier of all, however, was the climate. More dangerous than the savages themselves were the conditions of savage life, for it is impossible to shoot or to cajole a microbe. Foul water, food produced and prepared in filthy fashions, infections and fevers and contagious skin complaints, disease-carrying mosquitoes, sunstroke, chills from the

---

[1] *The Narrative of Robert Adams, a Sailor, who was wrecked on the western coast of Africa in the year 1810, was detained three years in slavery by the Arabs of Great Desert, and resided several months in the city of Tombuctoo*—Murray, 1816. Adams imposed on many learned men and was given a Government grant. Another prevaricator whose travels were the subject of a book was James Riley, also an American, *Loss of the American Brig Commerce, wrecked on the western coast of Africa, in the month of August* 1815. *With an account of Timbuctoo* by James Riley—Murray, 1817.

steaming dampness—few white travellers survived. As an instance of what Africa could do to white men, Mungo Park on his second expedition left the coast with thirty-eight men and reached the Niger, which according to plan was to be the mere beginning of the journey, with seven.

Caillié got safely across because he had deliberately prepared himself in advance. He accustomed himself to living as natives did. He inoculated himself by habit.

Of course all this talk of danger merely attracted the adventurous and romantic of Caillié's generation. Thousands of boys dreamed of winning the great African victory and of coming back home to tell their amazed friends all about the forbidden black city with the gold roofs. By a marvel it was to small, almost sickly René Caillié, a poor peasant boy, that the dream came true.

One other ambitious visionary and hero of the same generation, the Scot, Major Alexander Gordon Laing, reached Timbuctoo twenty months before Caillié, though this Caillié did not know when he started on his journey. Had Laing got safely home, Caillié's exploit would have had little value. As it was, Laing's tragic sacrifice had none, except to prove the Scot's great bravery, which needed no proving. Indeed Laing's expedition, but for Caillié's swiftly following triumph, would have done more harm than good to the cause of African exploration, for it would have seemed to prove that Timbuctoo was not only nearly impossible to reach, but impossible to get away from.

3

IF RENÉ CAILLIÉ's exploit had been easier he would be more famous. In the years after his moment of great triumph the world almost forgot him because no one was able to follow him. His great feat became legendary, even in his own country. The boy explorer in Arab dress—he might be found in Larousse, or perhaps in Jules Verne; the average Frenchman-in-the-street would not be sure which.

Caillié did something almost impossible to emulate. France interested herself in the comparatively easy developing of those rich African lands which were just across the Mediterranean—the campaign for the conquest of Algeria was undertaken within two years of Caillié's penetration into Timbuctoo.

The second in the Timbuctoo race, the second man to get into the forbidden city and away safely, in fact the next white man to get anywhere near the place, was scarce out of his baby clothes at the moment of Caillié's triumph. The third in the race was not yet born. It was sixty-five years after Caillié's visit before any group of white men dared venture into the city. At last, in 1894, Timbuctoo was occupied under Joffre.

The printing-press did not keep Caillié's name alive. For years he was not a popular subject for authors because nobody knew anything about the sweep of wild land and the secret city which was the setting for his adventures. Lately two books have appeared about Caillié in French —*La Vie de René Caillié, Vainqueur de Tombouctou* by Lemandé and Nanteuil, which dwells especially upon René's unhappy boyhood and on his life in France after his triumphant return, and *La Prodigieuse Vie de René Caillié* by Briault.

Probably no one has yet written about Caillié who has personal knowledge of all the Caillié Road. Two years ago, after much travel in Morocco, I travelled over practically all of this route, crossing the Sahara by automobile, staying at Timbuctoo, proceeding by steamer

along the Niger, and by car to Kankan in French Guinea
and to the coast—Caillié's route in the reverse direction.
By this pilgrimage, thrillingly interesting but rough going,
I gained a shuddering notion of the hardships and the
ferocious determination and courage of the lone traveller
who tramped this way over a century ago, when the
natives were unsubdued and fanatical, and the land a
roadless, and often foodless and waterless wilderness.

Caillié's own published record of his journey is the
best story, provided one can obtain a copy and also
provided that one is a patient and leisurely reader. The
*Journal d'un Voyage à Temboctou et à Jenné dans l'Afrique
Centrale, précédé d'observations faites chez les Maures Braknas,
les Nalous et d'autres peuples; pendant les années 1824, 1825,
1826, 1827, 1828* was published by the French King's
orders at the *Imprimerie Royale* in 1830[1] and was dedicated
to His Majesty by "The very-humble and very-faithful
subject, R. Caillié". It is in three fat volumes. The later
half of the third volume is made up of additional explanations by E. F. Jomard, a very distinguished geographer of
the period. The front of the first is embellished by a
portrait of René himself, a frail and thoughtful-looking
man, big-eyed, with a mass of dark hair, a forceful, heavy
nose, large, well-placed ears; the face both helped and
harmed by a noticeably clever mouth.

In these three volumes is the story of his early life and
the story of his great achievement, all told in Caillié's
own words and printed, by his own insistence, *just as he
wrote them*. In the manner of the writing as much as in the
matter itself we see Caillié's queer character. He tells of
some awful danger or almost unbearable hardship in
half a sentence, and he writes with almost comical detail

[1] The *Journal* was immediately translated into English and published that same
year in London. A much compressed version was issued in French in 1932.

of minor things, of meagre native meals and of greedy natives grabbing for strings of coral. He writes like the peasant he was. Occasionally he tries to "write", setting down his experiences pompously and with a flourish.

But through it all shows Caillié's honesty, his desire to tell everything with sacred accuracy. Tactlessly and passionately he expresses his indignation at those in authority, French and English, who refused him the pitiful sum of 6,000 francs, which he estimated would finance his journey. Coldly he tells how he financed his adventure himself with money saved from the generous salary paid him in the English colony of Sierra Leone, and how he plunged alone into Africa. The reader must guess at Caillié's bravery; he himself makes no parade of the dangers run, nor any claims to courage. He does not need to, for the bravery, and most particularly the moral bravery, of his adventure would be clear to a fool.

Outstandingly we see on every page indications of shrewdness—French peasant shrewdness—and proof that he was a great actor with an unfailing ability to control his tongue and his actions. He carried out his complete journey disguised as a native and pretending to be a Mohammedan. A single slip might have meant his death. He showed an infinite capacity to trick and lie his way out of every peril and trap, a ready ruse for every emergency.

There is heart-rending pathos in all his frankly confessed twisting and squirmings, humiliations and grovelling misery. He reveals everything to his reader. He is without shame. He would eat mud and let negroes spit upon him so long as he got forward along his road, and he would admit it all without reserve.

Yet there is wild untamable vanity about him, a pigheaded determination that he should be the one to capture Timbuctoo's secret.

From childhood he consecrated himself completely to

the attainment of a queer ambition which seemed to be altogether beyond his capacities and which, notwithstanding, he had the grandeur of imagination to know he could accomplish. His is a story of unceasing struggle to make a dream come true.

His was probably the most remarkable example of a specific fixed longing in history. Most men of accomplishment have had in extreme youth an ample and rambling ambition, desiring—let us say—power, or wealth, or victory at arms, or spiritual beauty and saintliness, or achievement in one of the arts, or adventure, or travel; and they have fixed upon some special goal, as the years passed and circumstances suggested. But in Caillié we have a lad who in his early teens decided to go to a remote undiscovered city—just one special city—and, leaving home while yet a child, never wavered from his ambition. He was like someone bewitched or hypnotized.

Let us admit from the beginning that, boy and man, René Caillié was a crank, an eccentric with a fixed idea. But he was a glorious crank. And so perhaps are most men and women who accomplish great, strange victories.

4

RENÉ CAILLIÉ (HIS name, by the way, is locally pronounced *Ky-ay*) was born in Mauzé in the Department of Deux-Sèvres. Mauzé is a quiet little place of some fifteen hundred inhabitants, in flat country twenty-five miles back from the Biscay coast. It is about a hundred miles dead to the north of Bordeaux.

Caillié himself did not know the correct date of his birth. In his autobiography he says "I was born in 1800" As a matter of fact he was born in 1799, on the 19th of November, a date described on the local register as

"28th Brumaire of the year VIII". The translation of a date from the Revolutionary Calendar into the normal calendar is difficult, and Caillié, like many others, made a mistake.

René's childhood encompassed one of the most dramatic periods in the world's history—the French Revolution, the rise and fall of Napoleon. Probably Caillié actually saw Napoleon in the flesh, for the defeated Emperor passed through Mauzé after Waterloo on his way to Rochefort and the *Bellérophon*.

But Caillié himself played a part in a drama which excited the folk of his little village more profoundly than all these great historic happenings, for he had the misfortune to be born into a scandal which set all the countryside talking. At the very moment of his birth his father, François Caillié, was on trial for grave crimes of which he was found guilty and for which he was condemned to a cruel sentence.

François Caillié was that most troublesome of relatives, the man who, unable to carry liquor, must be always drinking. He was not a bad man, which made him only the more trying, for—as it was—his unfortunate wife could not justify herself in loathing and leaving him, but must needs pity his weakness and be faithful.

By persistent drunkenness and persistent mischance François Caillié found himself accused of robbery, and, bad luck dogging him, was ill-defended and pronounced guilty. The sum involved—six francs, no more!—makes the tragedy almost absurd. But François Caillié was armed with a gun,[1] he was a guest in the innkeeper's house, he was drunk—very drunk. Incredible as it seems, he was

---

[1] From the Archives of Charente-Inférieure, quoted by Lamandé and Nanteuil, François Caillié received eight years in chains for committing a theft in an inn, two years because the theft was done at night, and two years more because he had a gun with him at the time. These authors suggest he was not guilty, being a victim of a series of misunderstandings while in drink.

condemned to twelve years in prison, a term which the poor man did not live to finish. So René never knew his father.

It is a byword that great men are born of interesting women, and no doubt René's mother, Anne Lépine Caillié, was a person of unusual character. Her father was a master baker at Mauzé. The young man, François Caillié, whom she was destined to marry came from the Vendée to work for Anne's father. The girl who marries her father's apprentice often has an unhappy time of it; the Cophetua role is best played by a man, wives preferring to look upward rather than downward to their spouses.

Anne Caillié had six children in all, René of course being the youngest. These children seem all to have been delicate. One girl, Elisabeth, who was called Céleste, was lame. René was not robust. Three died in childhood, and the only other surviving son, François Junior, died in early manhood.

A dying baby. Husband drunken and brawling. Poverty. Another baby coming, born of a drunken father. Illness. The contempt of neighbours and relatives. Poor Anne Caillié. And yet she must have dreamed. René was Anne's dream come true—a boy of hers who would be great and brave and famous, a boy of hers who would do something no other man had ever done.

Today there is fixed upon the ruins of the house in which she gave birth to René a plaque which reads:

ICI NAQUIT,
RENÉ CAILLIÉ
LE 19 NOVEMBRE, 1799

And every year a village festival is held in her boy's honour and all the good folk of modern Mauzé stand in a crowd and salute respectfully the Caillié monument at the bridgehead across the street from his birthplace.

She would like that. She would like, too, the queer little boat on the River Niger which bears her son's name, and the fact that many streets in Africa and one in Paris are marked: *Rue René Caillié*. And that René was named Chevalier of the Legion of Honour. And that he once dined with the King of France and told a round-eyed Princess the marvellous story of his adventures. And that a book all about his achievements was published in three fine volumes and dedicated to the King's own Majesty.

But perhaps proudest of all she would be of the monument at the place which Caillié knew as Kakandé on the Guinea coast, which marks the spot whence he set out on his perilous journey, and of the little clay house at Timbuctoo which sheltered him in his moment of secret triumph.

And what, one wonders, would she have thought of the Caillié centenary celebrations: the blare of negroes' trumpets and the clash of cymbals, the proud pageantry of France, the yelling, black crowd—she who perhaps never saw a negro in her life. She would have marvelled at the bravery of this son of hers who ventured all alone amongst such leaping savages.

But her timid gaze would have consoled itself as she saw scores of faces that were different from her own merely in colour—the faces of gentle, devoted mothers, so proud of their quaint, sleek children, young women with generous mahogany bosoms and old negresses whose breasts, like Anne's own, were worn with nursing babies. She would have known them as friends, especially had she realized that her René could never have got to victory but for a certain old negress such as these who had saved his life.

But Anne, I hope, grasped her dream. I like to think that she always knew her boy would be wonderful, that she saw the promise in René's dark ardent eyes.

5

ANNE AND RENÉ did not have long together. The mother's life was shortened by sorrow and shame and poverty. Soon after she rose from childbed she quitted the home village of Mauzé, taking baby René with her and leaving the elder children with their grandmother. She went to Rochefort where François had been sent to serve his term, working as one of the chain gang at the port.

It was natural enough that she should desire to get away from the scorn and pity of those she knew. It is hard to live in a village whose fifteen hundred inhabitants all know that your husband and the father of your children has been condemned to twelve years in chains. It is hard to meet eye to eye in the affairs of daily life folk who have actually seen your mate fastened to a pillory on which was inscribed "in big letters his name, his business, his domicile, the cause of his condemnation, and the sentence inflicted."

That Anne should have chosen Rochefort as her refuge might seem odd. Knowing nothing of her reasons, we can only guess that in weakness and tenderness, she blamed herself for some part of poor François's tragedy. No doubt she told herself: "If I had been gentler . . . or if I had been firmer. . . ." The situation typifies the needless cruelty of conscience, the harrowing cruelty from which genius often sprouts. Little René, sensitive and frail, bit young into acid, tonic fruit. His was no roly-poly childhood, red-cheeked and laughing. His days were days of worry and wondering, fearing to ask, fearing to find out.

When he was nine years old his father, still a prisoner, died. When he was eleven he lost his mother. René then returned to live with his maternal grandmother, and to rejoin his elder brother and sister, François and the lame

Céleste. He remained in Mauzé for more than four years
—physically a most uneventful youth, but psychologically
a period of turmoil.

To Céleste he transferred the sympathy and affection he
had in her lifetime given to Anne Caillié. She was, as he
said years afterward in his *Journal*, the sister whom he adored.

He loved to read and he longed to travel. Africa held
his dreams and "the city of Timbuctoo became the
continual object of every thought", as he quaintly puts
it in the first paragraph of his autobiography.

René received hardly any education, being early removed
from the village school to be apprenticed as shoemaker,
a trade which he loathed. After his African triumph,
when he set himself to the difficult work of writing a book
about his life and adventures, he complained bitterly about
the sparseness of his book learning.

Somehow in that primitive community he found books
about far places. He wallowed in the story of Robinson
Crusoe—a hero with his own initials—what a fine moment
it must have been when first he noticed the coincidence!
René longed for a life of marvels. "I burned to have
adventures like Robinson Crusoe's", he says, "Already
I felt in my heart the ambition to make myself famous
by some important discovery. I borrowed books about
geography and maps. The map of Africa, where I saw only
desert country, or lands marked unknown, excited me
especially. Soon this taste became a passion for which I
renounced everything. I ceased to take part in the games
and amusements of my comrades, I shut myself up on
Sundays so as to read any travel book which I could
procure."

While his comrades played and shouted René planned
out his life. He would be an explorer. He would make a
great name for himself.

His restless ambition was bred out of romantic longing
by a -sense- of inferiority. He was terribly irked by his
shameful parentage. The humiliations of his short past
produced a longing to leave home and all these folk who
knew he was the son of a convict. His sensitiveness and
vanity cried out for a chance to rehabilitate himself, to
do something wonderful in this wild unexplored land
which had captured his fancy.

The boy René trudged along the familiar roads of the
home countryside unhappy as a spirited dog led on a
leash. It was so usual, so repulsively safe. He crossed and
recrossed the wriggling, little local river, the Mignon,
"the Darling". He yearned for the great rushing rivers
of Africa.

Mauzé was a pleasant enough little place, but it cramped
him. He counted every minute till he should be old
enough to shake loose from this commonplace homeland.

One day—probably he was fifteen years old—he could
wait no longer. He says: "I spoke to my uncle, who was
my guardian, of my desire to travel. He disapproved and
painted for me with energy the dangers I should run at
sea and the regrets I should suffer far from my country
and my family. In short he neglected nothing to turn me
from my project."

A queer interview—the frail, earnest boy, soberly
pleading: "Please, Uncle Barthélémy, I wish permission
to go to Africa and discover Timbuctoo!" Useless for
Barthélémy Lépine, the innkeeper, to bid René go back
to his cobbler's bench and work hard at the situation to
which le bon Dieu had called him. The boy could not
put away Africa.

René persisted, braved the ridicule of the village, the
opposition of Uncle Barthélémy, the tearful pleading of
poor Céleste. At last Uncle Barthélémy gave his consent,

influenced by the colonial movement toward Africa which was then in the air, and perhaps also by a suspicion that this young nephew of his was a mad sort of youth who would never be a credit to Mauzé and the family, so had better be got out of the way.

Sixteen-year-old René Caillié left Mauzé, full of boyish rapture, and with sixty francs in his pocket. He had never been more than twenty-five miles from home before. Now he was going to Africa. He was on his way to Timbuctoo. On his way—why, he was there! Pattering along the French highway with his sixty francs jingling in his pocket and his little bundle on his back, he saw the golden minarets before him.

René started for Africa on the 27th of April 1816. It was twelve years—all but seven days—later that René, on the 20th of April 1828, "just at the moment when the setting sun was touching the horizon, arrived happily" —I quote his own words—at Timbuctoo.

6

RENÉ HAD THE luck to be transported free to the chosen starting-point of his adventures.

France was resuming possession of Senegal on the West African coast under the provisions of the Treaty of Paris. England was to move out; France was inaugurating a great "Plan of Colonization", a gallant but over-ambitious effort on the part of a nation which was just emerging from a long period of disorder and trouble.

Caillié went out to Africa as a very humble part of what might be described as a collapsible colony, which was shipped aboard a fleet of vessels and needed only to be unpacked and set in place upon the African shores, like a toy village.

It was a human Noah's Ark. Under the direction of the "High Commander for the King and Administrator of Senegal and its Dependencies and the Island of Gorée", whose name was Colonel Schmaltz, was a band of subordinates and technical experts, an assortment of workmen, and a little army of about two hundred soldiers with three captains, and minor officers. There was a naturalist, a geographer, a mining engineer to investigate the gold prospects. There was a school-teacher. There were two surgeon-doctors, three assistants and a pharmacist: it was this group, alas, which was destined to be the most useful to Schmaltz's little colony! There were four bakers. There were blacksmiths, butchers, coopers. There was a pair of official record keepers. A *préfet apostolique* was to see to the religious welfare of the colony. His work must have been at first mostly at burial services. There were numerous women and children. As preliminary spending money the sum of 90,000 francs was carried, packed in three little barrels. There were vast and various stores of material.

Colonel Schmaltz was taking out to Africa a community in miniature. The leader was full of enthusiasm, saw in his mind's eye a new tropic empire. Everything had been foreseen. The "Plan of Colonization" was perfect.

And so it was, except for two defects. These two defects, which may not have been the leader's fault, were very big defects indeed. One of them was that the command of the transporting fleet was given to a loyalist incompetent —a man who had been as a youth in the Royal Navy, had become an *émigré*, was recalled to the service by the grateful monarchy and given a command which he had not the experience to handle. This sentimental choice resulted in one of the most hideous disasters in maritime history. The other defect in the "Plan of Colonization" was that, when Schmaltz did at last reach Africa with the remnants of his battered and butchered colony, there was—through a cruel misunderstanding—no place to install it.

Four ships left France with the colonial enthusiasts, and of all the men and women the happiest and most hopeful was that sixteen-year-old adventurer, René Caillié of Mauzé, shipped as officer's servant at a salary of just eighteen francs a month. The others may have looked back wistfully toward their homeland on that June morning, wondering would they ever see it again—and indeed few of that ill-fated company ever did—but René had no regrets or fears.

Caillié sailed on the transport *Loire*, 550 tons. The other ships were the *Argus*, the *Echo* and the *Méduse*. This last was the leading ship of the little fleet, on which rode Colonel Schmaltz, the most important members of the party and the naval commander of the enterprise, Monsieur Duroys de Chaumareys of evil memory. For his incompetence and cowardice this man was later court-martialled and sentenced to three years in military prison and was ignominiously deprived of the Legion of Honour.

Caillié's ship, the *Loire*, carried food for five and a half months. She was the safe matron of the fleet, made a slow and cautious start out of harbour, did not distress herself to keep up with the others, and proceeded on her prudent way southward. She passed in due course Madeira and the Canaries, and crossed the Tropic of Cancer with the farcical demonstrations which in these more widely travelled days we reserve for the Equator—clownings and forced baths and so on as "Father Tropic" came aboard.

Then one day Caillié saw that thin line on the horizon which is so beautiful to the traveller by sea, the line marking the land of his desire. There was Africa! Flat sands, Saharan sands, barely rising above the level of the sea. The *Loire* came to the Banks of Arguin, bad weather and a dangerous coast, shallow, rocky and treacherous. The prudent ship went carefully. At Portendik, a now forgotten little roadstead midway between Capes Blanco and Vert, she came close in and anchored for a time, and so Caillié had his first real view of Africa. Portendik was a poor place, with a harbour of sorts to which European ships came sometimes to trade with the Moors of the desert.

René studied it with delight: this flat and torrid shore, this squat little native town with huts and tents instead of houses, the Moors in their tattered draperies, the women veiled in scraps of blue guinea cloth, negro slaves almost naked, a camel—the first camel Caillié had ever seen— and there, rolling off into an endless background, the treeless sands of the desert.

It was too wonderful to be true. He was actually looking at the Sahara—could almost touch it. Over there eastward, far, far off but rising from these same sands, was Timbuctoo. He was studying the battlefield where he was to be a victorious hero.

On July 9th, after a voyage of twenty-three days, the good ship *Loire* reached the harbour of Saint-Louis— principal place in Senegal, and selected as the *rendez-vous* for the four vessels, since it was the destination for the major part of the miniature colony.

The *Loire* was three days behind the appointed time. She was prepared to apologize for her careful, slow voyage. But the reliable *Loire* was not scolded. To the surprise and dismay of her company there was only one ship waiting at Saint-Louis, instead of three. They learned that the *Méduse*, master ship of the fleet, had been wrecked on the cruel Arguin Banks. Schmaltz, her commander, and certain others had just arrived before Saint-Louis in two of her small boats. Hundreds were missing. The *Argus* had been sent back to hunt for survivors, and a rescue expedition had been dispatched overland.

Details of the disaster were communicated to the horrified company aboard the *Loire* who, for reasons we shall discuss later, were not permitted to go ashore as yet, and it was bloody and shocking news indeed which came to them.

This is what had happened. M. de Chaumareys had managed by a miracle of carelessness to run the *Méduse* fast on the rocks at quarter-past three of a fine summer afternoon. It was inconceivable but true.

The *Méduse* was badly damaged and out of contact with the subordinate vessels of the fleet. Her small boats were inadequate for transporting the whole company of 396 persons. Schmaltz and his wife and daughter, his technical advisors and experts—the "white collar" part of the group, in a word—*and her commander* embarked in the small boats, after supervising the construction of a single great raft about 65 feet by 23 feet in size, on which the small fry would travel.

From the place of the wreck to Saint-Louis was relatively a short distance, less than three hundred miles, and Schmaltz, who suggested the raft, thought, or tried to think, all would be well.

Those who were ordered to ride upon the raft were less optimistic. Some even declined to leave the *Méduse*. They were wise. When they were subsequently rescued, one old tar, hearing of the horrible fate he had avoided by his refusal to leave the *Méduse*, had this to say: "I have been nine times shipwrecked. It is really my profession! How many wretches have I seen perish on rafts and small boats. So long as a ship floats, you should stay on board her."

Amid scenes of disorder, fury, terror and despair the poor creatures who did not have the old sailor's shrewdness —147 persons in all—were lowered aboard the raft, their weight nearly submerging it. They were almost all soldiers —the scum of the army, poor devils recruited from prisons, ex-criminals, branded men, men of all races whose harsh

lives led them to expect the worst. With them, as commander of the raft, went a twenty-three-year-old officer.
Amongst the civilian passengers were two young cabin-
boys—one of them was only twelve years old—and one
woman, an *ex-vivandière* travelling with her husband.
They possessed scarcely any provisions. The main items
were wine and a twenty-five pound sack of biscuits. Most of
what they had planned to carry had been lost, having
been tossed into the sea by the frightened men when the
overcrowded raft showed signs of sinking.

One of the small boats, itself, of course, also overcrowded, was to tow the raft. It was an impossible task—
Schmaltz's plan had been madness. The destiny which
these poor wretches had foreseen from the inception of the
scheme was inevitable. The tow-line was lost. The crowded
small boats looked back, hesitated helplessly, tried to
believe that the raft could make port with an improvised
sail, and went their way. The raft—helpless under a tropic
sun, rolling on the waves of an especially vicious stretch of
African coast before a desert peopled by cruel nomads,
scantily provisioned and loaded with 147 persons so crushed
together they could barely cling on—was abandoned.

Such was the first chapter of the story told to Caillié
and his mates on the *Loire*.

Nor was that all. Beside the poor creatures on the raft,
of whom as yet there was no news at all, others were
missing—officers and ladies and persons of distinction, for
many of those who had found places on the small boats had
insisted on being put ashore on the desert coast, hoping to
reach Saint-Louis on foot.

Day by day new and shocking details came in. Caillié
had wished that he might come close to adventures. Now
he was getting his wish; every day he heard of happenings
almost too distressing to record, heard them from the

lips of the survivors—the pitifully few surviviors—of the disaster, some of whom were quartered on the *Loire*.

In the hope of meeting the officers and ladies and others who had insisted on being put ashore from the small boats, a rescue caravan was sent northward from Saint-Louis by the English governor of the place.

This caravan, mounted on camels, was under the direction of an Irish colonist, who was described as a "trading captain". His name was *sir Karnet*—just that; and he was the type of person we all may hope will be sent to rescue us if ever we be stranded on a desert shore.[1] With tireless energy "sir Karnet" scoured the sands, consoled successive groups of poor wanderers, fed them and got them safe to Saint-Louis.

First to be rescued was a party which included the Picard family, wife and pretty daughters who discreetly disguised themselves in male costume to avoid the dangerous notice of Moorish nomads. Though the Picards were captured by Moors, their sufferings were less protracted than those of another group saved by the brave Irishman after they had stumbled about hopelessly in the desert for thirteen days. They had left six dead behind them and were themselves near death. They were famished, covered with awful sores and tortured by thirst. By day they had reeled under the tropic July sun. At night wild animals snarled and roared nearby—panthers and wild cats ready to kill them, hyenas waiting for them to die. They fell into a sort of stupor, seeing mirages of green, shady places and running water. One man thought himself in the Alps. When they came upon an occasional spring they fell upon it like beasts, scooping away the moist earth with their hands, jamming their noses into the holes and fighting one another off savagely.

Fatherly "sir Karnet", who, by the way, charged and

[1] The oddly-written name of the rescuer, together with the story of the *Méduse* disaster, told sometimes with harrowing frankness, is given in *Le Radeau de la "Méduse"* by Armand Praviel.

was paid just 187 francs for all his devoted and efficient work, nourished the poor sufferers with sugar and "little American biscuits" and managed to procure from the natives in an oasis a scraggy ox. A gigantic negro "twisted its neck as if it were a chicken", and the ravenous people fell upon meat half raw. Indeed one poor creature, an Italian, gollopped down so much tough meat into his empty stomach that "he swelled up to horrible proportions, and could not walk. They dragged him out of the way and there he died next morning ".

One lone survivor crawled back to Saint-Louis without "sir Karnet's" help—poor half-crazed Corporal Guérin, old soldier and loyal husband.

Guérin took with him on the voyage to Africa his wife Clotilde. They put ashore together in the desert. Clotilde's strength failed and she begged Guérin to leave her, but this he would not do. Guérin stayed behind at her side, while the others crawled off on the weary way southward along the line of the ocean. Night came on, and Clotilde died. Guérin was digging a grave with his bare hands when from nearby came the growl of a great cat. Guérin rushed into the sea for safety. With the dawn he saw a terrible spectacle. Leopards had devoured his wife's body. Only her head was left. Guérin swore that he would carry this poor relic of his beloved to Saint-Louis and give it decent burial, and this he did. With a sort of mad grandeur he struggled alone over a month of desert, his dreadful treasure wrapped in rags torn from his shirt, and—a crazy skeleton himself—arrived at last to carry out his vow. He too was buried ten days later, having died in hospital.

So much for what befell those of the *Méduse's* company who sought refuge on land. As for the 147 persons who were left on the raft, fifteen survived and were saved by the

Argus after thirteen days of such physical suffering and moral degradation as seldom even the awful annals of shipwreck can parallel.[1]

The poor creatures of the raft went through many moods. To the stupefaction which they felt when the towline broke and they found themselves floating helplessly on that absurd platform, succeeded a certain optimism. They put up a make-shift sail and hoped for rescue. It would be perhaps a matter of hours. No rescue came. The night was stormy, the raft rolled so that all were drenched, some were half smothered, and some were lost overboard. Those last were the lucky ones, for they died swiftly, and innocent of the horrors and crimes that were to come.

Hallucinations now. Some saw the lights of phantom rescue ships. Two cabin-boys and a baker leapt overboard, telling the others not to be afraid, for they were going to fetch help and would be back soon. Others became violent, and some turned childishly peevish, asking to be served luxurious meals—"the white meat of chicken". Others saw a fine harbour. One officer announced soberly that he had written a letter to the authorities telling of their plight and that inside a few hours an answer would arrive and they would be safe.

The second night they fought amongst themselves. It was again wild weather. Some were swept overboard, some crushed and smothered to death. Some in despair tried to sink the raft so as to end their misery. Others were thrown overboard, and when they clung to the raft, their crazed opponents cut off their fingers. Between sixty and sixty-five men were lost that night.

Then everybody on the raft went mad. They were tortured by the exaggerated nervous hunger and thirst which comes to those who know there is no food nor

---

[1] A painting in the Musée du Louvre, *Le Radeau de la Méduse* by Géricault, shows the frenzied scene on the raft when the fifteen survivors spied the rescue ship.

drink to hand. Most of them were men of low type to start with—former criminals and ex-pirates. They had but one thing in common, a ferocious sense of grievance and hatred. First chewing bits of leather, cloth and hatbands, they soon were ready to accept the offering made to them by a black soldier—pieces of corpses that had been killed in the night's battle.

This was not all. One of the whites in authority, aided by the black who had taught the first lesson in cannibalism, decided to reduce their numbers and get rid of those so weak that in no case would they have survived much longer. The motive was probably to conserve the small quantity of wine which remained and some flying fish which had come aboard and could be eaten raw after draining their stomachs of the precious milky liquid. There were fifteen men left alive after this weeding out— an act relentlessly logical and inspired by the cold reasoning of brains made extra-lucid by starvation.

These fifteen made a pact among themselves. There were no more killings. They dealt together in loyal misery. One day they found a lemon tucked away somewhere in a pocket. One day they found a head of garlic. These they shared scrupulously. It would have been death to cheat. They sucked scraps of metal, buttons and the like, thinking that it calmed their thirst. Their bodies were so covered with sores produced by alternate soaking in sea water and burning of the tropic sun that they cried out at every movement.

On July 17th they were rescued, carried to Saint-Louis, and lodged there in the primitive hospital. Six died almost at once, including the negro soldier who had found it so pitifully easy to lead whites back to savagery.[1]

---

[1] A curious bit of psychology is that one of the fifteen survivors of the raft, a man named Correard, went back to Paris and opened a bookshop over which he hung the sign: "At the Shipwreck of the *Méduse*". It is agreeable to record that he soon failed in this morbid enterprise.

All of this grim story was told on the decks of the *Loire* as she bobbed and ducked before Saint-Louis. It was strong stuff for a boy's ears, a frightening and nauseating story for a lad just out of a country home, just away from a simple fireside. It was stuff to make a boy shudder. How Caillié reacted we can never know. But he was not discouraged.

In telling of this time, he says merely this: "Our transport, having happily for us separated from the route which was followed by the *Méduse*, arrived without accident in the roadstead of Saint-Louis." Caillié was never one to gush!

7

Days passed and still the *Loire* rode at anchor before Saint-Louis.

Something was wrong. Solicitude for the *Méduse's* sufferers changed to uneasiness for themselves. René heard the impatient mutterings of men eager to go ashore and get started at the business of colonizing, the romantic business which had lured them from prosaic, workaday France. Africa to them meant a lounging life under the palm trees, negro slaves to do all the hard labour, laughing black girls to fan them with ostrich plumes and slip exotic fruits into their lazy mouths, and perhaps—with luck—a gold patch in their very back-yard! Like all colonists, in those days when the world was untracked and mysterious, they had dreamed of this unknown land as a free picnic ground, a place where they might enjoy a honeymoon with a rich virgin Earth for bride. It would be everything for nothing—better than Eden.

Then the decks of the *Loire* blazed. Bewilderment. Dismay. Indignation. The English declined to leave. The French colonists had nowhere to go!

Why they were in this fix nobody seemed to know. It

was two years since the treaty gave them a right to Senegal. Had Paris blundered? Or London?

There were angry words on the *Loire*. The English are grinning at us. The English know we are too weak to insist. The English want to keep us out of Senegal till they get all the profit on this year's gum trade. (Gum-arabic was the wealth of the country, and the trade season at that moment in full swing.)

Embarrassment and amazement in the little English trading-post ashore. Wherever the fault lay for the mis-understanding, it was not with the English Lieutenant-Colonel in charge. Impossible to give up the post, so he declared, without orders from his superior at Sierra Leone.

The sudden French arrival in such pompous force— clergymen, women, experts, scientists, tradesmen—flabber-gasted the English. Fancy taking Senegal so seriously! To their notion Saint-Louis, which had changed hands seven times in fifty-seven years and where the Lieutenant-Governor had been camping in part of a ruined factory, was quite unworthy of all this fuss. Perhaps the English *did* grin!

The villain of the affair, according to the French was one "Lord MacCarthy" of Sierra Leone.

"Lord MacCarthy" (then a mere Colonel, not yet knighted, but ennobled by certain French chroniclers in that polite fashion so frequent when the French speak of distinguished Englishmen) was really no villain and presumably was not to blame. MacCarthy was in fact a saintly figure. His fate was so gruesome that it would have distressed even the angriest Frenchman on the *Loire*, if he could have read the future.

MacCarthy for ten years governed with fine devotion the land which was the "White Man's Grave" and super-vised a wild undefined sweep of tropic West Africa that was said to stretch "from 20 degrees North to 20 degrees

South". He was, to quote the pidgin English tribute of one of his black subjects, "a good man too much" who caused "everybody have much work, much money, much laugh". He was called the "Good Father of Sierra Leone", He even sought to import into his unwholesome domain, by the way of matrimony, of course, a Good Mother, "a lady of good sense and good nature, capable and assiduous in superintending . . . civilization" (This from a letter which he wrote to Zachary Macaulay). But MacCarthy was killed by the Ashantis, and his skull was made into a drinking cup. Sixty years after his death this ghastly trophy was still paraded through Kumasi with a red rag bound round the forehead to represent a bloody bandage, its porter leaping and dancing and shouting the while.[1]

Until such time as London, or cruel "Lord MacCarthy", should instruct the English Lieutenant-Governor of Saint-Louis to move away, the French leader, Schmaltz, was in a tragic and ridiculous fix. He had a colony on his hands and no place to put it. Literally no place. Saint-Louis was closed to him. Little Gorée Island was closed to him. And that was all there was to Senegal, so far as whites were concerned. Senegal was not such a square of territory as we think of today when we use the word "colony". It consisted of just two points.

It was decided that the forlorn and homeless French colonists should seek refuge on the mainland of Cape Vert as paying guests of the natives. Their position would be ticklish. They had no real rights at Cape Vert and the natives there were known to be particularly independent. Schmaltz gave instructions that immediately upon arrival they should assure the natives that their stay would be only temporary.

The *Loire* sailed off to the southward and anchored before "the village of Dakar".

---

[1] *The Tshi-Speaking Peoples of the Gold Coast*, A. B. Ellis, 1887.

Dakar has developed with startling rapidity. Eighty years ago it was an unknown black village (the French did not take possession of it till 1857). Today it is the seat of the Governor-General of French West Africa, a territory of nearly five million square kilometres with a total population of fourteen and a half millions.

At Dakar village René Caillié set foot for the first time on the soil of Africa. It was July 21, 1816. René was sixteen years old.

The Presqu'île du Cap Vert, to give the place of Caillié's first African sojourn the name by which he knew it, was on the day of his arrival in its full dangerous beauty, lush and feverish, for it was the time of the rains. It was the place of "limpid brooklets, flowers of a thousand colours, trees of a thousand forms, birds of a thousand species" which an early French governor of Senegal, the poetic Chevalier de Boufflers, described to his dear lady love. A few months later this changeable land would become an arid red brick, and would justify the scorn of Christopher Columbus, who when he passed the Cape Vert Islands said plaintively that their name was "false" and that there was not one thing to be seen there of a green colour.

René must have been delighted by his first glimpse of Cape Vert. It would have seemed the real Africa of his most imaginative childhood dreams—a place of unearthly beauty, very fantastic, almost capable of sheltering fairies and goblins.

Out of bright red soil sprang exotic trees—date-palms, papaws, pineapples and baobabs. René, who know only the demure trees of Mauzé, poplars and honest oaks and fruit trees, must have shivered when he looked at his first great baobab—a huge thing, big as a castle, with a trunk thirty feet in diameter. The baobab is "the most monstrous object in all the vegetable world" to quote the words of a startled eighteenth-century traveller. It is the monkey-bread tree, the *Adansonia digitata*, named after Adanson, the French naturalist who first studied the flora of Senegal—and what a tree to bear one's name through the ages! The baobab is a department store and a hotel. Its fibre makes rope and cloth. Its fruit is of agreeable taste. Its leaves flavour native stews and beverages. It supplies a useful primitive medicine. And many a negro family lives cosily in a scooped-out cave in its trunk. But when the baobab's leaves fall and it stands in giant nakedness, squat and with its enormous trunk big and bare as a windowless house, it is the most desolate thing in nature, unforgettably strange and terrible.

The native here was at his very blackest—the Wolof, renowned for his brilliant ebony skin, his great shining teeth, and because he is the most garrulous and the most hilarious of all the negro races. These folk, who have a roar of laughter and a whirlwind of gesturing for life's smallest incident, must have gone into a frenzy at the sudden arrival on their shores of a shipload of white men and women.

A frightening scene of welcome it must have been to these tired and demoralized people, with the Wolofs bounding and galloping to meet them in their dusky near-nudity.

But the Wolofs of Cape Vert were no negligible band of savages. They were a peculiar community, a group of rebels who had revolted and formed themselves into a small black republic some ten to fifteen thousand strong, living in five villages which they operated according to the laws of the Koran under a headman learned in sacred things. It is easy to sympathize with their rebellion. Their former king, the Damel of the Kingdom of Cayor, had—like the other kings of West Africa—believed himself entitled to "the right of life, death and pillage", and hunted his subjects as if they were beasts, selling them to the slavers for their poor value in rum and brandy. (A slave's "weight in drunkenness" was variable, running from a scant jugful of diluted spirits to enough fine bottles to keep a village merry for a week.) With grim resignation the major part of this kingdom of poor savages seriously described themselves as "the Damel's slaves" and submitted to their ruler's cruel method of keeping up his wine cellars, but the population of Cape Vert—their independence both fathered and favoured by their geographical position on a rocky promontory—revolted.

Shocking indeed was the state of things from which they sought to free themselves. Let me quote from a contemporary traveller's account of the native scene when the Damel was on a rampage:[1]

"Gandiolle, since the Damel had been there, resembled a city which a conqueror had pillaged. What a difference from Europe where the presence of the sovereign usually brings pleasure and plenty! Most of the huts were abandoned or destroyed. . . . He had demanded of Gandiolle a contribution of eighty-three slaves, and taken them by violence. . . . Desolation reigned at Kelkom where we arrived at midday. The Damel had pillaged the village, alone were left the crippled negroes and they gave us terrifying pictures of the ills which their families had suffered. Many of their relatives had perished in resisting the cruel orders of the King, but the greater number now groaned in irons. . . . Bedienne, which we passed next, was waiting momentarily to be ravaged by the Damel. . . . Terror of the Damel had led the greater part of the population to desert Niakra where I arrived at sunset."

Sons sold their fathers. A certain King sold his Prime Minister and all his family, thirteen persons in all. In one year, 1793,—and it was not an exceptional one—the different European Powers landed in the New World 74,000 slaves, says Robert Brown in *The Story of Africa*. It was, of course, the development of America that caused

[1] Mollien's *Voyage dans l'Intérieur de l'Afrique aux Sources du Sénégal et de la Gambie fait en* 1818.

the slave trade to become so vast a horror over Africa. Till then the export slave trade had been a luxury affair, a mere matter of supplying occasional negroes to be the showy and pampered servants in rich men's establishments.

The blacks viewed the whites as villains. Said one traveller in the early part of the eighteenth century: "the natives say it is the Christians who invented the commerce in slaves and that before their coming we all·lived in the most profound peace!" The official suppression of the slave trade by the various white nations in the early years of the nineteenth century led to a yet more horrible secret trade. The profit to be made by handling contraband slaves was so huge—sometimes 800 per cent—that conscience and decency wilted. In those awful days "a slaver's vessel contained in a limited space the greatest mass of tortures and atrocities it would be possible to accumulate"—such was the admission of a man himself a trader. Squashed together—the space allowed in the slave decks even for a tall man is stated to have been from twenty-three inches to two and a half feet in height—the poor blacks were a confused *mélange* of arms and legs, filth and misery. Many were crushed to death each day of the voyage.

Luckier were the slaves whom the negro kings now dared not drive openly to the coast and who were mercifully killed. Nine hundred were once killed in a single batch.

No wonder that the Wolofs of Cape Vert rebelled and caused the sport of man-hunting on their neck of land to become so dangerous that the thirsty Damel left them alone.

No wonder they were vigilant in their independence. Almost under their noses was a daily warning. Cape Vert was a short canoe ride from the infamous slave depot of Gorée, that scrap of rock where slaves, captured in the interior, and dragged to the coast along paths "marked by skeletons" were stored, awaiting shipment overseas, in the homes of rich traders—each house having as a matter of course its gruesome iron-barred "captivery" in place of the usual cellar.

The Cape Vert natives frequently visited the island to deliver supplies of fresh water to the desolate place, to offer fish and other matters for sale, or to carry away Gorée's many dead—there being no burial-place on its rocky surface. Then they stared in horror and self-congratulation toward those awful *barracoons* into which they too might have been packed in misery, "waiting for the Christians to eat them", had they not had the courage to rebel. With what sympathy and delight they must have observed the slave mutinies of 1763 and 1777, when the Gorée fort was blown up, the town burned, white masters trembled, and slaves—free once more—danced high carnival and swilled rum. And with what a mixture of mystification and relief they must gradually have got it into their woolly heads that these whites from over the water were giving up the slave trade and that black men were no longer to be game for white hunting—that there had commenced a "closed season" for negroes.

Beside their grim dealings with Gorée the Cape Vert natives had enjoyed another and very profitable contact with white folk before ever the *Loire* sailed into their harbour.

They were professional salvagers. Shipwrecks were frequent. Every sail was a prospect and every storm spelt hope. They studied the horizon when the hurricane blew, for a wrecked ship was as truly an offering from the generous gods as a fine catch of fish. The ship—or what was left of it when it ran upon their rocky shores—was their prize. The crew, if they could be saved, were their prisoners to be held for ransom.[1]

[1] Later a treaty was arranged between the Dakar chief, Moktar Diop, and the French—a truly comical document,—whereby it was agreed that instead of grabbing wreck and survivors, the natives should aid in rescue work for one-third the cargo and the then colossal wage for African natives of two and a half francs a day. *Histoire de la Presqu'ile du Cap Vert et des origines de Dakar* by Claude Faure.

Clever savages these, quite able to see that there was much to be gained by supplying Schmaltz's wandering colony with camping space and odd supplies.

Chief Moktar Diop showed himself most friendly. He was under the influence, it was said, of a certain old negress who loved all the French because long ago, when she was slim and sleek, a Frenchman had loved her and made her his temporary wife.

Moktar Diop did his meagre best and was subsequently rewarded by a life pension of a pound of fresh bread every day (to be supplied by the baker at Gorée) and fifty-four francs every month, "as a token of the services he had rendered".

Despite Moktar's good-will, Caillié and his companions were very uncomfortable. It was no moment for al fresco life, being the wet season, which is surprisingly called "*hivernage*" in the French African colonies although it occurs in the summer. (The name means the winter period when ships are laid up.) The *hivernage* is not really a season but a catastrophe!

To René it seemed, when the tornadoes broke, as if the roof had been jerked off the world. The rain fell not in drops but in mile-wide waves, cloud-bursts that knocked men to the ground, crushed native huts and broke off trees at their roots. Thunder crashed—the "tremendous thunder" at which Mungo Park marvelled, the thunder of Africa "of which no person can form a conception". Great trees fell splintering. Everything was in a continuous blaze of blinding light. No time to count the seconds between flash and crash, for the flashing and the crashing never stopped. Nature was in a convulsion, she seemed—like a maddened scorpion—to be trying to bite herself to death.

Then suddenly the rain ceased. There came a cold wind, cruelly chill on damp bodies. And after the wind

dank heat till the next tornado broke. On the ground
near the villages, where natives had tossed all manner
of domestic filth—garbage, sewerage, dead animals—
a noisome mud formed, which boiled wickedly in the
tropic heat and bred germs. Flies and mosquitoes, in that
democratic way of theirs, distributed the various resultant
sicknesses and fevers. Almost everyone fell ill, and that
old quip, typical of the pathetic bravado of the West
Coast, "Well, how many died last night?" became the
usual cynical morning salutation.

Of adequate shelter, at this season when camping out
was so particularly unsuitable, there was none. The
natives could offer no accommodation, their own homes
being only sufficient for themselves and, at that, mere
bee-hive shaped huts made of rushes, so flimsy that
visitors talked to the occupant through the walls, not
bothering to go to the door. They were tiny things into
which one went bent double, every man—even the poorest
—having two, one to sleep in and one as a kitchen.

There were only four houses on the Cape, houses which
had been built as country houses by people at Gorée.
These the colonists rented, and in them—without furni-
ture—lodged the big-wigs, including Caillié's new master,
Lieutenant-Colonel de Foncin, named by Schmaltz as
Commandant of the camp.

René had been promoted to work for this important
personage. We wonder what his work may have been
in serving the Commandant in his wretched house "without chairs or table, which the tornadoes inundated",
and where every comfort was lacking. De Foncin was
effusively thankful for a gift from Schmaltz—some quinine,
some flannel and some "English biscuits, which were good
to dip in coffee". But the quinine did not save Caillié's
master, who was an elderly man and feeble. He died
after two months in the Dakar camp.

The rank and file of the colonists lived in the straw-covered sheds which had been hurriedly run up, leaning against the houses and which, as might have been expected, lost their roofs at the first tornado. Mercifully the English major in charge at Gorée consented to let women and children and the very sickest of the sick move over to the comparative civilization of the island.

Disorder and disaffection grew. Thirteen soldiers deserted with their arms, setting off across country in the notion that the unknown interior of this awful continent could not be worse than the Dakar camp. These adventurers were promptly captured by the natives and sold back to the command. No wonder that certain desolate young officers wrote a pitiful appeal to be allowed to go home to France. The Captain of the *Loire* might ship them in any capacity he liked, they wrote, so long as they were carried back to France and their dear families. For ever they would view him as "their liberator". These poor young men had been through the *Méduse* horror and then this awful period at the Dakar camp. One can understand their longing to go home and forget Africa for all time.

Another officer wrote: "this Africa produces only monsters and poisons and slaves. . . . Not a single good day, sun hidden in a thick veil of black clouds or behind whirling sand. Worse climate than England. Nature is alive with insects, ferocious animals and reptiles—nothing else to mention."

Amongst all these disgruntled people Caillié purred like a happy kitten. He alone was enjoying himself. What did it concern this adventurous boy that the sober Plan of Colonization—this rash attempt to harness Africa in a jiffy—was in a tangle? He was wallowing in adventure. Physically, it is true, the frail lad must have suffered

intensely. What horror to be swept at night by a tornado
—he who in his stuffy peasant home in France had
probably never admitted a breath of air into his sleeping-
room, winter or summer! But every morning he woke
to the glorious realization that he was in Africa, really
and actually in Africa. He had craved Africa, and he was
getting it in its most characteristic form. And still he asked
for more.

Caillié was learning to stand hardship and live. Nowadays we inoculate men against fever before sending them
on tropic service. But we have no method of inoculating
them against the dreadful discomforts of wild life. Caillié
was inoculated by boyhood experience. Just out of childhood, an unimportant person and presumably the least
petted of them all, he had survived where so many
perished. Perhaps it was his boyish enthusiasm that saved
him. He had lived through the worst which the tropics
could offer—a disordered and demoralized amateur
expedition camping out in the bad season alongside dirty
native villages, constant drenching, underfeeding, contaminated water, deadly contagious fevers all about him,
no hygiene, the bites of disease-bearing mosquitoes, terrible
heat. It was a true apprenticeship in misery, and of
immense value to Caillié's future. No other explorer ever
received such boyhood training.

At last, seven months after the imposing departure from
France, Schmaltz was able to move the battered remnant
of his colony away from the Dakar camp.

Caillié, insignificant little hanger-on, left with the rest.
If he could have looked forward a century to the Dakar
of today he would have seen a port into which great
liners come to tie up, a railway terminus whence trains
plunge out across eight hundred odd miles to the Niger,
a Cathedral with the beautiful name *Souvenir Africain*.
But, being very human, the finest thing in all Dakar to

him would be a certain enamel plaque which marks a main street running into Dakar's market-place, a plaque which reads:

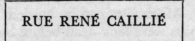

RUE RENÉ CAILLIÉ

8

FRANCE TOOK OVER her inheritance in Senegal on January 25, 1817. At noon on that impatiently-awaited day the British flag was hauled down and the white flag with its *fleur-de-lys*, the romantic flag of Royalist France, run up on Saint-Louis fort, and there can be no doubt that young René Caillié, one of the few of the new-comers who was not ill in bed, did his share in the huzzaing.

And then with the miraculous courage of pioneers and colonists, who, the world over, are never quite normal people, everybody forgot the months of waiting and misery, forgot the dead, and turned their faces hopefully toward the hard new endeavour, the effort to transform this uncouth lump of Africa into a prosperous colony. Schmaltz, their energetic and unlucky leader, showed almost fantastic optimism and pronounced the climate, which must be one of the worst known to man, to be "salubrious".

Now, more than a century later, we see that the courageous hopes of the early colonists were well based. Senegal is the most important part of France's empire in tropic Africa. By its prestige it has given a name to that rollicking group of black soldiers, the "Senegalese", although these splendid black fighters are by no means all from Senegal, being some of them Sudanese, Mossi and Dahomans, and from Chad and Guinea. And of the native civil population of Senegal some thirty thousand possess the title of French citizens. The colony has turned out as well as those who formed the Colonization Plan could have hoped. Their only mistake was one which is common to whites who invade Africa—they were in too great a hurry. Africa is not to be hustled.

These colonists were long dead before Senegal began to prosper, and of all the fine party who went out on the *Loire* and her sister ships—the officials, and scientists, and army officers, and mining engineers, and experts in this and that— none made the fortune of his dreams. Nor did any of them make an important reputation for himself in this new land.

The names of the important men of the group—even down to the specialist gardeners—are recorded in the archives of the period, but one may search in vain for the name of René Caillié. Yet of them all it was to Caillié alone that Africa gave honour and greatness and a big reward.

Proud Schmaltz, for instance, "the Commandant for the King and Administrator of Senegal and Dependencies", went back to France disgruntled and a job-hunter and finished his career as consul at Smyrna—certainly not a grand destiny!

In Caillié's day Saint-Louis was the only white city on the Atlantic coast of Africa, the only point of white civilization for nearly seven thousand miles.

Even today the white cities of tropic West Africa are quickly counted. Then there was only Saint-Louis. The other white settlements, strung along sparsely on coasts of desert sand and dank forest, were mere trading-posts, slave stations, small forts. And of course there was queer, idealistic Freetown.

Far and wide—up into the Sahara and out across the Sudan—this little white town, a poor thing to Europeans, was a marvel to Moorish and black Africans. To them it was known as N'Dar, which means simply "The City". Awe can go no further than that!

To the native mind N'Dar was the epitome of white culture, a glimpse of the puzzling white ideal. At Saint-Louis they could study these mysterious white men "who lived always on the sea in boats" and who had stepped ashore to construct at the mouth of the Senegal, betwixt the desert and the Atlantic, a permanent city of stone and great logs of wood—stone that must be fetched from way up-river, and wood from America!—an amazing place to the West-Coast African, whose custom it was to live informally in flimsy buildings made of clay or straw and to build fresh huts as whim and circumstance suggested.

Saint-Louis was a town with a settled population, a town with a past four centuries long. Saint-Louis had a history as romantic and exciting as that of many an old town in Europe, had seen many masters, wild gaiety and tropic luxury, and had fought off bravely the attacks of a hundred bands of jealous Moors and negroes. Of all the adventures which Saint-Louis knew, the oddest was that she remained for years the unique colonial possession of the deposed French Royal Family! Louis XVI appointed a governor to the town in 1788 and, though Paris cut the King's head off, it forgot to change the King's arrangements with regard to his namesake city. It shows how remote Africa was from Europe in those old sailing-ship days. So General Blanchot went on governing year after year, fought off the Moors and the English, became the idol of the native population, who knew him as "*le brave Général*", their white father, and "set an example of the ideal fusion of the white and black races by contracting a marriage "*à la mode du pays*"—which means a union with a handsome black girl to endure as long as he remained in Africa.

Saint-Louis had become with the years a pretty place, a gay place, such a place as one might expect where the

French temperament was warmed by a torrid climate. Its whites had been through the generations adventurous and reckless, and the mulatto population, a gallant, picturesque lot, immoral, gay, luxurious.

Life was hectic in Saint-Louis, hectic and usually short —the climate saw to that. Days were feverish and unreal. It was a year round grim carnival—a city dancing on pie-crust. Who could deny himself the extra drink, the night of love, the rowdy banquet which might be his last? Death came so quickly there in Senegal. One should carry no regrets to that sudden grave!

So few scrupled to form "Saint-Louis marriages", choosing girls with velvet black or soft brown skins, supple as young panthers, with big eyes full of swiftly alternating passion and greed, and lithe bodies which squirmed ecstatically into the clasp of unfamiliar corsets and the smooth caress of silk dresses and Paris bangles. "*Signares*" they were called, these enticing brides. It was a name of Portuguese origin. The "marriage" was solemnized solely by the ceremony of a nuptial dinner-party graced by other lovely *signares* in colourful plumage and officers in uniform—and by the priest, who accepted African morals as he found them. Afterwards a ball, dancing on the enclosed terrace—for the houses of Saint-Louis were of Oriental style—and flirting out under the great African stars.

To René Caillié, Saint-Louis showed a different face, stranger and more savage. This humble working boy had no chance to attend glamorous fêtes and dance with satin-clad *signares*, and probably no wish for it. He was not like the others. He had no wish to pretend that he was not in Africa. He rejoiced in Africa. Just to be here made every day a holiday.

He watched wild negro dances on moonlit nights—

half-naked black men and women with wide white teeth and rolling eyes who broke suddenly and unaccountably into rhythmic stamping and hand-clapping and lascivious wrigglings, while the crowd beat on little tom-toms and uttered sharp queer cries.

He wandered into the native market on the sands at Guet N'Dar—the native suburb—a negro ant-hill with natives scrambling over one another, and pot-bellied naked babies rolling under foot, and crippled and leprous beggars crawling hither and thither, moaning and pleading. There were naked women and veiled women, boys in rags and men in fine white robes, mothers with tiny babies strapped to their backs and old crones with breasts that hung down like the teats of cows. There were more flies to every square yard than there would be in all Mauzé for a whole summer. There was a sickening stink of dried fish. There was all the colour and clamour and stench of Africa spread out to thrill the senses of a curious boy.

Camels stood with one foreleg tied to prevent their running away while their insolent masters, Moors from the desert, chaffered gloomily for trinkets and millet. Wealthy merchants measured gold-dust with infinite care on little scales, *midioni*, using seeds of the carob tree as weights. Each carob seed weighed as much as four wheat grains. Canny merchants, when buying, gave their carob seeds an over-night bath!

Everything conceivable was offered for sale, from sweetmeats to the hair of dead negresses. A dozen different races, strangely dressed and undressed, shouted and quarrelled and stank.

And there was the desert, the glorious, terrible Sahara, stretching out to the North: smooth, quiet sands, full of mystery. Sometimes he walked out to the desert's edge, actually walked on the sands of the Sahara. He stooped and patted them with his hand, passed grains between his fingers, looked to the horizon and wondered.

The river bank, the bank of the mighty Senegal, was splendid too, a river of danger and delight to a thousand queer beasts—beasts which came to drink and beasts which came to kill.

He watched gazelles bounding away through the brush on swift, brittle-looking legs with their small tails impudently twinkling. They invariably ran in a zigzag course, he noticed, and the soft markings of their beige and white hides merged into the dazzling landscape so that almost at once they became invisible. This was a trick they had learned to dodge the pursuit of lions, he was told. Lions—yes; people talked casually of lions, and crocodiles, and ostriches.

At night hyenas called out mournfully, and by day groups of motionless vultures stared down fixedly from the branches of the baobabs—"waiting for us to die, and they won't have long to wait!" grim old settlers told him. Even the wild birds were startling. They had none of the timid daintiness of little French birds. They were garish things—livid metallic blue, or burning red, or harshly black and white in stripes.

And the strangest thing of all was impalpable. It was the light and the sunshine, which made it seem as if he was on another planet, as if Senegal was much nearer to the sun than he had ever been before. Its rays shimmered and leapt like dangerous wild creatures, and the gleaming sand seemed to wriggle and rise and fall like the sea. It was like walking on waves. It made everything seem unreal and magical. Sometimes he felt as if he had only to shut his eyes and then open them again and there he would be at the gates of Timbuctoo, the golden and the secret!

Neither the French nor the English were forgetting Timbuctoo and the gold of inner Africa. A continent lay there waiting for the nation that could first push into her mysteries and plant its flag. The opening up of Africa was a competitive business, a race between England and France.

Saint-Louis observed jealously the preparations for a new English expedition with its hundred men and two hundred beasts of burden, its expensive equipment, its artillery and its distinguished leadership. Young Caillié felt a jealousy of a far more burning and personal kind. These lucky men were getting the chance to do what he longed to do, what he had come to Africa for. He listened to every scrap of gossip which came his way. The pious care with which he recorded in his *Journal* the fine hopes and the tragic finish of the English expedition proves how close it all was to his heart.

The appointed leader of the expedition, Major Peddie, was probably known personally to Caillié, for Peddie had been stationed at Saint-Louis and had been in Gorée during the period when the French were waiting to take over the colony.

Peddie had won French affection by his goodness to the survivors of the *Méduse* when they lay in misery in the primitive hospital. An old lithograph shows Peddie, handsome and gracious, standing beside the cot of one of the survivors, and indicating with a gesture that the kneeling negro at his feet brings offerings of food and drink for the comfort of the sick and almost naked Frenchman.

The Frenchman's costume, incidentally, is better suited to the climate than the ceremonious uniform of Major Peddie, who wears high collar, heavy long-tailed coat, woollen trousers and thick boots. It is a curious circumstance that it took Europeans many generations to venture to adapt their dress to tropical conditions. One finds repeated complaints in the reminiscences of old-time travellers of "the obligation to button yourself up to the

throat in the African climate" or of the misery of dining
in "a cloth coat, dignified and uncomfortable". Although
it was then an almost exclusively male society, none
dreamed of relaxing the conventions. One English gentleman—a real desperado !—confesses that when he was
alone in the forest with two black guides, he dared to walk
along "released from the restraint of sartorial bondage,
the neck no longer tight bandaged, the limbs independent
and the feet emancipated from a leathery vice."

The Foreign Legion seems to have set the fashion of
wearing lighter clothes for African service, so far as the
French were concerned. In 1841 newly arrived soldiers in
Algeria were "scandalized to observe old Africans, who had
substituted the kepi for the shako and a cotton neck-cloth
for the stiff collar" (*La Conquête de l'Algérie* by Pierre de la
Gorce). The sun-helmet for French troop came later still.

Major Peddie, to return to his unhappy story, assumed
charge of an imposing body of men and beasts, artillery,
fellow officers and experts, and proceeded to the mouth
of the Rio Nunez (in what is now the colony of French
Guinea). He hoped to lead his men inland, over the rib
of the Futa Jalon mountains and on to the Niger banks,
but Peddie died of fever on New Year's Day, 1817, before
he had been able to proceed a single step along his adventurous road. Captain Campbell then took charge. During
the months of his ensuing misery he must often have wished
that he too might have been laid in the grave by the side
of his leader on that New Year's Day. The expedition
went from one trouble to another—sickness, terrible
paths over mountains, native treachery and plundering,
loss of pack animals, imprisonment by the Almamy (or
ruler) of Futa Jalon. After months of delay and persecution the Almamy turned the English back to the coast,
first charging them a heavy sum in goods for the privilege

of retreating. So big an expedition, said the Almamy, could only have come with hostile intent. Encouraged by their ruler, the natives harried the English back over the cruel mountain passes and Campbell in despair burned what was left of his outfit to make the going lighter, abandoned cannon, broke muskets and threw gunpowder into the river. It was a rout, a complete disaster Campbell got what remained of his men back to the coast, and then he died. African had triumphed again.

Perhaps the French at Saint-Louis smiled grimly in their turn, as the English had done at the time of the *Méduse* catastrophe. But René did not smile. In his heart he felt that he belonged already to the explorers' guild—a guild above international jealousies. Peddie and Campbell were his brothers.

The bulldog British never dreamed of quitting. Scarcely was Campbell buried than a new expedition, or rather an improved and enlarged edition of the old expedition, was planned. It was to be led by Major Gray, who, though he had been through all the hardships of the Peddie-Campbell fiasco, still possessed the vigour and courage to tackle Africa again. Gray was evidently a glutton for punishment.

News came to Saint-Louis of Major Gray's plans and preparations. His expedition would be even more important than the first, a *de luxe* affair, and to avoid the rapacious Almamy, the English this time would take another road inland, starting from a point up the Gambia River.

It was more than Caillié could bear. Here were men pushing again into Africa, while he plodded along on dull jobs in this safe little city, and listened to gossip about the gum trade and the pretty brown girls round the corner. He might as well be back home cobbling. This Englishman might win through, might prise Africa open, and leave it a hollow shell.

Further news came about Major Gray. He had reached

Bathurst at the mouth of the Gambia and was getting his company into final shape for the plunge into Africa. Fifteen camels had gone down from Senegal. It was said that he was ready to engage more men if suitable fellows presented themselves.

When René heard this he lost his head completely. He was practically penniless, without money for ship or caravan. He decided to *walk* across savage Africa to the Gambia and offer himself to the Englishman. It was one of the maddest ideas which ever came into a young man's head, and the fact that René succeeded in carrying out even a part of the project is proof of a tenacity and endurance that seem miraculous.

The total distance was some three hundred miles. The way lay at first to Cape Vert, about one hundred and sixty miles across semi-desert,[1] rough country of sand, salt marshes and scrub, then incredibly dry and desolate, for it was the season of complete drought.

René discovered a pair of negroes going southward and persuaded them to let him join them. The party set off. There were days of torture and nights of torment. There was no shelter from the beasts which prowled and the beasts which crawled: hyenas, jackals, occasional lions, and armies of crabs. They took the only possible way—very close to the sea so as to have ground firm enough to walk upon. Therefore they were far from oases and from wells of fresh water, and suffered atrociously from thirst.

---

[1] Not far from the line of Caillié's absurdly heroic tramp, but making its way over slightly better country, now runs the first railway which every startled the eyes of negro Africa. (Saint-Louis to Dakar, 163 miles, first rails laid 1882, inaugurated two years later.) The negroes were instantly tickled by the trains, and crushed delightedly and without fear into the open box car provided for them. In the early days an accident killed a whole car-load of natives. It was supposed that the new entertainment would become unpopular. Not a bit of it! Next day the black pleasure-seekers crowded back, but they had all equipped themselves with talismans of safety. Their *marabouts* (holy men) had sold every negro a "*gris-gris* against the railway trains". (*La Mission Hourst* by Lieutenant de Vaisseau Hourst.) It seems a pleasant variant on the white man's travel insurance to substitute peace of mind during the trip for a depressing promise of compensation after a disaster.

The two negroes were in a desperate hurry. Some clutching motive—fear, greed, or turbulent savage love—drove them forward at a rush. Even for them it was hard going, though they were used to this climate which is so notoriously torrid that on old French thermometers its name figured as a special rubric almost at the top, a little above 100°, "*Température du Sénégal*". So scorching is the heat of the South-Saharan belt that the native used when possible to turn night into day, rising to eat *couscous* at two in the morning, opening the Koranic schools at three, and setting all the village life in movement before the rising of the cruel sun.

René's two companions strode along on feet that were tougher than leather. To René they seemed like inspired demons loping ahead of him, always ahead. He panted and staggered after them at a jogging run, half dead with thirst, teased by the unceasing desert wind, his feet blistered and cut to bleeding ribbons, his eyes dazzled by the shimmer of the dried salt marshes and the glitter of the sand and the sea. He fell asleep as he walked. His head reeled with fever and he was full of delirious dreams of the adventures and triumphant discoveries which awaited him when he joined Major Gray on the Gambia.

It was no feat to boast about. Caillié himself afterwards recalled it with shame. But it was a consoling proof of grit to remember in hard days to come—the first notch on his gun. And proof of a fanatical longing to get started on his chosen career which presaged for René either success or an early death. It was as if he were voluntarily submitting himself to one of those tests of manhood such as African natives inflict upon their young males at initiation time—as if he was deliberately torturing himself, trying to see what he could stand.

Certainly this first African adventure of Caillié's would

have satisfied the ordinary plucky boy and sent him home to reminisce hair-raisingly for the rest of his days. The fact that Caillié went back again and again to let Africa pound him is significant. Evidently Caillié really wanted Africa, craved and thirsted for Africa.

At last—it must have been after a week or more of struggle through the sands—René and the two negroes reached Dakar. It was about half way to his goal on the Gambia. Caillié got himself ferried across to the Island of Gorée, thinking there perhaps to find a ship going southward.

His state was pitiable, and men who saw him, and most especially the Commandant of Gorée, Gavot, took him in charge. René told his story, protesting that he must go on. To the Commandant it seemed hysteria, the waste of a brave boy's life. Appalling hardships were before him. He was already at the end of his strength. Major Gray would have no use for a skeleton such as he would be, if ever by a miracle he did reach the Gambia. Such was the burden of Gavot's persuasions. Gavot, by the way, was a Colonel of cavalry, very oddly cast as Governor of a small horseless island, who was at the moment expressing his impatience by indulging in a spot of smuggling. Caillié owed him his life.

For René listened to his new friend. Caillié was an enthusiast, but he was not a fool. It is a quality of the genius as opposed to the crank that he can distinguish between mad effort that might win and mad effort that must fail.

René wanted to live. He wanted to get to Timbuctoo. He bit his lip and bade good-bye to hopes of becoming Major Gray's right-hand man, not knowing that he and the Major were destined to meet after all, and before so very long.

Gavot, with that almost maternal understanding of a

boy's disappointment which a man can sometimes show, found a new interest for René, procured him a free passage to Guadeloupe, and shipped him off on another voyage.

But Caillié was not a lad able to forget the old love in the arms of a new mistress. He was loyal to Africa, and as his ship carried him away westward across the Atlantic to Guadeloupe, his thoughts were all of the arid desert there to the East, and the hidden city he meant to discover some day.

9

RENÉ CAILLIÉ IN Guadeloupe, working in what he admits humbly in his *Journal* was "*un petit emploi*", a poor job, had an emotional experience which was like a re-conversion. By a miraculous accident he came upon Mungo Park's book, that wonderful, fresh account of his journey into Africa for the African Association, which is as readable and exciting today as it was when Park's 1795–7 voyage was news. It gave the French boy his first authentic and detailed information about the interior of Africa.

Caillié was stuck in prosaic exile. Guadeloupe, though first presented to white knowledge as the excitingly gruesome place where Columbus's men found human flesh roasting in routine fashion at every family hearth, was in Caillié's day dull and workaday. René fell on Park's book. He seems to have been born to be influenced by books; or rather, in some queer way, he attracted into his hands, which did not handle many books, just those volumes which he craved for inspiration. First it was Defoe's romance, then Park's realism.

Park's book wrenched his heart with a pang of physical jealousy. It was as if he read another's letters to his beloved. Park on his knees bathing his hot eager face

in the Great River and crying: "She runs to the East!"
—for till then no European knew her course—it was an
unbearable, thrilling taunt to the French boy.

René bit his knuckles and cried out for Africa. He read
phrases like: "Timbuctoo, the great object of my search"
and "Timbuctoo, altogether in possession of that savage
and merciless people (the Moors) who allow no
Christian. . . ." He read how Park was told that the Niger
"went to the world's end": Mungo Park's Niger, "broad
as the Thames at Westminster"—patriotic, homesick
Mungo to drag in the relatively miniature Thames!

Park was to look upon the great river where she was
many miles across, when nine years later he sailed down
her course to his death—a splendid, odd figure in long coat
and large gloves[1] commanding a crazy, patched *pirogue*,
"His Majesty's schooner *Joliba*", whence he shot at every
black in range, and gave an unfortunate impression of
Christian civilization to the mystified natives.

Heat-maddened, tortured by tropic sickness, and
horrified by the deaths of his friends and associates—
"The Wild Beast" he was named by such Niger natives
as could get out of his path. He wrote in his farewell:
"though I were myself half-dead I would still persevere,
and if I could not succeed in the object of my journey,
I would at last die on the Niger," and then set off to ride
over the brink of the world, taking a retinue of black dead
with him, like any African potentate. Africa, grand and
terrible, had made a madman of a decent Scotch doctor!

As Caillié read Park's story and wondered what Park's
fate had been—for the tragedy of it was then but dimly
known—all the wonder and colour of Africa came up

---

[1] So did an old chief on the Niger describe Park to Barth nearly fifty years later.
Barth had dealings with an old man who had been wounded in the leg by Park's
shots when a boy. "I was therefore rather afraid," says Barth, "that he might
take an opportunity of revenging himself upon me." And adds that there was no
doubt Laing's murder was instigated by such feelings of revenge.

before him. Africa played on his young nerves, rousing biting nostalgia and longing. Crimson and burnt orange, dank, dangerous green, and sinister ebony—colours he had glimpsed; heat in gusts and waves; the dramatic crash of African thunder; the tender emerald of brooklets moistened by the first days of the *hivernage*; the throb of Saint-Louis's tom-toms; the ungainly, awful strength of an ostrich's giant leg; the little wistful monkeys in the trees near Dakar; negresses smiling in innocent provocation; pot-bellied black children; that noise far-off that made men shiver and cross themselves, whispering, "*lions!*"

"I must go back!" cried Caillié. "I must go back to Africa!"

So, after six months in Guadeloupe, Caillié turned his face to the East. By those fortuitous and undefined methods which enable poor young men in a hurry to get somewhere, working at this or that or anything for their passage, he got back across the Atlantic. He passed by Bordeaux and went to Mauzé. It was probably an unpleasant visit—"Well, René, found Timbuctoo yet? Brought back an elephant? Or a lump of gold?" How youth hates home sometimes!

He must have contrasted himself enviously with his hero, Mungo Park, not only as to accomplishment but as to natural advantages. Park, a huge, strong man who stood six feet high, was a trained physician and botanist, an educated man with influential friends. Caillié no doubt knew that for his second expedition Park had been entrusted with a little army of white helpers, that £5,000 was put at his disposal.

Caillié stood up in his fortune—a single suit of clothes —and he had not an influential friend in the world. He looked in the glass and saw a small, frail youth, inside whose earnest forehead he well knew there was a world of ambition but hardly a scrap of education.

Undismayed, he set off for Africa once more.

It was the autumn of 1818. Caillié was just nineteen years old. "Nothing discouraged me", he writes in his *Journal*. "Everything seemed possible to my adventurous spirit, and luck seemed to be serving my destiny."

This was quite true. Luck *was* serving René's destiny, for when he got back to Senegal he found that during the months of his absence, which had seemed so long to him, exactly nothing had happened in his chosen work. Neither Major Gray nor anybody else had rushed in and found out all about Africa! Not a bit of it. Africa was locked up just as tight as ever. Major Gray had made no real progress and was still "ready to engage more men, if suitable fellows presented themselves". He had merely shifted the scene of his misadventures; after a series of mishaps on the Gambia—illness and death of his men, loss of animals—he had with many delays got what remained of his expedition as far as Bondou, a native kingdom lying south of the Senegal River, where he was in more trouble.

The Almamy of Bondou had observed the expensive equipment of the white stranger. He believed that Gray carried with him a silver service which he proposed, when he reached the Niger, to offer to the King of Ségou. He shrewdly inferred that a white man travelling in such magnificence should be able to pay high for the right to traverse his lands, and detained the Englishman, inviting him to buy the right to go forward.

Native demands had so reduced Gray's goods, and death, the number of his men, that he had sent a representative to Saint-Louis to buy supplies and recruit personnel. This messenger was a clever man named Adrien Partarrieu, a mulatto, or an *Enfant du Sénégal*, as the offspring of unblessed mixed unions were gently called in those days. Partarrieu had been with the Peddie-

Campbell fiasco. He was an experienced traveller, knowing how to speak Arabic and many of the negro languages as well as French and, I infer, English. He was—as we shall see later—very resourceful, full of cunning, and a person of character and dignity. Gray in his book always refers to him as "Mr. Partarrieu", and does not dwell on the fact that he was a coloured man.

Partarrieu's shopping trip to Saint-Louis coincided with René Caillié's arrival "*avec peu de ressources*", as he delicately puts it. The fact is that René must have been penniless. Here again "luck served his destiny". Eagerly he rushed to Partarrieu and demanded to be allowed to go to Bondou as a member of the relief expedition.

The mulatto, very busy with his shopping—he bought thirty-two camel loads of goods and recruited some sixty odd men while in Saint-Louis—hesitated. This slim, inexperienced boy of nineteen did not appear to be of the type his employer would welcome.

Caillié held on, pleading. The Child of Senegal had a kind heart. Brusquely he indicated that if René insisted on joining the expedition at his own risk and without pay—which was the boy's own sporting suggestion—he would not interfere to stop him.

To the enthusiastic young man this reluctant permission was as good as a cordial invitation, and when the party set off toward Bondou Caillié went with them. He was very happy. He had at last got his chance to go into the interior of Africa. Probably he set off on this first journey of his with dancing toes. Certainly he did not feel like dancing for long.

10

HERE AND HOW is where René Caillié thought that his life began.

The account which he wrote of his adventures proves this. Caillié's three-volume work, written after his triumphant return from Timbuctoo, is preceded by a twenty-nine-page autobiographical section entitled "Introduction" which tells all the things he thinks worth telling about his life previous to the immediate preparation for his Great Journey. With that contempt for the trivialities of his boyhood which is common to men of action, he skips across the first nineteen years of his life in six pages, of which space a third is given to describing the Peddie fiasco and Gray's false start. Thus it has been necessary for me to find in other sources such detail as I have so far set down about his boyhood and about Africa as he first saw it.

But on that splendid day when, for the first time, he was able to plunge into the African interior he begins to feel that his experiences are worth recording in some detail.

Almost all the rest of the "Introduction" is devoted to what befell him on this, his first journey into Africa.

It was February 5, 1819. The caravan, which consisted of between sixty and seventy men, half black, half white, like the leader himself, formed for departure at Gandiolle, a village near Saint-Louis. Thence they marched off with their thirty-two camels, dead to the East. They cut at right angles the way by which Caillié had gone stumbling southward at the heels of the two negroes.

René, a grown-up explorer now, part—a very small part—of an important expedition, must have felt that superiority which youth feels toward its own self when a little younger, must have looked back patronizingly on the folly of the desperate boy he was a year before. No doubt he found opportunities to brag a bit to his present companions, pushing out his thin chest and telling how he had been this way before and what a rough time he had had.

The caravan faced a hard journey. As it turned out, it was to take them just three months and a day. The distance in a direct line was not over four hundred miles, but the caravan could not go in a direct line, for the land was marbled with little deserts and the way impeded by bad natives. Major Gray had been travelling nearly a year and had got no further. A party of French who had gone to the same general region by way of the Senegal River the year before, with the intention of fortifying the little trading-post at Bakel, had been sixty-three days *en route*. (From *La Compagnie de Galam au Sénégal* by Saulnier.)

The caravan's destination, Bondou, where Gray, virtually a prisoner, awaited them impatiently, was a famous little kingdom—famous because it had gold-fields. Gold in this region grew in the ground like a crop, it was believed.[1] Naturally the country had been through the ages the scene of bloody native struggles and snatchings, and—since Europeans had begun to come to Africa—the object of white curiosity and greed.

Several white travellers had visited Bondou—certain Portuguese, a few French, and some English. Queerest figure of them all, perhaps, was Brother Appolinaire, the priest-explorer. Later came Houghton, Park's murdered predecessor, and Mungo Park himself. It was in Bondou that Park was despoiled by the then reigning Almamy of his fine blue coat with yellow buttons, "the only good one in my possession", and subsequently got even by flirting with the monarch's snub-nosed wives, who insisted that Park's mother had whitened him by daily baths of milk when an infant, and who listened with giggling disclaimers when Park praised "the glossy jet of their skins". Still another European traveller had visited Bondou a bare year before Caillié joined the Gray relief expedition. This was the Frenchman Mollien, who had been rushed this

[1] "Gold commences to sprout every August at the moment when the Senegal River is in flood." From an old Arab work called *Massalik*, quoted by E. F. Gautier in *L'Afrique Noire Occidentale*.

way by the jealous French to steal Gray's thunder—
unnecessary move, for Gray turned out to be more like
Job than Jove! Mollien himself had a rude time of it, was
poisoned by natives, held prisoner and cruelly ill-used.
His ambition to reach Timbuctoo came to pathetic failure,
but he did discover the sources of both the Senegal and
Gambia Rivers. And he is probably unique amongst the
African explorers of those days in that he lived to be a
really old man and died in a European bed.

Through all Caillié's story of the caravan's slow struggle
toward Major Gray runs one preoccupation. It is water.
"Our camels had been so heavily laden with merchandise",
says Caillié, "that we brought only a small supply of
water." No one has ever heard of a caravan which brought
enough! It seems almost a physical impossibility for
camels to carry enough water for their own needs and those
of their masters across African bad lands.

It was the dry season. A series of little deserts lay on
their road. "Soon we were reduced to a tiny ration. I
suffered extremely from thirst. Sometimes I felt myself to
be at the end of my strength, for—having no mount—I
was obliged to follow on foot."

"People have since told me", he records, "that I had
haggard eyes, that I was panting and that my tongue
hung outside my mouth. For myself, all I can remember is
that at each halt I fell prostrate to the ground, without
even the strength to eat."

Sometimes when at villages they were able to buy
water—for naturally only a madman would give water
away—swarms of thirst-tortured bees would envelop them
in a cloud, disputing their right to the water they had
purchased and stinging their lips and faces cruelly. The
bees of Africa have tigerish courage. The attack of
bees has put a stop to native battles. They constitute a

very real danger. One cause for Campbell's disaster was the loss of so many pack animals through bee stings. Mungo Park had an encounter with bees which almost wrecked his second expedition. The animals stampeded, and a fire followed which threatened the whole of his outfit with destruction. A wise caravan which meets bees on the move takes refuge if possible in woods or in water, for if a nearly nude negro falls victim to bees he is likely to die atrociously in a few hours, "swelled up like a water-skin".

Thirsty Caillié did not whine. With a fairminded-ness not usual at moments of awful discomfort, he realized his plight was nobody's fault but his own. "Could I complain?" he writes. "I, a useless mouth! I was there only by the complaisance of the leader!" This attitude pleased Partarrieu. He gave René some of his own water ration. He introduced Caillié to the charms of a novel native fruit, the *néoe*, a fruit with an exterior just like a potato but a cool juicy pulp that was a delight to a parched throat. The *néoe*, or Senegal apple, is, as anyone may find out today by a visit to the Dakar native market, so like an Early Rose potato as to be uncanny—form, size, colour, even "eyes". The only difference is in weight; the *néoe* is heavier. Whimsically one wonders if the *néoe* of Senegal is a relic of the proud days in vegetable history when "the apples of the earth", *pommes de terre*, now degraded to live underground, were allowed to grow on trees.

One member of the party found himself a native fruit similar in appearance and ate some of it, immediately to begin crying out that he was poisoned. Thereupon the others, no doubt at Partarrieu's solicitation, each con-tributed a few drops of their scant water ration to the sufferer. Says Caillié shrewdly: "He seemed so soon cured that I have since thought that his malady was but a ruse

to get a little extra water." He adds: "I saw several of the
men drink their urine."[1]

Then between deserts came a little relief. The caravan
pulled up for a few days at Boulibaba, a Fula village, where
limpid water was to be had in abundance—at a price.

The Fulas were, and are, the oddest people in Africa.
Not odd in the sense of being freakish or hideous: human
monsters were a commonplace in Africa. Travellers have
always prattled about such creatures as the "people
without heads called Blemines, having their eyes and
mouth in their breasts", the cave dwellers that "have no
speech, but rather a grinning and chattering", pygmies,
man-monkeys, women with platters in their mouths, and
so on. What has always made the Fulas so surprising is their
startling beauty and dignity. They possess patrician
delicacy of face and body. Their skins are daintily bronzed.
Their hair, as Mungo Park quaintly remarked, is "soft
silky". Their manners put white travellers to shame. They
seem like the survival of some forgotten aristocracy, like a
race which has passed through all civilization's phases and
returned to near the starting-point, carrying back with them
certain ineradicable elegances and graces. "The gentlemen
of West Africa", snobs call them.

The typical Fula is a wandering herdsman. Some say
that he has a mystic kinship with his humped cattle, that
certain Fula families inherit the ability to understand the
language of their beloved animals. (This is seriously
suggested in a work by Former Colonial Governor Gaden,
issued by the Institut d'Ethnologie.) The herds are masters
of the men. Cows lead and Fulas follow. Up and down
grassy Sudan between the Land of Thirst and the Land of
the Fly—between Saharan sands and the tsetse belt—the
Fula accompanies his cattle. Some writers say that in

[1] A not unusual occurrence. Donald Cameron as recently as 1928, in his *A Saharan
Venture*, tells of the fate of one of his men, a native, who drank his urine with deadly
results.

prehistoric times the Fula followed his kine all the way from Egypt.[1]

Wherever he goes he is graceful, dignified, proud and inconceivably tricky. Many a white man has broken his teeth on the Fulas! There is no hope of bossing and cajoling and coddling them like the big, fat-faced, over-grown children who are their negro neighbours. And it is very hard to handle them by force of arms. Fulas have swayed the destinies of mid-Africa. Great names of Fulas and of men of partial Fula blood stand out in the history of the tropics: mighty warriors delighting in holy wars and the bloody conversion of the idolatrous, wise emperors, cruel saints—fanatical, singing Othman Dan Fodio who carved the name of Allah across the face of an empire in letters of blood; enlightened Bello, an intellectual giant for his place and time, who mapped central Africa—a funny map, but little less comical than the maps of con-temporary white men; El Hadj Omar, the Pilgrim, who commanded the Red Sea to be calm and won its obedience in Biblical fashion, who was not convinced till 1860 that he could not push the Christians into the sea—"only merchants!" he said of the whites contemptuously, adding: "*Il faut bien donner à manger aux poules de mon père!*" A promise to feed God's chickens, the vultures, on French corpses. And there was Ahmadu, who had just made the Fulas masters of the region when René Caillié pushed his way into Timbuctoo.

A powerful and a queer race, the Fulas, who have puzzled and tricked and fooled white men from the Atlantic to the Chad. There was never—search the world over—such a subtle people, touching life with reluctant finger-tips, as if through a veil, adoring dissimulation and lying for the very love of the art.

---

[1] Discussion as to where the Fulas came from has produced a "literature". The various theories are summed up in Louis Tauxier's *Mœurs et Histoire des Peuls*—1937.

Wilfully they make life complex, like a race of dark Prousts. Frank simplicity disgusts them. A Fula mother will not pet her child in public, nor say that she loves it. A "double-language" of paraphrases and proverbs conceals ordinary things. How much more elegant—according to the Fula notion—it is to call water "the willow tree's breeches". Or to replace the conventional brusque refusal to purchase useless goods by the harmonious syllables "*Bornoto wutte ko dogido walabo*", which are a supposed quotation of the snake's scornful answer to the draper; "Let him who has shoulders buy himself a shirt!"

In physical matters the Fula is very brave. No boy dares complain at the torture put upon him at puberty. Flagellation is to be accepted with a smile. A moan, a tear or even a wincing contraction of the face and the boy is dishonoured for life, insulted by men and ignored by women. A terrible threat this last to the amorous Fula temperament!

These women, it is said, know how to rouse a frenzied devotion quite different from the animal and utilitarian sentiments usual with savage African men toward their womenfolk. Fula males are passionate lovers and jealous husbands. Says the Fula husband: "The only man whose jealousy is calmed is the man who has divorced his wife!"

Whatever may be their intimate relations Fula women are certainly lovely to look at. They wear their gay dress and complex coiffure with a sort of faint pathos and wistful fragility which is quite un-African. No traveller can have a more charming memory picture than that of a group of Fula girls at the moment of their own special and terrible festival. They are so daintily coquettish in their gala clothes, their hair arranged with such care and so curiously—the meshes being strung across an oval frame from forehead to crown, the effect being like a Spanish comb which has been given a quarter turn so that it runs from back to front instead of from side to side. They are draped in *pagnes* that are rainbow brilliant, patterned with queer designs. They are brightly jewelled as Christmas trees. Yet the fête they are celebrating is—by one of those typical Fula contradictions—the completion of the cruel and deforming excision operation ritually performed when each maiden comes to her age.

While Caillié, shortly after his arrival at Boulibaba, was studying his first Fula group from a comfortable place beneath a baobab tree, he was approached by a local "confidence man".

Said the villager, speaking deferentially in the Wolof language which Caillié understood, he would be so very proud if the white gentleman would be kind enough to write him out a *gris-gris*, or lucky paper, to bring him riches.

Caillié was flattered, thinking to himself complacently; "What a simple fellow this poor savage is, to be sure!" So he wrote out a bit of gibberish and accepted in return a drink of milk from the humble native. During René's preoccupation, the Fula had stolen his precious black silk cravat!

It was a lesson for René, a lesson which he assimilated. His eventual success, where so many failed, was based on his having learned through a series of such incidents that the people of Africa—be they bronze, black or beige —were not "just natives" to be bamboozled and patronised but exceptionally slick customers in their own way. He learned to put aside his instinctive notion of white superiority and to deal with the local inhabitant with all the respectful precautions that his French peasant forbears used on market-day.

René wrote down one silk scarf to valuable experience, and after a few days' rest duly left Boulibaba with the caravan. Another desert, and a turn to the South to avoid Futa-Toro. This region was inhabited by Fulas known to be especially harsh in their dealings with travellers, although one of their own legends might well have made them kinder to strangers in distress. A band of Fulas wandering, were, it seems, lost in the desert. They and their herds were near death. Beneath a stunted tree men and beasts bemoaned their plight. Amongst them dropped suddenly some grains of *green* corn! Above them sat a parrot. Green corn in the desert, in the dry season! "Follow the parrot! Run! And keep on running!" cried the Fula headman. And so into the verdant valley just south of the Senegal River the Fulas followed the parrot and there established a new Fula country, Futa-Toro.[1]

At the frontiers of Bondou the caravan saw at last their English master. Major Gray came riding to meet them and gave orders that they should follow him back to Boulibané, the capital of the native kingdom.

Caillié may have fancied that he was seeing the seamy side of Africa, but what was now coming was to make the past look like a pleasant cross-country walk.

I I

THE THIRTY-TWO CAMELS which Partarrieu had led from the coast carried across their humps Major Gray's Letter of Credit. Their loads of guinea cloth and trinkets were to pay his travelling expenses as he pushed further into Africa. It would be fatal if the greedy old Almamy of Bondou saw them, for what the Almamy looked at he asked for, and what he asked for he got. Partarrieu urged that the caravan should avoid the Bondou capital. Gray disagreed. They travelled to Boulibané, but so timed their arrival that it should be after dark. The Almamy turned over in his sleep. Next

[1] From a study of the Fulas by Guebhard in the *Revue des Études Éthnographiques*, 1909.

day he looked with pained surprise at what Major Gray had hoped would be acceptable as a farewell present, and suggested that the white man must be joking. There followed a fortnight of bickering.

Of course it was the Almamy who won. After grabbing all the gifts he could squeeze out of the Major, he told him that he might depart, but laid down definitely that Gray might not go eastward—Niger-ward, Timbuctoo-ward—as he longed to do, nor even might seek refuge with the French at Fort Bakel, but must go either into Bambouk or back to the coast by way of Futa-Toro.

The Almamy's motive was transparent. Along the ways he had indicated lived his friends and allies. They could further despoil the Major. Why send this generous English-man with the remainder of his thirty-two camel loads to be the benefactor of outsiders? Little he cared where Gray wanted to go. He was all for extortion, and to the devil with exploration!

Gray argued. He tried to resist, saying he would go where he liked. Now he paid for one of his blunders—a blunder which quick-eyed Caillié had remarked before he had been an hour in the Major's camp. It was that it contained no well within its four-foot palisade.

The Almamy put guards round the wells of the town. It was the usual native method of convincing an obstinate visitor of his error. Gray, after a period of suffering for himself, his men and his beasts, was blackmailed into submission. He would go to Futa-Toro, as the Almamy had told him. In the back of the tenacious Englishman's head was the plan that he might manage to get somehow to the Senegal River, cross it and double back upon Fort Bakel, whence he would make a fresh start toward the interior. Fort Bakel was dead north of Boulibané and not more than fifty miles away.

Caillié was gaining in experience every day as he watched Major Gray's misfortunes and mistakes. Gray,

he thought, should never have brought his camels to
Boulibané. Gray was indeed over-credulous. Gray's own
story, as he tells it himself,[1] shows a sanguine, bluff, brave
man, insensible to disappointments and unconscious of
his blunders—in short, thick-skinned.

The Almamy sent the English expedition away from
Boulibané on May 22nd like a herd of cattle. His men rode
round and round them like cowboys, and the seventy-year-
old Almamy himself went with the convoy during the first
day's journey and personally delivered the valuable Major
into the hands of the Fulas of Futa-Toro. Gray sighed, knowing the Fula of old, from the dreadful Campbell disaster.

There followed a most ridiculous and humiliating
scramble. The white men were driven like beasts and
watched day and night, whilst they travelled round in
meaningless circles and scallops, the Fulas seeking to
keep such profitable "guests" as long as possible, Gray
seeking to wriggle free. They stopped at occasional hostile
villages—groups of huts on the fringes of regions even now
described on a large-scale map[2] as *Haute Broussaille—
Région Non Parcourue* (High brush—trackless country)—
villages whose names Gray noted down phonetically as
best he could, Gwina, Loogoonoody, Looboogol, and so
on, where rapacious natives sold water at heart-breaking
prices. The year of Gray's passage, 1819, must long have
been remembered as the Boom Year in Futa-Toro. They
sold water at six and even ten francs the bottle—or rather
that equivalent in goods. Lucky were the camels who
could draw on their humps!

Gray finally lost his head and announced that he would
escape alone by night and push through to Bakel and
fetch help. Partarrieu protested, saying that the Fulas,

---

[1] *Travels in Western Africa in the Years 1818–21.*
[2] *Carte de Reconnaissance* issued by the A.O.F. Government, "Bakel" sheet on a scale
so generous that every kilometre is a centimetre long.

as soon as they observed the leader had disappeared, would fall on the party and massacre them. Gray would not listen. Next dawn the expected almost occurred, but Partarrieu calmed the native fury and suspicion by a shrewd lie—the better told since it was based on a genuine emotion. He said: "I have quarrelled with Gray and hate him! I have thrown him out."

Gray met with his usual bad luck. He got safe to Bakel where he was not altogether popular, partly because of international jealousy, more especially because the Englishman, having unlimited money to spend, had been paying hand over fist for supplies during the many months of his stay in the neighbourhood, hoping so to curry favour with the sulky natives, and as a result the French fort had been humiliated and deprived of food. But Major Gray was preoccupied with his own troubles. He hired eleven Moors and eleven "carrying bullocks" and persuaded some volunteers from "His Most Christian Majesty's Brig *Argus*", which was at Bakel, to join him, and then he set off to find Partarrieu and the rest of his expedition and fetch all hands to Bakel. On the way Gray was captured, and ill treated. The Fulas, he relates, "attempted to tear the clothes off the men's backs". Partarrieu came to the rescue again, but blarney, presents and threats were useless. Partarrieu, "poisoned with grief" (as René puts it), watched helplessly as the Major was led away in captivity.

Partarrieu decided to get through to Bakel somehow to seek further assistance and try to rescue the Major. Again he gave out that the Major had no charms for him. This, finally, had the desired result. When the natives realized that there was no bidding for English Majors, they eventually turned Gray loose.

Meanwhile Partarrieu, who in Gray's absence was in sole charge of the expedition, thought out another ruse. He was really a very clever mulatto, and he was also,

I suspect, aided in some of his dodges by the shrewd brain of his protégé, René Caillié. They wormed their way toward the river. It was useless for Partarrieu to expect to be allowed to cross: the Fulas did not want to lose so profitable a guest. After establishing a camp, he said: "I have some sick men"—which, alas, was but too true —"I want to get them to Bakel where they may be taken care of. Then I will come back here."

The chief of the nearby village snorted refusal.

Then Partarrieu added: "The trouble is, anyhow, that I have not enough carrier animals, so—even if you had agreed—I should have had to leave all my cases of heavy merchandise behind here in your charge." At this there was a sudden readiness to see them go.

That night they filled the cases with rocks and locked them carefully. They fastened bundles of their choicest merchandise upon their pack beasts and they slipped away, leaving the camp-fires burning and the cook-pots bubbling deceitfully. They hoped to get well along their way before the village chief had prised the boxes open and set off in pursuit.

They plunged and stumbled through the night. Suddenly they smelt the river, and at dawn they rushed toward it, the splendid Senegal, the blessed sight of water you did not have to buy or beg for.

A ford was found, and, it being not yet the season of high water, they were just able to get across, their clothing and what little remained of their possessions on their heads. The water was at times up to their necks. There was the ever-present danger of crocodiles, so sluggish and yet so swift. They crawled panting on to the other bank. Whites and blacks thanked their gods.

Then they looked back at the shores whence they had come. There were the duped men from the village, racing down the river bank in a fury. They wanted vengeance, but, armed with only home-made weapons, they dared not pursue. The guns of Bakel were close.

Naïvely they suggested a parley, beckoning the Europeans to come back and talk things over. Partarrieu grinned. Let them come to him at Bakel, he signalled.

It must have made a good scene: angry natives chattering fury on one side of the mighty Senegal; on the opposite side Partarrieu, nude leader of nude men, indicating an invitation with an ironical sweep of his hand.

Bakel received the wanderers with "generous eagerness", gave them "affectionate care and refreshing food". And a few days later, Caillié adds, "our joy was overflowing when we saw arriving Major Gray, whom the natives had set free".

Major Gray's fate no longer concerns Caillié's story. But it is rather splendid to record that the Major announced his intention of muddling through yet another expedition! He bought further supplies and attempted to follow the route which his dying associate, Dochard, had taken toward the Niger. Then in 1821, after three years of ineptitude and misfortunes courageously borne, Gray gave up the cause of African exploration where all his sufferings had been so useless.

12

SAFE AND AT peace after four months of danger, strain and discomfort, Caillié relaxed and realized how tired were his young nerves and his immature body. The rains were starting. Caillié came down with fever.

But a pleasant thing happened to René while he was ill. He met one who, for him, was probably the most interesting person in the world. This was Isaaco, who had been Mungo Park's native guide, and his man of affairs on his second fatal voyage. It was Isaaco who procured for Park the old *pirogue* on which he set off to try to find out where the Niger went to. Isaaco, having said good-bye to his white employer, carried back toward the coast Park's infinitely plucky letter to his wife: "I think it not unlikely I shall be in England before you receive this. You may be sure that I feel happy at turning my face toward home." And it was Isaaco who was picked to search for traces of Park when it seemed clear that Park was lost.

Caillié himself does not write about this meeting with Isaaco, but Gray mentions, in passing, that at Bakel he found Isaaco, "the same individual who accompanied Mr. Park on his last attempt", and it is inconceivable that René would not have sought the friendship of the old Mandingo, who, having been associated with two failures in exploration, must have had some caustic comments to make about the folly of white travellers.

This absurd scramble in which he had just taken part was no way to explore Africa, René must have told himself. This unwieldy mass of men, always thirsty, losing one another in woods, or getting ill and having to be pulled along by their comrades—what good were they? They hampered, without protecting. They transformed the explorer into a worried leader of a useless gang, the superintendent of a wandering hospital. These heavy loads of goods roused black cupidity. The white man's luxury and swagger alarmed and antagonised the native. It was not exploring. And it was not done on a big enough scale to be an armed invasion. It was just silly.

A man alone, now? . . .

Caillié, gravely ill, left Bakel on the flat of his back. It was a sad end to adventure—lying on the bare boards of the *chaland*, hiding himself as best he could from the drenching of sudden rains, a makeshift cover of boughs keeping off part of the terrible July sun. Through the stifling daytime hours he longed for the night to come and rest his hot head; then through the steaming nights of soggy dampness and tropic chill, mosquito-tortured and feverish he prayed for the morning.

It was a lively time on the Senegal. The gum trading season was just drawing to its exciting finish, white and half-breed traders from Saint-Louis competing crazily, Moors bickering, clawing for presents and free entertainment, discussing "customs". Customs were the official payments made by the whites to the natives for the trade concession.

The shores, deserted for the rest of the year, were spotted with tents where the Moors had come to camp during the season. The gum trade was their main, their only business, and they came in thousands, from all the South Sahara, Douaichs, Trarzas and Braknas—these last "the worst of all the African races", in Pierre Loti's words. The men were tall and proud, and greedy beyond imagining. The women were incredibly fat, their flesh hanging to their bodies like billowing drapery; they were artificially fattened when young and were really too unwieldy to move, so that sometimes they were to be seen supported by human crutches, a little slave beneath each armpit. Some of the men were practical enough, despite their habit of celibacy, to bring as companions for the annual trip to the trading-posts women whom they called in all simplicity their "travelling wives", women of lesser dimensions than the legitimate portly chatelaines of the tent, of inferior caste, plebeian and unfattened—Porognes, the offspring of unblessed Moorish matings with negresses.

Trading ran along all the lower reaches of the river, from Podor—115 degrees in the shade, "the hottest town in all the world"—nearly to Saint-Louis. At each of the *Escales*, as the trading-posts were called—the Escale du Cop, the Escale du Désert, and the rest—Moors squabbled bitterly with traders, quarrelling over the price of gum.

Gum was the gold of Mauretania. It grew wild on the desert's edge on a variety of acacia tree, and the Moor, who never degraded himself by work, caused it to be collected by his slaves and dragged to the Senegal banks, where the Christians came clamouring for it. Some years as much as six million pounds of gum changed hands. The price was paid in trinkets and in "the money of the river", which was "guineas"—strips of Indian cotton goods, each strip sixteen yards long, immensely popular with the native.

Never satisfied, the Moors were always screaming for higher prices and more presents—"the *bonjour* present" when the traders arrived, "the anchorage present", "the gift of a new costume", "the supper present", "the good-bye present". They did not know what the white folk did with the gum, but the wild competition suggested that these little balls of yellowy tree sap must be, some-how, a fundamental of Christian civilization. (As a matter of fact, it was merely a variety of the well-known gum-arabic, a substance used in preparing medicines and confectionery, to give lustre to crêpe goods and silks, and for other commonplace purposes.) So, confident that they had the whole white world by the neck, the Moors sat on their leather bags and held out for the last *coudée* of guinea cloth (a half-arm length, about half a yard, the old-time measure in Africa). The Senegal River along the Gum Coast during the trading season was a tumultuous ill-natured fair.

Back in Saint-Louis Caillié lay for many weeks in the wretched hospital. He left there penniless and friendless, faced with the immediate necessity of finding himself a job. He became cook in a Saint-Louis workshop!

Caillié in a kitchen, trying to remember how Céleste did it: unlucky those who ate his meals! Timbuctoo's gold glittering at the bottom of the copper casserole, Mauzé's sneers in the fat sizzling in the pan.

13

FOUR YEARS PASSED. René Caillié worked in the wine business for a Bordeaux house and sometimes travelled on their behalf to the West Indies. It was the sort of gap which is usually described, in the life-story of a great man, by some such phrase as; "The next few years were uneventful". That is a phrase which should rouse pity; those "uneventful years" are cruelly hard. They were hard on René, smirking away his precious youth as a servant of commerce; "Yes, sir!" . . . "No, sir!" . . . "I have the figures here, sir!" Sometimes he must have wondered bitterly whether he was only another of the dissatisfied, who dream of great deeds and die with a servile smile on their lips and a pen behind their ears.

On the Bordeaux water-front he sometimes met men from Africa. He sought them out, eager to hear, yet wincing with envy when they told him gossip of the coast, spoke of Saint-Louis—always in a ferment, told of Roger, the indefatigable new Governor of Senegal, who "ran everything". With a grin they told him Saint Louis's latest joke that there wasn't a crocodile on the river dared flip his tail without the Governor's say so! But they boasted of the Governor's cleverness, eagerness, and quick sympathy for new ventures.

Caillié listened hopefully. He pricked up his ears too at tales about one Louis Duranton who had married the daughter of an African King, "gone native", and lived at Khasso, far up the Senegal, with the Princess Sadioba and their mulatto offspring. Duranton, sponsored by his black father-in-law, dreamed of travelling unopposed to Timbuctoo.

This interested Caillié. Not that—so far as we know—he hankered for a black bride, but because there was a resemblance between Duranton's scheme and a plan which was in Caillié's own mind.

In the spring of 1824 he sailed for Senegal.

He says: "I tried my luck with a little *pacotille*." This musical word meant a pack of trinkets and cloth for native trading such as would be accepted as part of a man's personal luggage. Caillié writes that his employer, Monsieur Sourget, "a merchant of very distinguished merit, had advanced me enough to buy it. He showed me paternal sentiments of which I shall always conserve the memory". Monsieur Sourget gave him his chance.

René, the old-timer, could strut a little on the deck as they anchored before Saint-Louis, brag to the new-comers. Yes, his third time out to the Colony, came out as a boy in the early days with Schmaltz, had been way inland with that unlucky English expedition, spoke Wolof (not that that was so difficult; the negro language had only five hundred words).

He looked across the stretch of glittering sands, the beehive huts of the native fisher-folk, the white city beyond, and felt he had come home. He shouted a Wolof greeting to the naked *pirogue* men alongside. He sniffed familiar air—not very good sniffing, mostly Guet N'Dar's "stink-fish" drying, and the musky odour of the negro crowd. He listened to the rhythmic clapping, the little tom-toms, the nasal high-pitched chattering. It was the tune of Africa again, the tune which had been humming in his brain for these four years.

Caillié was slightly over twenty-four years old on the day he landed at Saint-Louis. Before his twenty-ninth birthday he was safe back in France with the first account of Timbuctoo ever brought to Europe by a white man.

Caillié sought out the Governor of Senegal, hoping to get France's official backing. He must have known that he did not cut a distinguished figure, and that the task of "selling himself" to the Governor would be difficult, especially as Roger had the name for being a snob.

As a matter of fact, Jacques-François Roger, the bustling ex-lawyer, was at this time trying to himself the sound of the delightful words, "Monsieur le Baron Roger". During the year he secured a long-chased title. But though Governor Roger was a climber, he had balancing virtues. He had terrific energy and a real love for "my Senegal". He lasted five years as Governor—proof of phenomenal endurance, for in those days the career of a tropical African Governor, French or English, was usually but a moment in the sunshine. Roger's ambitions and interests were wide: experimental agriculture, based on the queer dream of transforming arid and torrid Senegal into a luxuriant garden; the study of folk-lore; the penetration into Africa. His administration should see, he said, "the economic conquest of the Sudanese regions". He befriended explorers.

The plan which René laid before the Governor was imaginative and original. His idea was to go alone amongst the Moors of the desert, the same fanatical nomads whom he had observed from the *chaland* with feverish eyes four years before. He hoped by some ingenious tale to persuade them to tolerate him, to let him stay among them, to teach him to be a Mohammedan. Thus he would learn how to impersonate a native. He would pick up the complex ritual of Mohammedan daily life, would learn native ways. He would so gloss himself with native varnish that his personality would be acceptable to inner Africa and he might safely travel, or try to travel, to Timbuctoo.

René asked Roger to give him France's blessing and aid in his venture.

Roger, appalled at the danger, tried to dissuade him, failed, and finally gave him a very small quantity of goods —another *pacotille*.

The assumption in Caillié's mind was that Roger and France were behind him. He says soberly that he "received instructions from M. le Baron Roger, who promised him the protection of the Government". This point is important, in connection with what happened later.

Caillié made his preparations. He realized that it was likely that he would never return: the Moors of the desert were in those days the most feared people in Africa. They were fanatical, cruel, intolerant, almost maniacal. It is said that people who live long in the Sahara become mad. These Moors had lived on the desert borders for centuries, half-starved, tortured by thirst, their brains beaten by the copper rods of the desert sun. No negro joy in life for them! They wandered about the wide, bad lands north of the Senegal River in restless gloom, looking like minor prophets of the Old Testament, tawny, wild-eyed, dressed in long robes, austere, intensely pious, a race of religious hysterics.

If they would accept him, he would learn authentic Mohammedan ways. For theirs was not the easy-going Mohammedanism of their negro neighbours who flirted with the paganism of their forbears. He would learn to speak a language—a bastard Arabic patois—which, like Latin in the Middle Ages, would be understood by the intelligentsia all over inner Africa.

Would he be able to cajole them into accepting him as a pupil? It would all depend upon his tact and swift wits. He would often have to talk for his life.

The country of the Moors, the unconfined stretch of semi-desert across which they roamed, is still today one of the least known and one of the most dangerous places on earth. Aviators have a horror of this stretch—the Rio de Oro and Mauretania (a modern name for the country of the Moors, not to be confused with the classic Mauretania of North Africa).

So remote is the Moorish country from the influence of the white world that it held, up until a few years ago, a minor Timbuctoo—a secret city of its own, Smara, into which a French youth penetrated in 1930 disguised as a Moorish woman, and returned dying. Young Michel Vieuchange was perhaps the victim of Caillié's glamour. He had been a writer of scenarios, a poet who wrote: "I have all the hungers, all the thirsts!" He declared: "I waked from a strange dream. I was searching for Smara . . . I knew that another was ahead of me searching for the city. And it was René Caillié. . . . I was well content to share with him my discovery of Smara." [1]

Mauretania became a French colony in the early years of this century, but the Moors are unwilling hosts. They loathe strangers and Christians. At present every man, woman and child has, according to the 1934 census, two square kilometres to himself. To the Moors this seems quite crowded enough.

The Moors of the Western Sahara do not love anybody; and nobody loves them. I have never heard or read praise of them—nor did Caillié, I can venture. Their negro neighbours south of the Senegal River, who dreaded their piratical visits, had a saying: "A Moor's tent casts its shade over nothing decent but the horse!" The survivors of the *Méduse* wreck recounted how they were tormented in the desert; when they fell exhausted on the sands, Moorish women and children would cluster round them and divert themselves by pinching the whites till the blood came, yanking out their hair and rubbing sand into their sunburn blisters. Mungo Park, safe in his Scottish bed, used to wake shuddering after nightmares about the Moors, thinking he was again their prisoner and that they were again threatening to cut off his right hand or to put out his eyes.

[1] Smara was not "discovered" in the sense that Timbuctoo was discovered. A daring military raiding party under Colonel Mouret had already penetrated as far as Smara in 1913.

I think no white man but Caillié ever voluntarily sought to live for a long time amongst them alone as one of them. I think no one but Caillié could have borne it. The notes about Moorish customs which Caillié secretly made on the spot, risking his life with every sentence he wrote—and he wrote a great many, enough to fill 161 printed pages in his *Journal*—contain much which is still, after a century, not superseded by any newly collected information.

14

IT WAS ON the 3rd day of August, 1824, at four in the afternoon, that René Caillié left Saint-Louis to go to the land of the Moors. He recorded his own birthday casually and incorrectly, as I have mentioned. But here was a precious date and time, his birthday as a serious explorer. He sets it down as the first line of the first chapter of his book. The summary "Introduction" dealing rapidly with the adventures of his boyhood is over. On that August Tuesday when, garbed in his flowing native dress, he left Saint-Louis his career began. Exact details mattered now.

He wore a *coussabe* (a rudimentary shirt without collar or sleeves), loose drawers, and a supplementary wrap-around called a *pagne*. For some reason which he does not specify he did not take a boat from Saint-Louis to one of the *escales* up the Senegal where he hoped to make contact with the Moors, but went inland on foot along the marshy country by the river's southern shores. Probably he avoided the easy way so as to break, from the beginning, any connection with the white world which would have embarrassed him in telling the story by which he proposed to fool the Moors.

The country was lush, for August was the wettest month of the year. Everything was green, underfoot and overhead. From tree to tree hung flowering vines which met and tangled into an arbour very pleasant to walk under. There were wide fields of high grass full of birds and wild fowls, and there were occasional native *lougans* where millet and cotton and indigo grew, and smooth water-melons, the adored negro *beref*, glittered enticingly. And there were stretches vivid with marsh plants. Caillié, full of optimism, unpacked his adjectives and then added boyishly: "So much beauty in nature forces the soul to turn toward its Creator, and to admire the profundity of His intelligence." This from a man about to disavow the Christian God.

The natives along his way were friendly. At the first village he visited the local treasure—a magic stone which, whenever the village was menaced, could he relied upon to walk three times round the palisades as a warning and a mystic protection. Once, when a particularly dangerous enemy attacked, the stone produced blue flames out of the earth which frightened the invader away. As a reward the natives of the village never passed by the spot where the magic rock reposed between its protective travels without pulling a thread from their garment and tossing it upon the stone as an offering. Sometimes they would bring the rock food, calabashes full of the best *couscous*. In the morning the calabashes would be empty: the magic rock had eaten. Caillié sagely suggests it might have been prowling animals who benefited.

Caillié travelled idyllically. True he was often obliged to wade through marshes with water to his knees and his bundle of goods on his head, and as an inevitable consequence was laid up with fever "with such pains in every limb I could not move". True, too, he was lamed with thorns, afflicted with a form of rheumatism in the left arm, and met other incon-veniences usual to African cross-country travel. But these were such little inconveniences when he was so happy!

After eleven days he arrived at Richard-Tol, the French experimental gardens on the Senegal, and there embarked on a boat going up-river. It was easier going now, except that his nights were tortured by fogs of ravenous mosquitoes.

Finally at Podor, after nearly a month of travelling, Caillié succeeded in getting into contact with Moors of the Brakna tribe, to whom he explained that he wished to be instructed in Mohammedanism. This was a matter for their King to pass upon, they said. They agreed, at a price, to let Caillié accompany them to the place—many days' march away—where the King was then encamped in the desert. The Moors, as soon as the season of gum trading finished on the river, always fled into the sands before the attacks of the mosquitoes.

Now Caillié turned northward, into the great desert. As he stumbled over the hummocky ground at the desert's edge— cram-cram, that dastardly pricking plant, tearing at his legs with its little fish-hooks, loose pebbles bruising his feet, the wide rolling sands of the Sahara in the northern distance—he rehearsed to himself the story he would tell when he reached the Brakna headquarters. And often he must have wondered grimly whether he would be believed or assassinated.

His trip was a foretaste of what Brakna life would be. The food was wretched, mostly a boiled-up porridge and a combination of sour milk and water—the former called *sanglé*, the later *cheni*. The water was often so muddy that it was barely liquid and had to be strained through the teeth. Caillié's companions added a little molasses to it, a most uncouth drink which they considered a real treat.

One day there was a minor sand-storm. One night there was a terrible storm, with driving rain. Having no shelter they all stripped off their clothes and put them under up-turned cook-pots, taking the cold rain naked—and bitterly cold it was after the burning day under the African sun.

Far worse, however, than nature's torments was the behaviour of the Moors themselves. As soon as he arrived at a Brakna camp the nomads would crush round this young man who had come amongst them to learn the beauties of their religion. Who was he? What did he want? The women, hiding their faces with rags of blue guinea cloth, peeped at him between the legs of the men. If René moved a limb they shrieked in mock horror and darted back. When René sought rest, lying on the ground wrapped in his *pagne*, the children jerked it off him, yanked at his feet, and pricked him with thorns.

After a week of marching into the Brakna country Caillié's companions led him into the camp of Mohammed-Sidi-Moctar, the King's leading marabout (that is, a man of the priestly class but wielding much commercial and political power, the Moorish counterpart of a medieval cardinal). It was for the chief marabout to decide whether this stranger was a suspicious character to be done away with, or a potential source of income to the tribe.

Marabout Moctar listened to René with patronizing affability, a Moor who spoke Wolof interpreting.

Caillié told his story, told how son of a wealthy French family—he had read the Koran in a French translation and "recognized its great truths", how his father had opposed his desire to turn Mussulman, how—his father dead—he had come with his heritage to Senegal, attracted by the world-renowned reputation of Brakna piety and wisdom, how on the way to Africa he had been shipwrecked and a part of his wealth lost, but that a part remained and was now safely lodged at Saint-Louis, and that he, René, eager for religious instruction, had come amongst the Braknas seeking aid in the way to Allah.

It was a good story. The best of it was, of course, the reference to the goods in Saint-Louis. To the Braknas this promised profit to come. For Caillié it was a sort of guarantee of protection. Nothing grave would happen to him, or so he dared hope, until the Braknas could lay hands on the property.

The Marabout listened, and evidently felt that it would be a goodly and profitable act to bring this wealthy and presumably weak-brained young man into the fold. He agreed to take charge of René's religious instruction and added that already he counted him "amongst the number of his children".

That same evening the Marabout informed Caillié that they would next day go to the camp of the Brakna King, Hamet-Dou. It would be necessary for Caillié to have a bath before the royal presentation. Says Caillié: " I consented with especial pleasure since a bath would be very healthful for me and would relieve me after the fatigues of travel."

It took twenty-four miles of hot walking after the bath before they reached the King's camp, but just before their arrival Caillié was washed down again by a serf, so that he might be "purified". Then he was led to the royal tent, where Hamet-Dou awaited his visit, attended by a negro who spoke French.

Hamet-Dou, according to Caillié's spelling (Ahmedou I. of the Braknas) was—for a Moor—a rather affable person. He had been formally "recognized" by the French Government, and was the first King of this wild tribe to enter into anything like friendly relations with the French. At the trading-posts on the river he had picked up some words of French, and like many another man, held an exaggerated notion of his linguistic abilities.

He greeted Caillié with the usual Arabic salutation. Then he plunged proudly into French: "How are you, *Monsieur?* Very well, thank you, *Monsieur!*" Caillié listened tactfully. Hamet-Dou contentedly repeated his little piece several times.

To Caillié this bit of monkeyish imitativeness was consoling. He had been mauled and pestered by Moorish women and children, had cringed to these barbarians and flattered them, had been refused audience with their

King until he was bathed and purified. And such a King, too—a personage who lived in a tent of which the only furnishing was six wooden dishes, three iron pots and two casseroles, and who had no change of costume, so that—as René later noticed—he had to let his clothes dry on him after it rained! It was consoling to have immediate proof that he was just a pretentious, absurd nomad kinglet, a potentially easy dupe.

René spoke up and told Hamet-Dou his story. The King expressed his satisfaction. He took Caillié by the hand and said "*Maloum, Abd-allahi!*" which meant: "It is well, Slave of God!" This name, Abdallahi, Slave of God, was the one Caillié had chosen for himself. Thus was he known among the Braknas during the period of his life with them, and by all the other natives who knew him during his great trek.

15

ON THE VERY next morning the whole camp packed up and moved.

At sunrise the tents of henna red were pulled down, rolled up with the poles on camel-back, one tent to each camel, and the household gear was packed on humped pack-oxen, patient beasts broken at calfhood by the artful use of a cord through their nostrils. Then the Moorish ladies mounted on camel-back, sitting two by two in the depths of huge baskets—and Allah aid the camels, for two Brakna ladies weighed a mighty lot!

Reposing in her *bassour* of scarlet and yellow and silk embroideries was Hamet-Dou's Queen, the same childless lady who, some years later, desiring to get rid of the protector of one of her husband's bastards, put poison in camel's milk, Hamet-Dou's favourite and practically his sole food, and murdered her royal mate by mistake.

Very splendid and colourful were Hamet-Dou's people preparing for the march, and a fine tangle they got themselves into at the first step forward. Caillié describes the King's departure as a crazy hubbub. The flocks bellowed and plunged, the women tumbled off their camels squealing, an indignant horse kicked up his heels, frightened pack-oxen dropped their loads, pots and clothing rolled on the sand. From baskets where babies were bedded down for the journey beside new-born domestic animals came howls and yaps and bleats of terror. Slaves ran hither and thither tripping over one another and shouting conflicting orders.

After all this fuss they pulled up at a new camp just three miles distant. As the place had no water, slaves were sent back to the old camp to fetch it. Other slaves went nearly as great a distance for firewood. Still another group prepared thorny enclosures called *saniers* to shut the flocks in at night.

Such was the endless cycle of Brakna nomad life. Everything was done with a maximum of discomfort and confusion. There seemed a set policy of making life as uncomfortable as possible. For these Moors were no gay gypsies. Their endless wandering expressed pessimism, inherent dissatisfaction. Each new camp displeased them, displeased them even before they had got the tents up. Petulantly they squatted down in profound inertia. Often the women spent all day lying down, slaves feeding them as if they were invalids. Everything was left to the slaves, and performed clumsily and with great fracas. When the camp was foul and the poor grazing used up, they all moved on gloomily—Caillié's *Journal* recounts one move after another—moving not because a new place attracted them but because the old place stank and was exhausted. All camps, they knew beforehand, were alike detestable, and life on this earth was acceptedly a poor affair.

The diet was sparse and unvaried, mush and milk. At first Caillié fainted with hunger. Should a Brakna commit the extravagance of killing a beast, he and his associates in this debauch hid away in secret to eat it and the festival had a special name, translatable as "A Party-at-Which-Meat-Is-Eaten". If discovered, those who surprised them would rush up snapping like famished dogs.

They dozed through this life in grim discomfort, all their thoughts on the joys to come. Never did a people more desperately need a belief in Paradise. They rubbed their ill-filled stomachs and consoled themselves by a study of the Heavenly Menu in that fine Hereafter where, as a marabout told Caillié, "four rivers flow; one of water, one of milk, one of honey and the fourth of *eau-de-vie* but this *eau-de-vie* is better than that which the Christians drink and which God forbids. It is the most exquisite thing you could drink!" Beside the four rivers of delight stood great basins of food, free for the eating. So fertile is Paradise that what is on earth an insignificant berry there becomes "big as a calabash".

Thus the Braknas gloried in their gloom.

It cannot be said that Caillié gained anything like real instruction in Mohammedan lore. The ramshackle ways of Brakna life precluded any serious study. But Caillié had no need for formal learning. What he needed was to become automatically familiar with the ritual gestures and behaviour of Mussulmans and to learn Arabic.

Also he needed to accustom himself to living in native discomfort. There would be no need for Caillié, after he had lived amongst these people, to break himself in as did Mungo Park, who—when he went to Africa for the second time—"took to living on the plainest food in preparation for the journey". Stagnant water would never make Caillié qualmish, nor filth turn his stomach. He was learning also how to bear cheerfully native prying and pushing and teasing. The Moors of the Sahara specialized in the minor torture of those who could not protect themselves. Sadism was the national sport. Caillié was to meet many bad natives but never any so wilfully cruel as these, and probably none more insanely curious and intrusive. There was no privacy for the Slave of God. Another explorer, franker than Caillié, tells how a crowd of "one thousand to fifteen hundred persons would sometimes follow him to the spot where generally one desires to be alone".[1] He taught himself to take for granted men "covered with vermin", women who "gave off a rank odour capable of incommoding a European". One of their fashions was to rub rancid butter on their hair from the calabash which held the cooking butter. Pityingly, but restraining his protests, he watched little girls being forcibly fattened, vomiting the milk, sobbing and rolling on the ground in agony while a slave obliged them to continue drinking by pinching and beating them. He saw Brakna mothers using primitive methods to embellish their daughters according to local taste, which demanded that women's teeth should jut out over the lower lip.

One item in the Moor's code Caillié must have found thoroughly understandable. The Braknas, from the King down, ignored Koranic privilege and never took but one wife. One such lady in the tent Caillié must have felt was quite enough! "They never kiss", he records, and probably that too seemed to him wise under the circumstances.

One of their habits which puzzled him, however, was the strict rule forbidding a son-in-law ever to have any dealings with the parents of the lady of his choice from the moment when the terms of the *dot* have been arranged. Should they meet they might not even look at one another.

He was amazed and shocked at their courtships, carried on unchaperoned and unhurried in the young lady's tent

[1] Captain Binger, *Du Niger au Golfe de Guinée.*

in the dark. "*Manière peu décente de faire l'amour*", said the young Frenchman.

René developed his plans. He decided that he would actually become a Brakna by an informal naturalization process. He would buy flocks, marry, no doubt, one of the specially fattened girls who smelt of rancid butter (René would do anything to get to Timbuctoo!) He would wander with his new people about the desert, would announce his intention of making the Mecca pilgrimage, choosing the Timbuctoo route, and he would—God willing —pass quite naturally into the secret city. Then he would somehow make his way back to Europe via Egypt.

It was a fine plan, and the more he considered it the dearer it became to him. The essence of it was that the Braknas should like and trust him and should see in him the promise of continuous profit. René hinted at his notion to settle amongst them, realizing that the shrewd Moors would gloat at the prospect of selling him crock animals at high prices.

He saw it was time he began to cut a better figure, he the supposed son of a wealthy Frenchman. He had long since given in presents all the goods in Governor Roger's small *pacotille*, and he was in rags.

Adroitly he obtained permission to go to one of the *escales* on the Senegal River, where he hoped to be able to get fresh supplies and to communicate guardedly his plans to the French. The gum-trading season was on and there were many Europeans on the river. He was disappointed in his hope of seeing the French officer in charge, and a letter which he sent down to Saint-Louis failed to bring a prompt reply. This disturbed him. But at any rate he did get some goods from a French trader, René Valentin, who "had the generosity to lend them without security".

Caillié, with his sparse little load of guinea and *birampot*,

which was an openwork blue cloth from Calcutta much
esteemed by the Moors to fend off mosquitoes, hurried
back to the Braknas. His prompt return made a good
impression. It convinced them that he did sincerely want
to become one of them.

He had now been eight months a nomad and a Moslem.
One night in the first week of April there rose a new moon
which was to put his piety to test.

It was the new moon of Ramadan misery, swift little
white knife that slashed off what small comfort and
happiness the tribe enjoyed. These poor folk who had so
little must stint themselves yet further, and Caillié —
seeking to acquire merit in their eyes—must join fully in
their sacrifice, inflicting on himself what turned out to
be a quite useless martyrdom.

Ramadan was the Brakna Lent. But no mere Lent of
Wednesday and Friday fish. No Christian saint's most
fanatical self-sacrifice could be so terrible a mortification
of the flesh as what was undertaken as a matter of course
every year by all the adult Brakna males. The women,
it is pleasant to record, were less strict. The Ramadan of
Caillié's year was especially hard, for it occurred in the
hot weather. During the long torrid days they deprived
themselves completely of water from earliest morn, "the
moment when one can distinguish a black thread from a
white", until sunset. They deprived themselves of food,
too, but this, in their climate, was of minor consequence.
It was the lack of drink which hurt.

Every man was his neighbour's torturer, watching him
like a hawk. What joy to chastise the weakling who sneaked
a drop of water. Or to report to the Marabout that such-
a-one had dared to kill a tickling louse during the hours
when even this small satisfaction was accounted impious.

The Ramadan of Caillié's apprenticeship was embellished by a special feature. All could watch Caillié, watch

how this unaccustomed ex-Christian would stand up to the hardship. It was fun for the Braknas, and hell for René.

He writes:

"My sufferings increased as my strength diminished. The sixth day I believed that I could not bear these dreadful privations any longer. The East wind blew hard, the heat increased. My thirst was insupportable. My throat dried up, my tongue was arid and cracked like a file in my mouth. I thought I was going to die. . . . At last the marabouts allowed me to bathe my face and head and part of my body, but I was observed with the closest attention and it would have been at the risk of being massacred had I been seen swallowing any water.

"My sufferings were a diversion (to the Moors). If they found me lying almost senseless on the ground, expiring with thirst they pulled my clothes and pinched me . . . finishing always by asking me didn't I want to drink some brandy and eat some pork, and then bursting into roars of laughter."

Yet Caillié did not weaken. He felt that he had found the ideal way of getting to Timbuctoo. Nothing else mattered.

With the consent of the Braknas he set off for Saint-Louis. There he intended to lay his plan before the authorities and to secure the financial help which he had been led to believe would be given him, as soon as he had completed his preparation amongst the Moors. He would ask for 6,000 francs.

A companion was deputed to go with him as spy, so that, as soon as the young Frenchman should take possession of his supposed inheritance, he might be escorted swiftly back with it for the enrichment of the tribe.

This man suggested almost before their departure that it would be suitable if Caillié were to give him, as soon as they arrived in Saint-Louis, "four pieces of guinea and a gun". The evening before Caillié's departure he overheard the words of a man in whose tent he was resting. "I hope", said this man, "that he will die *here*, when he comes back with his riches!"

On this rapacious note Caillié said good-bye to the Moors; a last good-bye, as it happened.

16

DISAPPOINTMENT CRASHED ON René at Saint-Louis. His patron, Governor Roger, was on leave in France, and had left no word about the claims of this young man whom he had encouraged to go a studying in the hard Moorish school. The interim governor, Hugon, snubbed Callié firmly.

To Hugon this young man in tattered Moorish draperies who asked for 6,000 francs and told a romantic story of strolling to Timbuctoo seemed either a lunatic or a charlatan. It really shows much courage that Hugon finally offered Caillié 1,200 francs worth of goods.

Caillié refused the 1,200-franc offer. He had represented himself as a person of means to his Brakna friends. It would have been silly and dangerous to return with a trifling sum to spend, especially since the arguments with Hugon had taken considerable time and the delay had roused suspicion in Caillié's Brakna companion.

Caillié saw that his plan was temporarily wrecked, that he must await Baron Roger's return. He was penniless, as usual, and for a time received hospitality at the establishment of a friendly merchant. He must have been an embarrassing guest, still persistently wearing his Moorish petticoats, and involved in mystery and intrigue and native suspicion. Presently he received a Government order for fifteen days' free living. His position was beyond bearing. He was humiliated, bitterly disappointed, an object of ridicule.

A steamer was leaving for Fort Bakel up the Senegal, where René had already been with the Gray expedition. He asked to be allowed to travel on board, hoping somehow to make his way inland from there. Another refusal. The reason was that at the moment there lay ill at Bakel a certain Monsieur de Beaufort, to whom the French had given very large financial support for a proposed expedition to discover Timbuctoo, and that the sick explorer would be pained to see Caillié push off inland under his nose! Caillié was indignant at this frivolous refusal. In his opinion he was being wilfully impeded.

René believed the French Government had given his rival 20,000 francs. Perhaps it was not as much as that. De Beaufort had complacently conceived and submitted to the Government a most sweeping scheme. He had suggested that he should be sent to the Niger with a band of helpers. There his little army would split into four parts, going to the four quarters of Africa and finding out not only just where the mysterious Niger went to but *everything else of interest* about the dark continent! His proposal was submitted to the able geographer Jomard, the geographer who on Caillié's victorious return aided him in preparing his notes for publication. Jomard said dryly that de Beaufort had better first get to the Niger. This the unhappy man never did, and his expensive expedition was of very little value. When he died at Bakel, it cannot be expected that Caillié mourned him, for certainly, had it not been for him, René would have got the encouragement he longed for.

Caillié, seeing that all hope was lost for the present, asked for work and was offered the repugnant job of overseeing negroes at the Richard-Tol, the experimental gardens up the river. He was to receive fifty francs a month and keep. On his way toward Richard-Tol, Caillié was seized by the notion to collect bird specimens—which perhaps seemed to the disappointed young man to have a certain pathetic kinship with exploring. His request for instruments for stuffing his collection drew from "one in high authority in the colony"—Hugon, I presume—the tart comment: "Willingly; in this way Caillié will at any rate be doing *something useful!*"

René, "rage in the heart", pushed on to Richard-Tol. But even in his anger he could not forget his ambitions. He began to study botany, profiting by the varied gardens of the establishment and the expert gardeners employed there.

The gardens, named after Richard, the gardener friend of Baron Roger's who inaugurated them (Tol being the Wolof for garden), represented a really mighty effort. Experts were brought to Senegal at high cost, a *noria* (water-wheel) was installed, the place was fortified with cannons. Roger procured special cotton seed from the French consul at Savannah and fetched out working gardeners from the Tuileries and the Jardin des Plantes of Paris.

Tropic plants from abroad were imported and tried out. Local plants that till then had "just growed" now found themselves petted and cherished. The natives marvelled at such solicitude. The Bambouk round pea was cultivated with respect, also the Senegal pepper, the succulent native tomato, and the humble calabash which provided the negro with his bowls and dishes.

Roger ordered that attention should be given to the familiar *soump* tree, from whose fruit a sort of oil was produced which the natives liked. And to the wild sarsaparilla, and the native dye plants—*fayer*, from which was obtained a handsome strong yellow, and *neb-neb*, whose extract gave a good black.

And always he sang a song of indigo. The good Baron was an indigo enthusiast. When the indigo crop failed it is a matter of record that he literally became ill. He asked that an indigo expert be sent from Bengal. He paid the colossal wage—or so it was then considered—of 7,500 francs a year to the man who organized his indigo experiments, and he sent representatives through the country to preach its proper cultivation and handling amongst the natives, who, though they adored blue cloth, had never, of course, developed the plant according to its possibilities.

Of all Roger's extravagances the pursuit of Perfect Indigo was perhaps the most costly. By a most curious freak of fate it was Caillié who reaped the profit! At Richard-Tol[1] Caillié learned what enabled him later to get the money for the journey to Timbuctoo.

Word came to Richard-Tol that the great "Borom Ndar", the white chief of Saint-Louis, was back from his visit to France.

Caillié was crazy with joy and excitement, "I rushed about," he says, "trying on every side to find a boat that would carry me down the river to Saint-Louis. If I could have, I would have swam. As soon as I was at Saint-Louis I hurried to the Governor. I gave him that same day the notes I had prepared during my stay amongst the Braknas, and I accompanied them with a new demand for help or for a salary. This was not granted. . . . It was a thunder-clap, but I tried again, and then it was that they had the goodness to promise me a certain sum upon my return from Timbuctoo. Upon my return from Timbuctoo!!!"

The three points of exclamation are René's—René, whose style was always so sober and dignified. M. Jomard must have deplored them. They must have pricked like a trident into M. le Baron's hide.

Roger in his handling of Caillié blundered woefully. After Caillié's victory the Baron found himself in a riling position. He was one of the special commission of six which was charged by the Paris Geographical Society to pass on Caillié's claims. How he must have winced when he signed his name to the Commission's report in which occurred the statement that Caillié had succeeded "without help from anyone!" And with what annoyance must he have listened to the polite amazement of some fellow Commissioner inquiring: "But weren't *you* out there at the time, Baron?"

[1] These facts about Roger's experiments at Richard-Tol I have found in the very careful book of Georges Hardy, *La Mise en Valeur du Sénégal, de 1817 à 1854*.

It was Roger's boast, based on his expensive experiments and feverish energy, that he had "given France and the King a new colony". But he had to admit that by his dullness of perception and his evasiveness he so antagonized the greatest explorer of his age—first encouraging Caillié by implied promises and then repudiating him—that he very nearly lost France and the King another colony. Several colonies. The wide lands of Western Sudan and the upper Niger. All the un-discovered country upon which Caillié, the first white man, set his foot is now French. Roger, by discouraging him did all he could to turn these discoveries into the hands of England.

One thing Roger did do which stiffened Caillié's nerve at this discouraging moment, though probably Roger did it merely to get rid of an annoying pest. He told Caillié about the prize of 10,000 francs offered by the Paris Geographical Society to the man who should clear up the Timbuctoo mystery. Afterwards Baron Roger found in this perfunctory act something to boast about. The report of the Geographical Society's Commission contains the proud words: "One of us who was at Senegal at the time and who saw him to be animated by a passion for travel communicated to him a copy of the programme."

The Geographical Society's "programme", which Baron Roger showed to René, is an unintentionally funny document. After telling of the various offers of money made by private persons and Government departments and by the Society itself, whose part was to promise a gold medal[1] worth 2,000 francs, it rehearses its demands.

The prize would be awarded to the man, who proceeding from the western coast of Africa, should reach Timbuctoo and bring back "a manuscript account" of the mysterious city. The traveller should tell exactly where the city was.

[1] To win the Société de Géographie's gold medal was, still is, a very great honour. It was first won by Captain John Franklin, of North-West Passage fame, in 1829. The second to win the medal was René Caillié. It was conferred on Lindbergh in 1927.

He should describe the neighbouring rivers, the trade of the town. He should give information "of the most convincing and precise kind" about the lands between Timbuctoo and Lake Chad and should tell the height of the Sudanese mountains. He should also report on the nature of the ground, the depth and temperature of wells, the speed of rivers and colour of their waters, and specify what were the products of the country. Furthermore, he was instructed to describe the wild animals and to make and carry home to the Society a collection of fossils, shells and plants.

While he was about it, he was invited to pick up a few details of a more personal and romantic character. I quote the last paragraph of the programme, which, by its grotesquely varied demands, typifies the stay-at-home's inability to visualize the traveller's difficulties. And, by the way, it is astounding to find that René Caillié really did manage to secure almost all the detailed information which the gentlemen in Paris desired.

The paragraph in question runs: "In observing the natives he shall take care to examine their manners and morals, their customs, their arms, their laws, their religions, the way they eat, their sicknesses, the colour of their skins, the form of their faces, the nature of their hair, and the different objects in which they trade. He is desired to record their vocabularies, translating the words and expressions into French, to give an account of their habitations, and to make plans of their cities wherever he is able to do so."

Although it must be admitted that the Society desired a great deal of dangerously gained knowledge for its 10,000 francs, we can imagine how their programme must have excited Caillié.

Now comes the hardest time in all Caillié's hard life. At a loose end, all hope of French backing lost to him, René clung with a snarling obstinacy to his Arab dress, all that was left of his dear project. He was not a pleasant fellow to deal with in those few days while he still hung about Saint-Louis, thinking he saw a sneer on every face.

And although René probably suspected sneers where none existed, there was much gossip and a certain amount of grinning at the plight of this odd little man. The discovery of Timbuctoo was a vitally practical business to the traders of Saint-Louis, not a "stunt" or a matter of satisfying unbearable curiosity. They believed Timbuctoo was the key to a great market from which they were being excluded by native pride and secretiveness. They believed that its discovery and the consequent smashing down of black defiance and intolerance would make everybody's fortunes. A limited company, in which most of Saint-Louis's business men held shares, had been formed, having as one of the main items of its charter "to organise a caravan to introduce French goods into the interior of Africa and preferably to Timbuctoo".

Every serious attempt made by anybody to invade the secret city was the subject of tense interest. Caillié's obscure efforts were hotly discussed and confused word of them even reached Paris. Jomard received a letter from Saint-Louis written by a prominent colonist and a rival explorer named Gérardin in which, after mentioning various travellers, the writer says, "and another Frenchman is joining a caravan of Arabs whose ways he is adopting in the idea of getting to the city by a new route".

Caillié felt anger, but not despair. He still had self-confidence. His longing to plunge into Africa was an obsession stronger than his patriotism. He claimed the pitiful one hundred francs he had earned at the gardens, tucked up his Arab skirts, and went to sell himself to rival England, France's enemy in his boyhood and the subject of criticism and cavil ever since he had first come to Africa. It was the English who had made them hang about in misery at

Dakar, it was the English who interfered with the gum trade by seducing the Moors away from the River to Portendik; it was the English who were always attempting to beat the French as explorers—Peddie, Campbell, Gray and the rest.

Caillié left Saint-Louis, never to see it again, and set off toward the English colony of Sierra Leone. But he was destined to give his life and his work to his own country after all, and to return to France by a wider route than ever any Frenchman had used for his home-coming.

17

GRIMLY HE TRUDGED along the same hard road he had walked eight years before with his two racing negro companions, crossed from the mainland to Gorée Island, and looked about for a ship to carry him southward. He dodged all contacts with the French people of Gorée.

From Albreda on the Gambia—fifty straw huts and four houses—the last French-controlled post in Africa that Caillié would ever see, he crossed to Bathurst, the rival English establishment, and took ship to carry him along the road Equatorward, toward Sierra Leone, seat of the English Governor.

It was a quite new world to Caillié, a different Africa. Out of the land of frank, brilliant, burning sunshine and gales of desert wind. Out of sandy lands so scorched and dry that the *harmattan's* blast breaks table glasses with a sudden pop, and once, so says Mrs. Bowdich, a contemporary of Caillié's, cracked the bell of Bathurst barracks! Into the dank green of the world's armpit, sweaty and secret. Dim clouded skies, the *pot-au-noir* of French sailors. Coasts wooded to the ocean's edge. Coves and the mouths of mysterious rivers up which slavers felt their way to hide their victims in masked *barracoons*, and pirates buried their treasure, where savages lurked with poisoned arrows, and stagnant water was deadly.

Here and there was a crouching trade-post, or some queer

little stranded group of white settlers and their cross-bred descendants.

On the Geba and at Bissao loafed the copper and beige and sallow inheritors of the old Portuguese adventurers, tinted like human rainbows, and carrying noble titles which nobody bothered to challenge. They lived as poorly as the jet black negroes whom they grew each generation to resemble more closely. Very chummy with the natives, and much beloved. As a mere act of courtesy these natives once massacred a neighbouring English trading-post, "lest its presence might incommode" Portuguese trade!

Posts where other whites had made their homes—Yankee and English slave traders who had married the daughters of native Kings and founded half-caste dynasties, little primitive kingdoms. They were strange folk: madmen some of them. One Ormond threw any slave whom he could not sell into the sea with a rock tied to his neck like an unwanted puppy, and burned alive in a barrel of tar a black couple whom he caught in unauthorized fornication.

Trading-posts that were more creditable: posts where white men worked hard in conditions of unimaginable difficulty and danger, and made well-deserved fortunes. At the mouth of the Rio Nunez were big "factories" run by worthy Englishmen and Frenchmen. Caillié would see the Nunez again.

He was nearing his goal, Sierra Leone, "the lovely charnel house". The air was heavy as steam from a boiling kettle. The shores were a dense green strip—"as if it had been cut with a pair of gardener's sheeres", said one of the travellers quoted in *Hakluyt's Voyages*. Sometimes at night phosphorescence made the sea a rolling mass of fire. Then a towering mountain rose abruptly from the sea, the Lion Mountain of Sierra Leone. They entered Frenchman's Bay, as it was called in the old days; a bitter name, no doubt, to the ears of the renegade Frenchman. There before him was Freetown, pretty as a Viennese waltz, and then considered the deadliest place on earth.

To Caillié all this unwholesome tropic beauty held neither romantic charm nor terror. To him it looked like one thing only—money! He was Dick Whittington going to London-in-Africa to make his fortune!

It must have required great moral—or call it immoral! —courage for a Frenchman to approach the English of Freetown just then with a request for aid. Freetown had fresh and indignant memories about the French and the visit of a squadron of *Sans-Culottes* which tested the courage and temper of twenty-six-year-old Governor Zachary Macaulay. Every house was looted, the church destroyed, and all the papers and books in the settlement tossed to the wind. If the latter "happened to bear any resemblance to Bibles" the Revolutionaries trampled on them. Offences less serious but almost as grievous to the infant settlement were that the French shot twelve hundred hogs in the town, killed "no less than fourteen dozen fowls" in the young Governor's poultry yard, and finally—to quote Zachary Macaulay's own record—"some of the sailors were actually seen in the act of killing a beautiful musk cat, which they afterwards ate". They put the final insult on the loyal English community by the insistent singing of "the Marseilles hymn"!

All this was only a generation away when Caillié presented himself at Freetown.

18

TWO STONE LIONS marked the entrance to Government House, a battery of cannon pointed seaward, the British flag drooped in the heavy air. Caillié passed between the British lions, saluted this new flag, and sought audience with King George IV's representative on the West Coast, Governor Turner.

Was René still wearing his ragged Moorish robe, or had he borrowed a pair of trousers? At any rate he must have seemed an unprepossessing little morsel, and it is to the credit of the Governor that he listened to his extraordinary proposal. A French writer, praising Turner for this, has said: "The English—and it is one of their fine qualities—have no sense of the ridiculous."

René writes that Governor Turner received him with "*bonté*". But, alas, he declined Caillié's proposal. He would not back Caillié. As René found out afterwards, Turner had a specific and excellent reason for his refusal.

Caillié turned disconsolately away. Turner called him back. He would retain him at Freetown. There were two specific and excellent reasons for this! One was very simple. Caillié had presumably mentioned his botanical experience at Richard-Tol. Governor Turner welcomed the opportunity to find out what the French were doing in those experimental gardens of theirs. The other reason Caillié was to learn later. And perhaps still a third reason influenced the English Governor—the simple wish to be kind to a young man in trouble.

He offered Caillié well-paid work, created a position for him at what must have seemed to Caillié a princely salary. Caillié, who had been getting fifty francs a month at Richard-Tol, was to receive the equivalent of 3,600 francs a year as director of an indigo establishment.

More gardening! Caillié shuddered. But what could he do but thank Governor Turner and accept?.

Presently—it was a tragic commonplace in Sierra Leone—the Governor died. Caillié approached his successor, "sir Nill Campbell". (This is Caillié's spelling. It was Major-General Sir Neil Campbell.) Again he told his tale of Timbuctoo for sale for 6,000 francs. Another refusal.

Now Caillié learned why the Governors of Freetown would have none of him. It was because Laing was trying to get to Timbuctoo. Major Laing, who had served in

Sierra Leone and accomplished fine feats of minor exploration, who was a Scot and a local hero, had received the
English Government's generous backing for his Timbuctoo
attempt. It was a clever move to keep this frantically
determined rival in safe inactivity in an indigo works.
Caillié understood now both the refusal to back him and
the main reason for his employment.

Again René found himself held back because of a favoured
rival. Moribund de Beaufort he had not feared. Laing, yes!

How Laing's venture was progressing Caillié did not
know. Laing had left Tripoli some eight months before
in the hope of reaching Timbuctoo.

After "sir Nill's" refusal Caillié came to the second important decision of his life. Oddly, both decisions were associated
with the English. The first came when he was in hospital after
the Gray breakdown and realized that he must wait and grow
strong before he could hope to start on his great journey. Now
he decided that he must pay for it himself: that he would
grow old before he found anyone ready to back him.

So, counting himself lucky to have been offered a salary
that made economy possible, he settled into his well-paid
niche and saved his shillings.

René Caillié after his triumph was taxed with not being
properly thankful for what was done for him at Freetown.
It is certainly true that a reader of his *Journal* cannot discern
an attitude of obstreperous gratitude to England, either in
Caillié's own words, or in the editorial remarks of Jomard,
who makes but the most fleeting references to Caillié's stay in
Sierra Leone. Peevish, in fact, is the burden of Jomard's
comment on Caillié's experience in the English colony: he
complains that Caillié there learned to write native names
with a *w*—that unfamiliar letter to the French—and that, in
editing his notes, Jomard had to alter each uncouth *w* to *ou!*

Yet by nature Caillié was not ungrateful, but was, on the

contrary, a conspicuously appreciative man, remembering every good turn done him in his hard life and recording it with almost childish care. His *Journal* contains many acknowledgements to persons who aided him, recording their names and the exact nature of their kindness and Caillié's high opinion of them. When his book was published one can imagine that many men who had quite forgotten the small service which they had rendered were astonished and touched to find their good deed so carefully set down in print. I do not say this about Caillié in order to idealize him. The real Caillié is far more interesting than any idealization. Caillié was so utterly different from the typical hero of romance and history. He was a human curio. But, whatever else one may say of him, anyone who studies his history must recognize that he was sensitive and grateful.

But also he was shrewd. His unemotional acceptance of the wage paid him for work which he evidently performed properly, for he retained his position and left by resignation, was the proper reaction to the situation.

He well knew that his English protectors had their own motives for making his stay in Sierra Leone attractive, so that it might be prolonged as much as possible. Further indication of this was given when he was treated with evasiveness on asking for an English passport to go inland. That the two English Governors realized his capacity, despite his shabby appearance and his ignorance, was proof of their good sense. Baron Roger showed less intuition. Caillié was flattered. But it does not follow that he owed England anything specific.

Caillié writes that he was indebted to the stranger nation for "a generous hospitality" and that, when the first disappointment was over, he was glad that he had been refused foreign backing as an explorer. Thus he was able to work as a free-lance and to offer the fruits of his discovery to his own people, a natural and normal action. It would certainly have been an absurd gesture had

Caillié attempted to present Timbuctoo to England because he had been given work in an English indigo works.

Freetown was, in Caillié's day, as queer a place as ever existed anywhere in the world. It was not a town but a philanthropic institution, a refuge for black men and liberated slaves, a kind of negro zoo, where specimens of almost every black race of Africa were sheltered.

It was, too, a psychological hospital where the blank-faced terror of the freshly rescued savage rapidly changed to comical and bumptious self-satisfaction. The fact that white men took such pains to import him or to liberate him went to his head. Sierra Leone was populated with immensely conceited negroes. The negro had no conception of abstract indignation. The fact that these white folk saved them could only prove they were especially valuable and superior negroes.

But why, many a woolly head wondered, save anyone from slavery? Slavery was a natural institution. Allah approved of slavery. The danger of being caught and made a slave was one of life's risks. Slave chasing was a natural sport, slave dealing a dignified business for enterprising men.

"Can a cat give up mousing?" a distinguished negro demanded, when the British told him to stop. "When I die it will be with a slave in my mouth!" The desire to catch and sell one another was as normal and respected an impulse as the modern white man's effort to better a competitor in business. As a matter of course little children did not venture far from their villages lest they be snatched up by passing collectors who went equipped always with a large wallet, specifically intended to be used as a human game bag.

Freetown's dusky social fabric had a very elaborate pattern. The underlying weave was made up of the original arrivals, of what one might call the negro equivalents of Mayflower aristocracy. These were, first, the "Settlers", a group of loyalist negroes who had opted for the English at the time of the American Revolution and naturally found themselves unpopular afterwards. They had gone to Nova Scotia and thence—some eleven hundred of them—had been transported to Sierra Leone, their protectors supposing they would flourish by the mere fact that they were of African blood and had been returned to Africa. Without shelter or provisions, they died in the beginning at the rate of half a dozen a day. When Caillié came to Freetown there were not six hundred of the Settler breed left, despite negro fertility.

Next amongst the First Families of Sierra Leone ranked the Maroons, rebel slaves from Jamaica, who also came to Freetown by way of Nova Scotia. The Maroons, a history of bloody revolt behind them, were tougher than the Settlers, and their numbers were on the increase. They maintained a chief who called himself the King of the Maroons, and, like the Settlers, had a quarter of their own, called Maroon-Town.

These two groups hated one another and regularly celebrated Christmas by desperate frays and mutual outrages. What caused them to choose the Yuletide season for their disputes is not explained by the travelling clergyman[1] who records the quaint custom. He adds, however, that "the benign and softening spirit of the Gospel" led to a better understanding and calm.

There was indeed no lack of Gospel in Freetown, which attracted a variety of missionaries. The city and the surrounding country were splattered with chapels and primitive meeting-houses. Many peculiar Christian sects had places of worship, some of them straw huts or shacks. The Established Church had a large edifice, said to be the only English Church on the West Coast in the old days, also said to have "resembled a barn", although it was years in the completion and the pet hobby of each succeeding short-lived Governor and cost altogether some £40,000. And yet, with all this choice of Christian facilities, the converted negro could not always shed his paganism. Some-

---

[1] Thomas Eyre Poole, *Life, Scenery and Customs in Sierra Leone and the Gambia*. (1850).

times pastors, visiting members of their flock *in extremis*, were shocked to perceive "an idol behind the pillow".

The only other "superior" blacks besides the Settlers and the Maroons were such as survived or descended from the "Black Poor". "Black Poor" was a name given in England to the embarrassed negroes who were suddenly tossed into freedom and destitution by the court judgment of 1772 which stated that a slave was free as soon as he set his foot on England. They were shipped to Sierra Leone, and with them were sent by ungallant whimsy a group of sixty white prostitutes, mostly shanghaied when drunk.

All these "superior" blacks wore European garb of a fantastic sort. It must have been in the Sierra Leone negro that old-fashioned comic artists found their inspiration for the savage in a top hat and one cuff. Their language was also a grotesque imitation, "talkee-talkee", pidgin English, common to the jumble of native races of Freetown. Part of the Bible was translated into talkee-talkee and made very remarkable reading.

These various immigrant groups of negro aristocracy who already knew white ways were swamped by a wild riff-raff, the captives rescued off the slave ships which the English seized.

Thousands and thousands of negroes, invariably naked, were dumped on the shores of Sierra Leone—natives of all the races of West and Central tropic Africa; proud, beautifully muscled Krus, Akans, Kissis, Susus, Ibos; men with tattooed faces, tribal cuts, carved backs; cannibals with teeth filed to points, "crocodile teeth", the other natives said.

Sometimes, even in Freetown, these cannibals so far forgot their civic duties as to eat their fellow citizens. At about the time of Caillié's visit to Sierra Leone one of the liberated Africans disgraced himself by returning to town "with human hands and other portions of human flesh in his wallet". Questioned, the man admitted that, wandering in the environs of the town, he had become hungry and had fallen upon a fellow townsman "weaker than himself", killed him, eaten most of him and fetched the rest back for a subsequent snack.

It must have required wisdom and devotion to handle these masses of frightened, filthy, sick and disorientated creatures. When a slave vessel was captured the slaves often supposed their position worse than ever. The British must have seized the ship to eat the cargo! So some jumped overboard and never reached Freetown at all. Of those who came ashore, all were scared and many were very ill, suffering from ophthalmia, fevers and skin complaints generated and exchanged in the suffocating filth of their ship quarters, sometimes even crippled for life by long crouching between decks.

As they landed to each was offered the bewildering gift of clothing, a yard and a quarter of coarse calico per slave. After that, they accepted the honour of adoption as free British subjects and the stronger men were led forth to be soldiers, which —because of the tight and heating scarlet cloth uniform, the weighty shako, stiff stock and cumbrous shoes—was regarded as a worse form of torture than confinement on the slave ship.

The newly liberated African women were married off to liberated African males—often males of other races, so that the courtship was very short and the married life in its early days quite silent. But every new-comer received a plot of ground, some tools, and a temporary allowance of twopence a day. To most this meant luxurious ease. The twopence made the tools superfluous. Hurrah for the British!

In those days living in Freetown was an adventure in itself—often a fatal adventure. Freetown then was a death trap, the subject of a score of grim jokes, and very different from the Freetown of today. It is said that 1,421 Europeans died out of 1,658 between 1822 and 1830, dates which include the period of Caillié's stay at Sierra Leone. The "Coffin Squadron" of police ships brought batches of slaves into port reeking with epidemics. From the swamps and dank forests near the little city came the stench of decaying vegetation, and at night a white mist came floating, which was known as "the malaria", an odd case of a disease and its source bearing the same name. Such horror did this deadly creeping mist inspire that the people of Freetown planned to erect a thirty-foot wall sixteen miles long to keep it away.

They were a gallant and fantastic handful of Englishmen, the "old-timers" on the West Coast. Or rather, Scotsmen; for, says a contemporary traveller, it was "a curious circumstance that the whole of the white residents, with a few exceptions, bear Scotch names". About a dozen wives pined and aged ten years in one. "A white woman was a phenomenon rare as a palm-tree in England." And there was just one unmarried white woman in all Sierra Leone.

The white man's ways were often desperate and mad. Once someone suggested cricket in the sunshine, as in Old England. In the shade it was 98 degrees. They cheered on the game with "abundant wines and liquors". After a fortnight only one of these sportsmen was left alive.

The drinking was stupendous. In the rainy season it was not unusual to find in the morning that the town drains were choked by the bodies of soldiers who had fallen intoxicated in the night. A bottle of rum could be had for a "cut money"—just over a shilling. It made death very cheap.

Genial Dr. Poole, on his visit to old Sierra Leone, deplored excesses which he noted. The good clergyman could speak advisedly, for he tells us blandly that he drank palm wine for his early breakfast as a pleasant "substitute for tea or coffee", and proceeded to a second breakfast at which he drank "ale or claret and water".

Caillié had no need for the crude drinking which deadened fear and heartache, for he felt neither. Keen to please his English employers and keep up the incoming stream of shillings, he put his best effort into his work. Undoubtedly he tried to teach those under his charge a better way of handling indigo. The native fashion was complex and lengthy. In Senegal he had observed the experiments in a simpler and swifter method, a method by which—the description reads like a glowing modern advertisement for some household appliance—"an operation which required great skill and several days' work could be accomplished in twelve hours by an ordinary person who had once seen it done."[1]

There can be no doubt that René had "ordinary persons" to do his work—very ordinary indeed. And very slothful. These pampered black men of Sierra Leone were almost invariably loafers. Their drowsy laziness is the subject of uncounted West Coast anecdotes. In a charming little collection of negro tales and songs and sayings, *L'Ame Nègre* by Maurice Delafosse, is a typical fable from Sierra Leone. Two dusky sleepy-heads met and immediately after saying "How-do!" fell asleep side by side. A python swallowed the first man, a crocodile swallowed the python and a mythical beast called a "water-leopard" snapped up the crocodile. The "water-leopard" was killed by a hunter, cut open, the crocodile within its stomach cut open, and the python cut open. The Sierra Leone negro yawned and said, "I must have dropped off!" and looked about for his companion. But the companion had been overgrown by the jungle and buried under earth and dead vegetation and it was only when a farmer dug into him with his hoe that he awoke to say, "I must have dropped off too!"

René's leisure was devoted to study and preparation. One lesson was peculiar. He taught himself to estimate accurately his rate of march, so that as he later walked across Africa he could keep track of his route.

Daily he used to walk the timed hour between mileposts in Freetown, learning to estimate the speed of his pace automatically, and to know the lapse of time by

[1] From a letter written by Baron Roger, quoted in Hardy's *La Mise en Valeur du Sénégal de 1817 à 1854.*

instinct. With only the sun to check time by and a compass which he would seldom dare use, he would still be able at the end of each day's march, to note the distance covered and the shifting directions.

Caillié, all his life an eccentric, can never have seemed odder than during these walking lessons along Water Street.

From behind the jalousies of their picturesque wide veran-daed houses the pallid ladies of Sierra Leone peeped out at the little Frenchman in wonder. Merchants stared at him from out of the shaded recesses of their cavernous "stores" and tapped their foreheads, thinking him another victim of the climate.

His negro acquaintances—his workmen and their families—marvelled too, wondering why their *pootah* boss, their white overseer, trudged along, indifferent to their "Daddee, daddee, how-do!" which was the "talkee-talkee" fashion of saying "Good day, Sir".

It was useless for the children, the *bobbohs* and *titties*, or for the old *gaa mammies*, or even for the pretty girls, *wanghy-kellens* and *ghynny din-a-dys* and *pusses*, to smile at him. Caillié, as he went back and forth from the Parade Ground to the wall of the "Liberated African's Yard," had no ears for the babel of the market-place with its clamour of twenty different languages, nor nose for its aroma of dried fish, palm oil and *fu-fu* balls, nor eyes for the comic native scene, the bride in white satin and bare-foot, carrying her white satin slippers like a prayer-book, the groom majestic with blue swallow tail and the indis-pensable nuptial umbrella. He was counting off his paces to Timbuctoo.

19

AT FREETOWN CAILLIÉ learned while he earned. With its ten thousand natives of twenty or more races it was an ideal museum for the studious explorer.

Some of these natives must have been hard fellows to become intimate with—and dangerous. I scarcely think René could have got beyond a nodding acquaintance with the Akans, who were believed to be fire worshippers, or with the Kissis and Susus, and the saw-toothed cannibals from the far South. Nor were the Krus genial subjects: grumpy men who never married whilst they remained in Freetown but lived apart in "a silent suburb of naked bachelor Krus, where a thousand men dwelt in heavy stillness, and no woman's form was seen or voice heard". When they had made their fortunes they went home and presumably resumed normal life. The procedure of the average white resident at Sierra Leone was much the same!

The Krus consoled their lonely leisure with wrestling matches, where splendid men challenged one another with animal leaps and spurnings of the dust, and by their national dance, the Krikkery-Boo, the Dance of Death, a sort of pantomime.

There was ample chance to watch all sorts of dancing. The native was always ready to dance, anywhere, at any time, if somebody would hit a drum. There were frequent Koonkings and Tallalas, forms of women's tam-tams. The negro aristocracy, the Settlers and Maroons, delighted in more formal dances, which they characteristically called "Dignity Balls"!

From the start Caillié made friends with the cleverest natives of them all, the Mandingos. This was not out of admiration, for René described this race as "liars, crawlers and boasters", but because he wanted to learn their language. He profited by the hint in Mungo Park's book to the effect that their language was "with a few exceptions universally understood", and that Mandingos "constituted the bulk of the inhabitants" in the countries Park passed on his way to the Niger.

Caillié's success was largely due to his knowledge of Mandingo. He eventually learned the language well enough to prepare a little Mandingo-French dictionary, which is included in his *Journal*. For eight months Mandingo was his sole form of human communication, and this at a time of peculiar and tragic crisis in his adventures.

There were plenty of Mandingos at Freetown, living in the "Mohammedan-town" with its little mosque, and supporting themselves as leather workers, metal workers, traders in gold and in black gold. For the Mandingos were the slave merchants-in-chief of the region and maintained that Freetown, here under the nose of the emancipators, was "one of the best places for kidnapping men along the whole West Coast".

In secret the trade went on. The liberated African, it seemed, was often ready to sell his fellow ex-captive back into the condition from which the English had saved him.

One day René visited Mohammedan-town on a special mission. He had made up a new story about himself, the story by which he planned to explain himself into Africa and to Timbuctoo as soon as he had saved enough money. It was carefully designed to endear him to native confidence, and like every wise liar he sought an early opportunity to practise it and see how it went.

He writes: "With a mysterious air I told them this story under the seal of secrecy:—I was born in Egypt of Arab parents, and I was taken to France when very young by certain French who had gone into Egypt with the army. Later I was taken to Senegal by my master as a helper in his commercial affairs, and he—satisfied with my services—had freed me.

"I added, Now that I am free to go where I like, I desired naturally to return to Egypt to seek for my family and to go on in the Mussulman religion.

"At first the Mandingos did not seem to give credence to

my story, and were especially doubtful of my religious zeal. But they no longer doubted when they heard me recite by heart some passages from the Koran; and when they watched me in the evening join them in the 'salam', they finished by saying to one another that I was a good Mussulman. Need I say that in secret I addressed the most fervent prayers to the God of the Christians, that he should bless my voyage?"

Soon Caillié's Mandingo friends became deeply impressed by his romantic and pious personality. He suffered from their oppressive hospitality, and was obliged to eat many a dinner of rice and water and palm oil. Then, as happens so often to those who seek the intimacy of natives, Caillié found himself the victim of greed. One of his Mandingos even attempted to trick him out of his silver-mounted tooth-pick, probably René's sole valuable possession, with which he may have made elegant play at the native dinner-parties. Caillié concealed his annoyance and gave away some small presents. Again he had learned an important lesson. He says, "I must above all and always feign to be poor. I must never awaken cupidity."

A certain Mandingo *cherif* now undertook to pilot Caillié a short distance into the interior. It seemed a chance to start. But, when Caillié asked for a passport, his request was ignored, and he could not leave Freetown. A disappointment, but, on second thoughts, René saw that it had been for the best. Also, through the incident he learned another lesson, for the friendly *cherif* set off with some of Caillié's luggage "by mistake"!

From this Caillié realized that the natives, though satisfied with his story, would always act rapaciously toward him so long as he appeared before them in European clothing. To the primitive native mind trousers spoke louder than words. He realized, too, that he could not safely make a start from Freetown, with negro companions who had known him in his white aspect.

He altered his plans. He decided that, when he was ready, he would go disguised to some other place on the coast where the natives would never glimpse him in white man's clothes, and so would have no conflicting physical impressions of him.

At last, shilling by shilling, Caillié had saved up enough. He had the equivalent of 2,000 francs. "It was my whole fortune," he says, "but I thought it right to consecrate it to carrying out my journey. I used 1,700 francs to buy powder (gun-powder), paper, tobacco, bits of glassware, amber, coral, silk handkerchiefs, knives, scissors, mirrors, cloves, also three pieces of guinea and an umbrella." The whole outfit did not weigh a hundred pounds. He could buy only tiny quantities of each thing, for prices were "very high".

The rest of his fortune, the remaining 300 francs, he would carry as a reserve in his waist-band, half in silver, half in gold.

Some friends at Sierra Leone gave him a farewell gift. This was a kind act, for Caillié was a rival in the great Timbuctoo race for which their local Scottish hero was favourite. There was still no definite news of Laing.

The farewell gift was a little packet of medicine, a thing to which men's minds turned readily in that climate. They gave him cream of tartar, jalop, calomel, "divers purgative salts", sulphate of quinine, certain ointments and nitrate of silver.

He possessed two pocket compasses. He carried many loose leaves of the Koran, for a purpose which will be seen later.

The simplicity of Caillié's outfit contrasts so very strikingly with the usual outfits of explorers that I cannot forbear to instance what a few other men took into Africa. Park, for example, for his second expedition, was given £5,000 for expenses and unlimited credit. Barth, the next

man after Caillié to get to Timbuctoo, spent £1,600 and
was praised for his "thrifty German" ability to make his
money go a long way. A large Niger expedition chronicled
by Captain Mockler-Ferryman gave the value of £145
to the chiefs of a single native state, and Speke in East
Africa made presents to a single potentate of everything
from telescopes and gold watches to beads and iron chairs.
Presents, of course, are an essential of African travel!
Hourst went in Paris to a "*spécialiste pour explorations*"
who offered prospective travellers bundles of stuff from
fire-sales and the like, and bought himself 27,000 francs'
worth of *démodé* clothes and assorted junk before he made
his Niger voyage. Stanley's stores in 1887 piled up "in
hundredweights"—in all, six tons of material. There
was in Stanley's case a total of 27,262 yards of various
trade cloth, 100 each of shovels, hoes, axes, bill-hooks and
tents. Some of the food and the medicines were supplied
free by dealers whose names appear in the opening pages
of *In Darkest Africa* with testimonials to the fact that
"the coffee was the purest Mocha" and that "Blank and
Company's Extract was of the choicest".

What a splendid testimonial, by the way, Caillié could
have given the English maker who supplied his umbrella,
had René possessed Stanley's journalistic enterprise. That
sturdy umbrella, the outstanding treasure of his outfit, was a
credit to old-fashioned English workmanship, for it stood up
with its master over a thousand miles of Africa and finally
secured for him his passage along the Niger to Timbuctoo.

Finally, one evening in March, everything was ready
and packed. Caillié's Arab dress was spread for the morrow.
Caillié doffed symbolically—and, he must have feared,
for ever—the trousers of his white manhood.

Next morning the ship *Thomas* carried him north
toward the mouth of the Rio Nunez.

BOOK II

René caillié disembarked at the mouth of the Rio Nunez in what is now the colony of French Guinea, on the 31st of March, 1827. Immediately he met someone romantic enough to delight in his far-flung plans. This man, Castagnet, was in charge of an important trading-post. He took the eccentric young stranger to his heart. He offered Caillié a temporary home and promised to help him to connect with a suitable native caravan going into the interior.

Impossible to start at once, he explained. It was the beginning of Ramadan. No native was moving. He himself was just starting for the Rio Pongo on a trading trip. Would Caillié be his guest? René was deeply touched by Castagnet's goodness, so touched that, when the time came, he parted from him with tears of gratitude and set down the solemn promise that "the generous hospitality which I received in the house of this estimable compatriot during my stay at Kakandé will always merit my gratitude".

Kakandé (sometimes spelt Cacaudé) was the old, affectionate name for the region on the left bank of the Nunez. It is not to be found on modern maps and can no more be rendered into words than a cat's purr. Variously translated as "The-Most-Beautiful-Country" or "The-Country-One-Does-Not-Leave", its name is the simple expression of native content in a plenteous and beautiful homeland.

Kakandé showed Caillié a characteristically smiling face during the twenty days which he spent on its lush green coasts.

There were several Englishmen at Kakandé and nearby. In those days the Nunez was a free trading area and its banks were dotted with the factories of French, English and American traders, who often used as stores what had been old slavers' fortresses. Each "factory" stood apart like an independent village. Many of these settlements bore, some still bear, garbled English names, as Wakéria (or Ouakaria) after Mr. Waker (Walker?) who lived and died there and whose wife was remarkable for the place and times in that she was "a real white woman", according to native tradition. Téléa, similarly, was named after " Master Tell".

Caillié mentions two Englishmen who were particularly friendly, Mr. Tudsberry and Mr. Bethmann. The latter was the same Mr. Bateman so useful to the unlucky Peddie-Campbell-Gray party, which presumably knew better how to spell an English name than René did. Peddie died in his home, and near it Peddie and Campbell were both buried. Mr. Bateman had a very intimate knowledge of the horrors of African exploration.

When Caillié confided his wild project to these two vigorous traders (for men did not run "factories" on the Guinea coast in those days without a strong arm) they must have exchanged a dismayed glance.

It was impossible to dissuade him. All they could do was to be especially kind, as folk are kind to a man condemned to death. So, for the first time in his life, Caillié was treated with a certain awe and as a hero. It was a glorious change from ignominy and indifference. It was a fine "send-off".

The two Englishmen took him to view the tombs of Peddie and Campbell, which would seem, everything considered, a tactlessly chosen outing! It was intended as a warning. Caillié admits that later he thought about the tombs and "shuddered". He knew he would probably soon lie in a grave far less beautiful and honoured. The fate of white travellers who tried to pretend to be Mohammedans was notoriously nasty. So many have tried—both before Caillié's time and since. So few succeeded in the deception.

Shrewd men and suspicious, the Mohammedans. In vain did some men cause themselves to be circumcised— Caillié did not do this, his story of a French upbringing being an adequate explanation. Some pretenders were caught because a tiny corn betrayed the habit of boots. Some because a stopped back tooth attracted notice. A gesture put others away. A very dangerous business pretending to be a Mohammedan in those old days of untamed fanaticism. No wonder Caillié shuddered when folk showed him tombs.

But I rather suspect that Caillié enjoyed shuddering.

On a spot in Kakandé there was put up forty-two years later a monument to commemorate his departure to Timbuctoo. It is a sugar-loaf of modest size done in light stone. It reads:

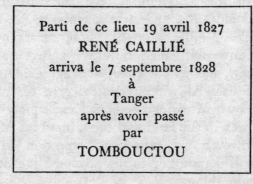

Parti de ce lieu 19 avril 1827
RENÉ CAILLIÉ
arriva le 7 septembre 1828
à
Tanger
après avoir passé
par
TOMBOUCTOU

On the monument's back is another plaque, stating that this stone was set up in the reign of Napoleon III. It was the great Faidherbe, creator of French West Africa, who inspired the gesture of erecting in this lonely place a tribute to René Caillié, the lone fighter. It would, I think, have pleased Caillié more than anything else that has been done in his honour.

But as a matter of fact that statement that Caillié actually began his journey from "*ce lieu*" is not literally true. Caillié left from Castagnet's "factory". The monument is lodged safely inside the grounds of the *poste* of Boké, the leading present-day French town of the region, two hours' walk up-river, a little place whose European population (I was told by the Commandant of Boké in 1935) numbers just fifteen persons. It is remarkably beautiful but hard to approach. In certain seasons its mails must come from the nearest railway point, about one hundred and fifty miles away, on the heads of native porters. At the time when the monument was erected it was thought unwise to put it out in the open country on the exact spot where the explorer started to step off his miles, for this would have been to court destruction by the natives.

Caillié presented himself to the local chief, Prince Macandé of the Landoumas, the then predominating tribe at Kakandé. Macandé was a genial pagan who liked strong drink. (Caillié brought home an account of a favourite native fermented beverage called *jin-jin-dhi*, a complex brew, having "a sweet and agreeable savour".)

Macandé listened with a cynical grin to the story— interpreted by a Mandingo—about René's piety and longing to get back to the land and the faith of his Mussulman fathers. However, he raised no objection to Caillié's presence in Kakandé nor to his proposed journey, which was the main thing.

But the Mohammedans of Kakandé gave him their hands "in sign of peace", and asked him to join them at prayer time. None doubted his bona fides.

Caillié put in the remaining days of Ramadan in study. The Geographical Society had asked for detailed information about the natives whom a traveller might meet along the road to Timbuctoo. Near Kakandé were certain very curious races—Landoumas and Nalous in the region itself, Bagas close by. Caillié set himself to investigating these folk, and amassed a quantity of quaint and ribald detail.

Very rollicking pagans they seem in the pages of his *Journal*. The Landoumas, he heard, had sometimes as many as two hundred wives: but, he adds cautiously, "this is a number which I believe to be much exaggerated". The splendidly fertile delta land fed them— according to their modest tastes—with barely an effort, and they beguiled their extensive leisure with palm wine, and wine made from wild plums, and with the "sweet and agreeable" *jin-jin-dhi*. From time to time a hideously cruel war gave spice to their loafing. It certainly was, according to male savage ideals, "The Most Beautiful Country".

Landouma women had a less agreeable life. It was evidently the men who gave Kakandé its name. Married out of hand to any men who would offer their fathers suitable gifts of rum, tobacco and kola nuts, they were expected to give incontestible proof of physical purity, which was a matter of public parade as is frequent amongst savage races. Their subsequent chastity was partially guaranteed by the local custom giving an injured husband the right to sell the discovered paramour into slavery and keep the price as damages.

The Bagas, a nearby tribe whose island and marshland homes at the mouth of the Rio Nunez Caillié did not visit, but whom he observed and heard about when they came to the trading settlement, show up very engagingly in his notes. The Bagas wore almost no clothing, were splendid swimmers, and delighted in war for the joy of combat. When it thundered they would drink palm wine and dance to the sound of drums, saying they wished to join in God's tam-tam. (I write God with the usual capital, but these blacks had then no inkling of the Christian or any other outstanding Deity.)

The Bagas menus left something to be desired, for they ate monkey meat, lizard meat and the flesh of serpents. But idyllic indeed were their marriage arrangements. They raised a boy and girl couple together from the moment of betrothal at the age of seven or eight. Every morning the boy was expected to give his little fiancée a calabash of palm wine, and, as Caillié delicately puts it, "they celebrate the marriage when they perceive that the young virgin has ceased so to be, which is ordinarily at the age of eleven or twelve years".

But do not -blame the earnest explorer for frivolity in his reports about these native people. The choice is mine from amongst a mass of details which he gives in his *Journal* about primitive agriculture, hut building, local government, trial by poison, and many other matters.

Beside his note-taking Caillié did another piece of writing, one which gave him vast satisfaction. He wrote to a friend in Saint-Louis that he was soon starting toward Timbuctoo. He must have delighted to think that the Baron Roger would surely hear this by way of gossip.

Ramadan was drawing to its close. Soon Kakandé's Mussulmans would see the crescent of joy. It was springtime, *la-siri* in the native calendar. The year was four moons old. This was the month called "The Beginning of Pregnancy", a happy time when dark women were full of hope.

And a happy time for Caillié, for it marked the opening of his life as a great explorer.

Castagnet returned. According to his promise the friendly Frenchman sought out a group of Mandingo traders of good repute and told them Caillié's story. The Mandingos listened with respect, being Mussulmans, but their interest increased enormously when Castagnet mentioned a present they would receive if they would permit Caillié to travel along in their company. A deal was made and cemented by a gift from Castagnet of "the value of an ox in goods".

The caravan would consist of twelve persons including René—five Mandingo free men, three slaves, a Fula porter carrying Caillié's *pacotille*, Caillié's "guide", Ibrahim—by which term was meant, as we shall see, far more than the word usually indicates to us—and the guide's wife. They would, it is needless to say, travel on foot. All except Ibrahim and his wife and Caillié would carry enormous packs on their heads. In these packs were goods from the coast—salt, guns, powder, beads, cloth—going inland to be exchanged eventually for gold, ivory, slaves. The caravan would eat and sleep as best they could. It promised to be a rough journey, and it was.

It was the 19th of April, 1827. René Caillié was twenty-seven and a half years old. Just a year and a day later, on April 20, 1828, he arrived in Timbuctoo. And after a total journey of 508 days he brought his great adventure to a victorious finish at Tangier in Morocco. According to his notes he had during this year and a half travelled in all 2,849¼ miles (I have suggested that this was a scant and incomplete estimate of the distance). He crossed what is now called French Guinea, cutting off a corner of the modern colony of the Ivory Coast and going through French Sudan to the Niger River. Along the Niger he had ridden by boat to Timbuctoo. Then he had crossed the almost unknown Sahara and fanatical Morocco and at last reached the sea, a few miles from Europe at the Straits of Gibraltar.

Caillié's route to Timbuctoo was in outline like an indecisive capital S reclining on its side and written from bottom to top. It was terribly round-about. It would have scandalized a crow. Had he been able to cut through directly from Boké to Timbuctoo he would have saved himself some six or seven hundred miles of agonizingly difficult travel. But like a river Caillié did not dispute his path but went round obstacles. And like a river he found his way.

"*Oulou-lou-lou, ko tiaygueul, so mayo hewi, deguiet*" runs the Fula wisdom. It means, "The Brook complains *Oulou-lou-lou*, the Great River is silent."

2

LEAVING THE NUNEZ and its white men, traversing the stretch now called the Avenue René Caillié, turning to the south-east along a native path, Caillié was away!

He tramped and waded across low-lying Guinea, the "Land of Death", sticky and tropically hot, heavy then with that special and hideous oppression which precedes the rainy season, when the air is, for hour after hour, like that single choking moment which in temperate lands goes before a thunder-storm. "Guinea grass" was so high overhead that he weaved his dark way through it like some little scuttling animal.

Then up along the jagged paths toward the mountains, climbing in blistering heat, crouching shelterless during sudden storms, swarming over great rocks, fording mountain streams up to his arm-pits.

Land of Death it was indeed, but of unearthly loveliness, perhaps the most beautiful part of Africa: a land of dappled rivers and cascades, of proud, untamed trees trimmed with big love flowers that only African bees would dare to fertilize. There were fruit trees with fruit that sang its way down dry throats like the gurgle of rippling brooks: forests of orange trees, bananas growing in prolific *regimes* in their quaint upside-down fashion, mangoes smooth-skinned as thick satin, strange native fruits, flaming with colour, bursting with juice. Nature on holiday, spending herself like a drunken sailor.

The first day they made twenty-three miles, lunching under a bombax tree off roast peanuts and boiled rice, all of them dipping the rice out in handfuls from the general calabash. They slept on the ground in a ravine. Next day they did sixteen miles and a half. The third day Caillié had an alarming dispute with a pair of fierce red monkeys who attacked him barking like dogs. Says he: "I admit I was rather frightened." This was no shame to Caillié. These strong-limbed and angry creatures had been known to drive all the inhabitants out of their trading-posts. René was saved by the arrival of his companions.

His adventures continued; on the eighth day he was swept off his feet in a mountain torrent and nearly drowned. Each mile had its risks. Danger and hardship were commonplaces.

It seems odd to the reader to find that Caillié's pages do not tell more about those hazards and feats which fill the books of African travellers who have been in far less danger over their whole journey than Caillié was in a single day. I confess it seemed odd to me. But reflecting I understood. The whole pattern of his life was danger. To him minor adventures were mere silly mishaps, tending to make him conspicuous.

He was like the animal trainer in the cage. Never allow the scent of blood; never make any sudden movement. Walk among tigers—travel across Africa—suavely, without commotion, without arousing antagonism or greed, without even arousing notice.

There were thrills in plenty, but Caillié minimized them. To his notion the far greater danger was detection or self-betrayal. Across slippery fords and up steep paths he carried the crushing burden of always and always acting a part. For seventeen months his life was one continuous subterfuge.

Sometimes suspicious people set traps for him; sometimes the mischievous teased him. Over and over again he had to hear disgusting references to Christians, even listen to attacks on holy names. Very hard this last on an ignorant man like Caillié. It took a queer moral courage to mock at all he had been brought up to reverence. He must have shivered in his soul, fearing that the God he was denying would punish him. When trouble came—and it was to come in plenty—it must have seemed a judgment for permitting negroes to speak ill of Christ's ways.

Unsupported by any real identity, he lied his way along, telling his story at each new village, watching anxiously to see how it "went", building it up by little details, reinforcing it by manifestations of Mussulman devotion—for soon he was in country where all the natives were Mohammedan.

Caillié never met doubts which he could not put at rest. He really did do what Abraham Lincoln considered impossible. He *did* fool all the people all the time. He fooled a continent.

But had he blundered just once, if just one village had been obstinately suspicious, or had he been recognized by some travelling native who had known him in earlier years, there would have been no Caillié to write about.

And Caillié it must be remembered, was not only a fake but a spy. His masquerade was made infinitely more difficult and dangerous because it had to be combined with a perilous sideline. René had to be a secret note-taker.

What would have happened had he been seen scribbling those notes of his on the loose sheets of paper which he kept hidden in his Koran? What if someone had caught him writing—writing from left to right in the fashion of the detested Christians—the carefully memorized count of miles and changing directions, the names of villages and rivers and hills?

Or if his inquiries about place-names had seemed over insistent?

Or if he had been observed using that mysterious thing, the compass?

In this country where the trade routes between great markets and the locations of gold-fields, kola groves and salt mines were the stock in trade of kinglets, he who was caught amongst them "writing the country", as they called it, would soon be dead.

Caillié became master of the art of guarded inquiry, the seemingly indifferent question about place-names which concealed an eager interest, quite out of keeping with his role of ambling pilgrim. He learned the technique of swift secret note-taking behind a bush. He forced himself to remember, to stow essential names and numbers in the back pocket of his brain whilst chatting with his companions or mumbling prayers.

What a memory he must have had! Sometimes it must have been several days before he could write down his route, his head bursting with difficult native names, casually pronounced, and with a list of shifting directions and of the number of miles travelled in each. On the second day, for instance, their path shifted its direction nine times. On the third day there were fifteen alterations.

Yet over all his long journey Caillié kept his record clear, and from these notes of his a map could be drawn —a map which was invaluable when along his whole route, there was not—from the Rio Nunez to Fez, that is from the start to almost the finish of his journey—one single place whose situation was geographically fixed, one place whose situation was other than a mere matter of native or Arab gossip.

It was an astounding performance. Just go for a ten-mile ramble through roadless country and by a record of directions alone bring back an account of your route intelligible to another to whom the country is quite unknown, such an account as would enable the other to draw a reasonable map. Do this over 3,000 miles. It is what Caillié did.

Apart from the compass, which he did not often dare look at, he had no instruments. He did not even have a watch. And, even if his masquerade had not been a bar, Caillié would not have known what to do with scientific instruments.[1]

It is possible to follow his route all the way from the Atlantic to the Mediterranean on modern maps, provided one procures maps of large scale[2] on which the names of the most minute places appear. On a series of such maps, of which I have procured enough sheets to carpet a room, I have spent many hours at this entertaining game—rather like trying to solve a detective story.

It is René's fashion of writing place-names which makes trouble. He jotted them down as they sounded to him when spoken hurriedly. Probably he hesitated to seem interested enough to ask for them to be repeated. I do not find, however, that he ever blundered so badly as did one learned explorer who, having asked a village name, painstakingly wrote down the answer, " *Mannawaji*", later to discover that the word conveyed an invitation to go to the devil with his prying questions. (This happened to the great German explorer Barth.)

Where Caillié seems to have blundered the fault is not always his. Names of native places had a way of

---

[1] Later, when misfortune held him long inactive in a tiny Sudanese village, Caillié did conceive the notion of making an observation of sorts by measuring as best he could the shadow cast by his cane at midday.

[2] For his first five hundred miles I have maps on the scale 1 : 200,000. Next thousand miles scale 1 : 1,000,000. For the Sahara as a whole 1 : 4,000,000. Certain Saharan sections on a much larger scale.

changing. Villages moved and took their names with them. Names were duplicated, for descriptive names were common. Villages disappeared. Names altered and realtered. Take the case of Kakandé itself. Bateman's place was known as Debucca originally. The name shifted to Robucca or Robugga or even Rebecca. Then to Débocké. And now it is associated with the name of the town Boké. All inside a hundred and twenty years.

But, though Caillié admittedly made hash of certain outlandish native names (or a different sort of hash from that made by modern cartographers —who can say how a name should be spelt where there is no written language?) his descriptions of the country were splendidly vivid and accurate.

It is easy to identify on the map that wriggling river of his that "snakes itself across the plain" or to locate that sudden jutting rock rising from a plain to the height of "one hundred and twenty-five brasses" (a brass equalled about five feet).

Hampered but happy Caillié pushed into Africa. His dangerous days were all the harder because on the surface he must always wear a mien of saintly calm. Never must he use harsh words or make threatening gestures. He must always maintain the attitude of a rather silly sanctimonious young man making his way toward a remote religious carrot. He wandered along in Oriental draperies without any romantic support or trappings.

He had no inner support either, no knowledge that if he met a cruel fate in his effort to open up a savage land to his country it would be reported to a sympathetic sovereign, to a cold-eyed, appreciative chief of secret service, even to a comprehending Foreign Office. Caillié was just an ace working on his own. He can scarcely have had the inspiration even of a really passionate patriotism.

His relationship with France was vague and embittered by much official snubbing.

René Caillié had the capacity to be the lonest of lone workers. He could do without everything—without comfort, without companionship, without sympathy, without applause or praise—even without adequate incentive. And he could keep up this life of mole-like solitude and deprivation with patience for more than seventeen months. There was probably never a queerer sane man than René Caillié.

3

IBRAHIM, THE GUIDE, handled Caillié's "press". As soon as the little caravan drew up of an evening, Ibrahim told René's story to the village chief and the people. He was a capable talker. As he warmed up to his work, Caillié's story improved. Soon Caillié became "an Arab from near Mecca", and "a compatriot of the Prophet". His long nose and pale skin puzzled observers. Sometimes folk suggested he was English which, of course, he denied indignantly.

The choice of Egypt as a place of origin had been clever, for though probably nobody in this part of Africa had ever seen an Egyptian or had any notion what an Egyptian was like, the name had a vague prestige. René was accepted as a mixture of crank and saint. While Ibrahim spoke his introductory piece, René looked his most pious and turned his big black eyes toward the East. Mecca to them. Timbuctoo to René!

After the presentation, the caravan fell to. Supper: René so hungry, and he got so little to eat. Mountains of mush, boiled millet, *foigné* or rice, bulging food that gave no comfort to a white man's stomach and little strength to his legs. Sometimes they had tough meat—goat, or, for a rare treat, fresh-killed beef. Occasionally there was a limb of chicken to gnaw, those little tough African chickens which look as if they had been prematurely hatched, and taste as if they had been nourished on straw and gravel.

Sometimes there was honey. But no more "sweet and agreeable *jin-jin-dhi*" to warm the heart of tired travellers. This was Moslem country.

At some villages there was the joy of fruit. Oranges and bananas at three beads a dozen. Native fruits with liquid, juicy names: the *caura* with its plumlike flesh, the *cobaï* fruit, no bigger than a hazel-nut but so delicious that natives say that whilst it is in season no one would wish to touch any other food, the delightful *sône*, and the *tekeli*, formed and tinted like a cherry but with little grains like a blackberry. These experiments with unknown fruits were minor adventures to René, delightful after mush and goat.

Another hard day done—a dozen miles further into Africa. (The average daily progress of the caravan here in the mountains was between eleven and twelve miles.) Study the day's damage to ill-shod feet, white man's feet not born to tramp in ragged sandals, or sometimes barefoot. Rueful counting of bruises and cuts and blisters. Gloomy thoughts of the morrow. Such a hard path, jagged rocks hidden in brooklets, traitorous submerged logs with limbs like needles.

And then to bed. Not under the stars, except in an emergency. It was considered very dangerous to sleep out. After torrid heat there came at midnight a treacherous chill to strike sweating bodies. Prudent natives slept inside their airless huts beside a smoky fire, stifling but safe. There was no real bed, of course. René stretched himself upon a mat with fleas for company and mosquitoes for a lullaby.

Now and then he had a touch of fever, but nothing serious as yet. It was even pleasant in its way, giving the momentary repose that goes with loss of identity. No more bruised feet, no smoke, no empty stomach aching for a decent meal, no worries. Voluptuous relaxation, the massage of gentle, consoling pain. Float and dip on the waves of mystery, pat the clouds, stroke the moon. Fever, nature's fairy-tale to tired travellers. And then the blessed coming of sweat. And sleep.

Next day, almost every day, they tramped on. Only twice did they pause for a day's rest between Kakandé and Ibrahim's home-town and destination, Cambaya. Their direction was generally south-east. Timbuctoo lay to the north-east, but Caillié had to go where the caravans went and be patient.

Every day the going was harder. Toe to heel[1] along the little beaten path they pushed through brush and through gummy marshes where their feet sank to the ankle-bones. They scrambled over fallen trees that impeded the way. They crossed rivers where the bridge was made of a single slippery log. They swam rivers where there was no bridge at all. They picked their steps over fords, leaping from one wobbling stone to another.

Then the mountains—they panted up the steep sides of cliffs, clinging to loosening bushes, crawling on hands and knees, skirting the lips of gorges on vertiginous platforms where branches of wood had been thrust out over the void and brush laid on vaguely. In this country villages seemed stuck to the mountainside like wasp-nests. The inhabitants climbed home by primitive ladders. Travel here was mountaineering all the time.

The caravan's porters were crushed with fatigue. Each man's burden weighed nearly two hundred pounds. The black porters of today are more modest in their

---

[1] Captain Binger, an important traveller whose route in part followed Caillié's sixty years later, says that the Great North-South Road, the most important thorough-fare in tropic Africa, connecting the Sahara with Sudan—salt and trinkets to the South to exchange for slaves and kola—was less than a yard across.

Most of the trade roads were no wider than a negro's foot. (*Du Niger au Golfe de Guinée.*)

exhibitions of strength and the usual load is fifty-six pounds.

Caillié felt ashamed because though he carried no load, he "was just as tired as they were". A cunning device, common in tropic Africa, aided them. The load was tight-laced in long, boat shaped baskets carried on the head. Each man had a pole. When unbearably tired he rested one end of the basket on the branch of a tree and the other end on his pole and stood from under. The clever negro who first invented the system should be the patron saint of porters.

At some villages René became a hero. People so poor that generosity was an emotional debauch offered him pitiful little presents—a drink of milk, a kola nut, a bit of fruit. Once he even received a pair of sandals—a glorious gift, for his own footwear had gone to pieces and he was walking barefoot. Women sometimes knelt to him. Old chiefs patted his face reverently as if to extract indirect benefit from the touch of so exaltedly religious a youth.

They asked René for advice about their sickness, and from his little store of English medicines he handed out simple doses, accompanied by constant recommendations to do a little washing. This last was not to the popular fancy. Having this unique opportunity to lay their troubles before a young man of such far-flung religious aspirations, they were not going to be content with the commonplace counsel to wash the affected part. They craved a dose, and so open-handed was Caillié with his precious store that Ibrahim interfered, saying: "They will take you for a Christian!" Possibly Caillié's real faith never received a prettier tribute.

The most embarrassing case presented to the amateur doctor was the delicate one of a man who—admittedly because of his own fault—possessed a wife who first complained, then became unfaithful, and finally presented the husband with a bastard baby. Young René listened sympathetically and "since ginger was growing nearby", urged the laggard spouse to eat a great deal of it, assuring him it would improve matters in the home. Again the remedy was too unpretentious. The unhappy husband wanted something from Caillié's magic medicine box— jalap was his choice—and Caillié adds light-heartedly: "I gave him some to get rid of him!"

A quaint picture is of Caillié examining a little albino baby, born to a very puzzled black father and mother. The negro mother had brought this freakish little thing to show to the traveller, perhaps in the hope that he could in his wisdom turn it black, for to her mind its paleness indicated illness. She laid the baby questioningly upon Caillié's knees and Caillié studied "its woolly white hair, its flax-coloured eyelashes and eyebrows, its face of palest rose, light blue eyes with fiery red pupils and perfectly white body". But its features were negro features. The baby's sight was feeble and it refused to play with Caillié's Mussulman chaplet and cried.

It was, on the whole, a bit of luck to be born a *founé*, an albino. For, though a few negro communities disliked their *founé*s—perhaps because of some old tradition of a negress who took too much notice of travellers—albinos were often valued and revered.

Some said that a black woman bore an albino because she had been frightened by a white man. Some counted albinos sacred to a goddess of human form who was covered with close white hair all over like a goat, and whose name was Aynfwa.

The counterpart of the albino problem fortunately does not bother the white world. No occasional coal-black baby comes without cause to white parents. A variant of the albino puzzle amongst blacks is the harlequin baby, the piebald, a poor little creature coloured like a two-tone map. One such freak, called "The Spotted Boy", was imported and exhibited to the delight of England in Caillié's day. Another problem in negro babies was the *bala*, a negro born dirt-coloured with dingy red hair, and named after the grey roan donkey.

As the caravan struggled up the Futa Jalon mountains, a ticklish situation arose for René. Their route was very close to Timbo, residence of the Almamy of Futa Jalon. Local custom was that a traveller should report to the big chief, or to one of the big chiefs, for Futa Jalon had developed a system of duplicate royalty—two Almamies who worked in shifts—so that, as the natives boasted, "if one Almamy treated you badly you could complain to the other one!" (From André Arcin's *Histoire de la Guinée Française*.)

René knew that any formal visit to the Futa Jalon court would be dangerous. He could impose on village people. But Timbo was a relatively sophisticated town, rich capital and fortress, where "one might see as many as one thousand horses". Timbo possessed, so rumour ran, a palace which was built of stone and was two stories high with stairs! Timbo loathed foreign intrusion. It lay in a most profitable situation—between the coast and its trinkets and the remote secret reaches of Africa where the gold and the slaves came from. White competition was not wanted. A hard scrutiny would be cast upon any pale-faced traveller with a romantic yarn. The clever Fulas of Timbo said that "the whites only wished to know their country so as to grab it!" Hospitality was a patriotic crime. Few whites succeeded in crawling up their mountain paths. Fewer still were decently received. Timbo was trail's end.

Caillié very wisely desired not to put himself to the test of the Almamy's sharp eyes. An official visit to the capital would have been obligatory upon a more important-looking traveller. Shabby René made one tactful excuse after another, that he was worn with fatigue and the road was hard, that the rains were coming on and he must get forward, that he was a humble person of no interest to the great Almamy. His omission to present himself before the Almamy nearly got him arrested on one occasion, but René talked his way out of the trouble and never went to Timbo.

Cambaya, Ibrahim's home village, was reached on May 10—226 miles from the coast, twenty-two days of travel.

René followed Ibrahim to his home, or rather homes, for Ibrahim was a multi-married man. Ibrahim's cordiality was perfection. He bedded René for the night on a tanned skin which he had prepared for him in the *case* of one of his wives. Hospitality could not go further. The wife herself slept in the middle of the hut ringed round by her children.

Ibrahim naturally desired to remain awhile at Cambaya to gossip with his wives and children, and—on the understanding that the guide would presently accompany him further into Africa—Caillié agreed to pause at Cambaya for a short rest. It was a most lovely spot near the great cascade of the Tinkasso, which was a small tributary of the Niger. Ibrahim's father was village chief, a kindly old blind man, who felt Caillié and said: "*El Arab, el Arab acagnie!*" (Arab, you are good) and then gave Caillié two kola nuts, a gesture similar in good-fellowship to pouring out a drink in our lands.

But the chief's subjects, who had their sight, were less credulous. Several of them had been to the coast on trading journeys. They thought Caillié looked like a white man. Amongst themselves they muttered: "*La forto, forto!*" which meant he was a white.

Ibrahim declared Caillié was a *souloca-tigui*, a hundred per cent Arab. Caillié redoubled his pious demonstrations. But Cambaya was not easy in its mind.

Then a most unfortunate incident happened. In Cambaya lived a certain Mandingo who had been accustomed to brag that he understood Arabic. To know Arabic was an elegant accomplishment.

The Mandingo addressed René in Arabic, halting and badly pronounced. René indicated that he was puzzled. Cambaya, standing round, watched the fiasco, and some whispered that their fellow villager was not so learned a person as he had been claiming to be. The Mandingo did what anyone would have done in his place. He announced, and he kept on announcing, that Caillié was no Arab at all but an impostor.

His attacks were dangerous to René, and René's way of dealing with him was characteristic—one of the many shrewd actions which won him through to victory. Instead of losing his temper or arguing with the man or protesting to the rest of the village, Caillié at a suitable moment seated himself on the ground before his hut with his little writing board in his hand and a few leaves from the Koran. He assumed a puzzled expression and waited. Presently the Mandingo walked by, pouting. Caillié called to him, engaged him in talk and finally begged his aid in writing out a *sura*, a passage from the Koran which, so he said, he desired to learn by heart. It was the apology magnificent.

The Mandingo expanded his chest and complied with a flourish—and probably a great many errors. He had been afforded a chance, there in the open road with all Cambaya watching, to prove that he really was a *karamoro*, which is the honourable title given by Mandingos to a man who can read.

After that, as Caillié gently remarks, "he became my best friend and stood up for me in the village and assured everyone I was an Arab".

The ability to conceive so simple and friendly a plan and to carry it out gracefully was typical of Caillié's wisdom in dealing with negroes. These people were peasants, masters of their own country. René, child of white peasants and far from home, treated them with sincere respect. Caillié had spent most of his grown life amongst coloured peoples in Africa and in Guadeloupe. He had a genuinely democratic attitude toward dark skins, and a complete sophistication toward dark customs.

Caillié was ignorant but he was wise. To this worldly good sense it is due that unlike so many explorers in Africa, he was never imprisoned or seriously molested by natives. They teased him, robbed him, drove him mad with begging and pushing and staring, insulted him and half starved him, but these were minor affronts. They never detained him, nor injured him, nor enslaved him, and—unlike a long sad list of less tactful explorers—he went where he wanted to and he got home alive.

René was scrupulously fair in money dealings—or rather in the handing out of those little gifts of trade goods which was the equivalent of money payment in these lands where no actual money existed.

No formal arrangement maintained for lodging or feeding travellers. Traders depended entirely on private entertainment. The private entertainer expected a reward. And it was usual to give the chief of each place a souvenir. If the traveller looked rich the presents should be large.

In the matter of repaying hospitality and services René used most exact care. He records every disbursement minutely, and tells how almost always a counter suggestion would be made that a little more should be added, which would be done. Payments were in goods—cloth, beads, tobacco, and so on, and, later on, usually in salt.

Not for long months would Caillié get into the cowry country where small shell tokens were, and still are in some remote districts, currency. He never had occasion to use certain of the queer sorts of money, such as *lemma* (tiny round mirrors), cotton money, *leppi* or *tari*, nor—very luckily—"iron money", which consisted of lumps of iron a foot long, very awkward for long-distance travellers.

Occasionally Caillié made his payments in the form of little scraps of "scarlet" (red cloth), an inch and a half square. One native host, for instance, received two such squares as recompense for two nights' lodging and two suppers—the one being sour milk with rice (to which Caillié added some goat meat of his own providing) and the other being yams. Another native next morning sold Caillié his "copious breakfast of rice to which was joined a chicken and some milk"—the price being a sheet of paper.

Poor as he was, Caillié let the natives with whom he had dealings imagine that he was yet poorer. He hid away certain of his best stuff—amber and coral and some gold and silver. Great was his annoyance if a drenching rain obliged him to open his bundle and dry his goods before covetous eyes.

Caillié began to suspect that Ibrahim was fooling him, that he had no intention of leaving his wives.

Delay was dangerous. The "mango rains" had begun, the intermittent damp period which precedes the uninterrupted rainy season. The weather was heavy and leaden, sun hidden, and at night lightning played round the mountain-tops of Kankan-Fodéa. Caillié tells how as he lay awake he would watch these lightning flashes, and would worry himself sick wondering how he would struggle across the wild country ahead of him after the continuous rains began, picturing the mountain torrents in rebellion, brooks boiling and rivers out of their course, and all in a shelterless wilderness.

It was madness to wait for Ibrahim to tire of family life. Caillié with difficulty found a new travelling companion, a Mandingo who was going as far as the Niger,

—now only a hundred miles away—and beyond. At the promise of a good reward he agreed that Caillié should be a member of his party.

This man's name was Lamfia and he was destined to cause Caillié much trouble. In fact, when Caillié left Cambaya, his troubles were going to begin—at first small, but gradually mounting.

Bustle of departure. First get the consent of the good blind chief. Then make ready some food, for the land between Cambaya and the Niger was desolate and had few resources. Native equivalent of tinned goods, food that was easy to carry and would keep. There was a big *cagnan* cake made of corn, honey and *pistaches de terre* (no other than the humble peanut!), and other cakes less luxurious, made of rice.

Then the paying-off of Ibrahim, guide, landlord and press-agent. Quite a business. René gave him "a fine present of amber, *indienne*, guinea, powder (i.e. gunpowder), paper (always a treasure and often mentioned as a trade article by Caillié), scissors (much in demand as a novelty), and silk handkerchiefs".

Ibrahim was delighted, but still had the appetite for more, and at the last moment retained surreptitiously a few trinkets—beads and the like—as souvenirs of Caillié's visit. This was an almost traditional gesture, and Caillié took it with good nature.

On May 30th Caillié left Cambaya. There were eight in the caravan, one of them being a wife of Lamfia, who came along according to custom to do the cooking. Their plan was to amalgamate with another caravan *en route* so that their band might be larger, for along their way there were dangerous forests infested with brigands. As far as the bridge across the Tinkasso some of Caillié's friends from Cambaya came to see him off. Ibrahim politely carried Caillié's umbrella and his *satala* (which was a small tin pot) wherein was packed the travelling provision of rice cakes, from which by force of habit he stole two. Yet Ibrahim liked Caillié and cried out farewell over and over regretfully: "*Abd-allahi! Abd-allahi! Allam-Kiselak!*" (May God take care of you on the way, *Abd-allahi!*) Caillié, in that sober language which he always used, described Ibrahim's behaviour in the matter of the rice cakes as "an indiscretion".

It was very much harder going now. The mountain paths, though rough, had been comparatively cool. Here in the open the heat was hideous. The rains were beginning, and often Caillié and his companions were wet through "to the very bones". At night during pouring rains the caravan crouched in the inadequate shelter of "*cahuttes*", a system for protecting travellers consisting of a line of branches with straw covering laid toward the western, "weatherside".

Caillié must have blessed his clothes and thought with horror of what must have been the sufferings of other white travellers in similar circumstances—Park, for instance in his blue stuff coat, and his soldiers in red wool uniforms, or Peddie collared to the throat and trousered to the instep.

At one village Caillié acquired a new name. He was dubbed "Maka", meaning one who is going to Mecca. To the chief who so baptized him René gave a novel reward—a dose of cream of tartar!

At another village René was moved to add a touch of verisimilitude to his narrative. He presumably felt the natural longing of an artist to improve a work of art. It was at Sancougnan (Sinkounian on the modern map) a village on the Bandiegué, a little stream, which—like René—was hurrying toward the Niger. As the villain for this new chapter of his life story Caillié chose an Englishman, "Monsieur Macaulay".

The name Macaulay was familiar even in the remote
interior, though probably Sinkounian had not the faintest
idea who or what Macaulay was. "Macaulay" meant
power and money and white folks. Many a Sierra Leone
negro proudly joined himself to the clan and called himself Macaulay. Native traders brought the name back in
their gossip from the coast. The great Macaulay business
house with its several branches conducted its affairs in
spectacular fashion and with a "profusion and revelry"
that shocked old Zachary Macaulay in London—keeping
open house and putting up salaries to five times the original
figure. With the name Macaulay went in the negro mind a
mysterious prestige. After this additional chapter of Caillié's
story had been repeated a few times "Monsieur Macaulay"
began to figure in the cast as "The King of the Whites".

This is what wicked "Monsieur Macaulay" had done:
He had taken a fancy to Caillié and had made a propo-
sition to him to accept an advance and to set up in commerce under his patronage. But would Caillié do this? No!
He had rejected the suggestion, so great was his repugnance
to staying any longer amongst the infidel Christians!

Caillié would then draw forth some leaves of the Koran
and read.

It went very well, being just the sort of story, with its
mixture of financial, religious and personal interest, that
was calculated to tickle the native fancy. And Caillié,
flushed with success, committed a blunder. An old man
in the crowd, wishing to make himself important, took
the Koran leaves from Caillié's hands, and, holding them
upside down, pretended to read. Caillié so far forgot
himself as to laugh. The old man, indignant, cried out
that Caillié was a white man and a liar. It was with
difficulty that Caillié won back local confidence.

"I promised myself," Caillié says, "to be in future
more circumspect with the negroes, who are generally

ignorant, touchy and vindictive. I had hurt the old man's *amour propre*, and it is always dangerous to offend the dignity of the ignorant."

A few miles further, at another Cambaya village, two days' time was lost waiting for the other part of the caravan. It was a gay little village where somebody gave René a chicken and the folk were "very gentle and hospitable". Of an evening the inhabitants danced in the light of the moon, assembled under a bombax tree (cotton tree or kapok). "I watched them with pleasure jumping gaily to the sound of a little Basque drum (tambourine) and of an instrument made in bamboo which resembles a flute and from which they extract very harmonious sounds."

Then Caillié's heart began to pound. Niger coming nearer. Twenty-nine miles away. Fourteen. Tomorrow—Niger, Mungo Park's Joliba, the most mysterious river in the world.

Of those very few whites to whom she had shown herself most were dead. On June 10, 1827, the Men-Who-Had-Seen-the-Niger Club would have been a very exclusive association. Its charter member, Park, was long since dead. So was Dochard. Clapperton had passed on while Caillié was at Kakandé, Major Laing was at the Niger for one brief midnight moment, but Laing was no longer available as member for this or any other earthly club. Lander, Clapperton's servant, survived.

On the morrow the Men-Who-Had-Seen-the-Niger Club was to have another member, its first Frenchman.

4

RENÉ'S WAY OF telling his readers that he has reached the Niger is characteristic. It is an example of the sort of thing which has kept him from his proper fame as a very great explorer.

What a tremendous moment it must have been in his life. It was a triumph for him as an explorer. As a suffering traveller it meant that one stage of his hard journey had been accomplished. And to the adorer of Africa it was a gorgeous experience to see for the first time her great secret river, and to see it at a point far from where any other white man had ever been.

Aware of what must have been René's state of mind on that June day, the reader, as he inches toward the dramatic moment, wonders what René will say. What he does say is as odd as anything contained in any published book. For he actually succeeds in making his announcement that he has reached the Niger in such crab-like and secretive fashion that only the most careful, painstaking reader, reading every word in a dense paragraph would grasp the thrilling fact at all.

René hides the news in the middle of a paragraph of four hundred and thirty words, fifteen sentences, forty-five separate statements of fact. The news is so carefully packed about with trifling details about this and that as to give an impression of wilful concealment.

The passage is too long for quoting verbatim. But here, briefly, is the manner in which Caillié tells of his victory and of a great emotional experience:—

1—He leaves the chief of the village where he had slept on the night of the 10th to 11th June, gives him three leaves of tobacco and the chief seems satisfied.

2—They go to the south-east.

3—Now follows mention of some men of the Sarakollé race who are now of the party, of their asses, of their goods, of brooks which make the going harder, of the great heat, of a storm, of fever which fell upon Caillié on the road and how he had a shivering fit, of how they waded across streams in water knee deep.

4—A change of direction to the east is recorded, and then follows a story of how the Sarakollé leader stayed behind and traced lucky signs in Arabic on the ground and assured everyone they could continue in safety. Then a statement about the varieties of trees, the sort of ground.

5—And *then*—I now quote verbatim—"About two o'clock in the afternoon we arrived at Couroussa (Kouroussa) village of Amana, situated on the left bank of the Joliba: a little before arriving a storm surprised us, my umbrella and the trees under which we took shelter protected me a little."

This marvellous moment did not even get a sentence to itself, but had to be bedded down with the umbrella and the trees!

After this Caillié goes right on—his paragraph is not yet finished—to tell of the party's fatigue, of how he found lodging and how he bought a chicken for supper for two "*coups de poudre*", of how his fever was better but he still had a bad headache. And then at last our modest author allows himself a little outburst. He writes: "I ran very fast to the banks of the river which had been for so long the object of my desires. I saw it coming from the SW. 1/4 S.; it runs slowly to the ENE. for the distance of a few miles, then it turns to the E. I perceived, a little to the N. of the village, a sandbank close to the left shore: the canal for the *pirogues* is more to the right shore. I sat down for a moment, to contemplate at ease this mysterious river, about whose characteristics the savants of Europe are so curious to learn."

This passage is typical of Caillié's style. His *Journal d'un Voyage à Temboctou*, so honest, ample, kindly, shrewd, and so woefully confusing, makes one realize what a gap there is between having something to tell and knowing how to tell it. Caillié was a brilliant explorer, but he was probably as bad a writer as ever had a book printed.

His bad writing diminished the fame to which he was justly entitled. Contemporaries and generations to come found his adventures too difficult to follow. Modern writers have not seen in him an easy subject. Yet—admitting that his jumbled style makes hard reading—there is something very winning in his simplicity. Anyone who has read every word of Caillié's three volumes will love Caillié all his life as if he were a personal friend.

René shows the enthusiasm and the transparent honesty of a little boy who cannot get the words out fast enough when telling his adventure to a kind parent, and who jumbles all his recollections together so that the big important things are often shoved in behind the little details. The trouble is that Caillié remembered too much. The reader cannot see the wood for the trees, cannot appreciate the real grandeur of Caillié's accomplishments for the trivialities in which he hides them.

His book—like many another—could have been improved by editing. But Caillié refused to have anyone "touch up" his notes and recollections. He was well aware of his inability as a writer. He apologized for "*mon peu d'habitude dans l'arte d'écrire*", and he begged public indulgence for the "*récit d'un voyageur sans prétention*". Yet he would not have his book put in shape by a professional writer. Jomard contributed certain general geographical matter at the end, checked the route, and prepared a day-by-day itinerary from Caillié's notes. He also attended to the business of plucking all the nasty English w's out of the fair French pages and substituting *ou*'s. But Jomard says that he had nothing to do with the writing of the *Journal* proper and includes in the appendix his own opinion that Caillié's writing is "naïve and artless", which unchallenged statement *in his own book* proves that Caillié, at any event, was quite without literary vanity.

Probably Caillié was wise to refuse editorial help. Upon his return great discussions broke out. This was natural and only to have been expected. Too many ambitions, both in France and in England, were disappointed by this unpretentious little man's success. Caillié was in certain quarters called an impostor. Some suggested that he had been shipwrecked on the Barbary coast, and had cooked up his Timbuctoo and Central African adventures. Consequently Caillié longed to fling full proof of his honesty in the public eye, and to tell every detail which he could remember. He turned "the fugitive and very laconic notes, written in trembling, and almost whilst running" into an enormously long and ill-arranged book. A graceful writer, necessarily ignorant of the facts which only Caillié knew, would have made a better book, but failed to achieve Caillié's absolute convincingness. As that odd brave woman and interesting African traveller, Mary Kingsley, said: "Anyone can criticize my writing, precious few what I write about."[1]

5

NEXT MORNING CAILLIÉ hurried back to the Niger banks. "I could not tire of admiring the river", he says. A young Niger here at Kouroussa, near to its source. Current, he estimated at two and a half or three miles the hour. Depth, he judged by the *pirogue* poles as eight or nine feet. Width, nine hundred feet. A baby giant!

There were many guesses as to what happened to the Niger. But like the Tuareg who lived beside its banks, the Niger veiled its mouth. Caillié's theory that it emptied into the Gulf of Guinea was proved right a few years later

[1] Stephen Gwynn, *The Life of Mary Kingsley*.

by Lander's courageous voyage. The Niger's course makes almost a complete circle; source and mouth are about a thousand miles apart.

Other suppositions were fantastic. Some said the Niger evaporated. Some maintained it was the headwaters of the Nile. Mungo Park himself identified the Niger with the Congo and expected that if his hazardous trip on "His Majesty's schooner *Joliba*" went on to a safe finish, he would at last find himself debouching into the Atlantic below the Equator. And one of the queerest suggestions of all was that the Niger went *under the Sahara* all the way to the Mediterranean.

René's correct guess was not because he enjoyed unique opportunities to question the natives. They knew nothing at all about their great river as a whole. No native had knowledge of the Niger beyond the limits of his own region. The river was known under many names. Each region christened the great river, considered it theirs alone and gave little thought to its vast wanderings through the lands of other tribes.

On flowed the Niger under a dozen names, but whatever the name was—Joliba, Mayo, Isa, Kwora, and so on—it meant merely the Big River, mighty waters. Its finest name was that cry of ecstasy. "The Sea!"—Eguerriou—by which desert men greeted its cool water, when it lipped up before their tired eyes in all its sudden loveliness beyond a dune of sand at the Sahara's rim.

Caillié always called it the Joliba, which he spelt Dhioliba.

Where the Niger rises in the mountains of Futa Jalon was a place of awe, home of a demon or spirit who lived under water in a house of gold. The priest of the source made a fat living by giving out his master's advice to the public. For the native laity to look at the spring which is the Niger's birthplace was sure death within a year.

Should a native be obliged to approach, he must go backward.

Natives living further along the Niger knew nothing about its actual source. Some, like the great conqueror El Hadj Omar, believed it came *from Mecca*. "To see it is to make a pilgrimage to the Holy City!" he told his hordes. "To bathe in it means that you shall go to Paradise!" Others, like terrible Samori, picking up the river at another point in its great coil, thought that it was going *to Mecca*.

Perhaps the most agreeable theory of all was that held by many Niger fishermen and sailors who accepted the Niger gratefully and said that, when it passed beyond the range of their individual travels, it was lapped up by the fishes.

As Caillié stood on the river bank that morning and watched the Niger flowing so effortlessly toward the city of his ambitions he must have wished that he might get himself a boat and float to Timbuctoo. How his feet must have pleaded for a boat, those feet which were destined soon to betray and almost destroy their master.

Caillié tossed a chip into the Niger, watched it float Timbuctoo-wards at two and a half miles the hour. The distance to Timbuctoo by river was about 825 miles.

In five days' time, if it kept floating, it would pass by a place he most desired to see—the fabulous gold-field of Bouré, reputedly richer even than the Bondou field and the Bambouk field added together—and Bambouk was "the Peru of Africa". To see "the gold of Bouré" and to carry back first-hand word of it to greedy Europe would have added another feather to René's well-plumed cap.

A visit being impossible, René angled for gossip and was able to collect the first detailed information about this place ever to reach the white world.

He tells us that the region was so rich with gold that the natives scorned all agriculture, though their land was very fertile, and—like a nation of aristocrats—*bought* all the food which the country needed. They gave their whole time to panning gold, and exchanged their nuggets for rice and millet and lesser comestibles, which the women of less favoured neighbouring countries delivered to their door.

It was a lucky native who was born in Bouré, and it was a very lucky man indeed who was their chief. His name, in Caillié's time, was Boucary. He was absolute ruler and received for himself one half of the gold that was collected.

Boucary was a Mohammedan with pagan leanings, a form of religious straddling which was rather common. He covered himself with *gris-gris* and he liked idols, while revering Mussulman ways and protecting marabouts.

Very naturally this king of the gold-fields could afford not only duplicate religions but multiple wives, each in a hut of her own. Suspicious, like so many rich men, he maintained a triple guard round his royal establishment, and further combined prudence with pleasure by sleeping each night in a different hut.

When Caillié returned to France, Jomard announced that the Bouré gold-fields would be "a new source of riches for our old Europe surcharged with debts and population". (*He said this in* 1830!)

So eager was "our old Europe" to get at the gold that a wild plan was discussed of cutting a canal between the Niger and the Senegal River. Thus the gold could be readily transported to Saint-Louis and on to Europe, once it had been coaxed from Boucary's subjects by the bedazzlement of "our old Europe's" trinkets.

Who was going to build this canal across lands where, as yet, white men dared not even march, had not been decided! Failing a canal, it was suggested that a fortified post should be established on the Niger and the gold

RENÉ CAILLIÉ

CAILLIÉ'S HOUSE IN TIMBUCTOO

VILLAGE IN FRENCH GUINEA, WHENCE CAILLIÉ STARTED FOR TIMBUCTOO

CAILLIÉ MAKING HIS NOTES ON A COPY OF THE KORAN

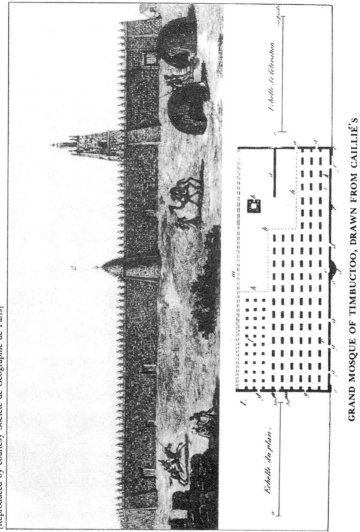

GRAND MOSQUE OF TIMBUCTOO, DRAWN FROM CAILLIÉ'S

OWN DESCRIPTION

THE NIGER, NEAR TIMBUCTOO

A LADY OF TIMBUCTOO

[Photo de l'Ofalac-Alger.]

"AT LAST THE BEAUTY OF THE PALMS AGAINST THE SKY"

carried across to the Senegal under escort. Caillié favoured this proposal. He urged that Bamako—then known only by repute to white men, except for Park's visit and Dochard's—should be the place chosen to fortify. From all reports its geographical situation was ideal, just where rapids broke the flow of the Niger, so that it could trade both ways, be a clearing house.

Caillié foresaw Bamako's bright future. It was then a native town, lyrically called one of the "Five Pearls of the Niger". Now it is the finest city in inland French West Africa and capital of French Sudan. When he returned to France Caillié spoke of its potentialities with such enthusiasm that he was named "resident at Bamako on the Niger" with a salary of 6,000 francs per year from the day of his arrival, and an interim honorarium of 3,000 francs.

But Caillié, had he survived, would have been eighty years old before he could have profited by the doubling of salary, so optimistically promised him by the French Royal Government against the time when he could actually take up his duties. Caillié was perfectly right in predicting a big future for Bamako, but it was a slow future. France met many checks before she pacified the Sudan.

Yet Bamako has not forgotten its spiritual grandfather who, on the 12th of June 1827, first planned its birth as an inland white African city. In Bamako there is another——

RUE RENÉ CAILLIÉ

6

THAT SAME NIGHT at Kouroussa Caillié saw something which touched him profoundly. "I noticed that thousands of swallows of the same breed that we see in Europe had made their nests in the wall (the ten-foot mud wall round the little town). They were just gathering in troops in the tall trees and I thought that they were making ready to go away."

Often in his home country the boy René had listened to old peasants as they watched the swallow's flight south-ward in the autumn, and had heard the whisper "Shall I ever see them return?" Here was René at the other end of the line.

Kouroussa was a town of polite idolators. Its chief, reputed a great warrior, received Caillié and permitted him to admire the arsenal—bows and arrows hung on the walls of his hut. Although the chief made his fortune by the tax he levied on men and goods that crossed the Niger at this point, he said that Caillié was such an interesting stranger that he should be ferried over the river free.

Next morning René was again on his way. Lamfia's caravan was making for the city of Kankan, to the south beyond the river. The stream was not wide, but the natives got all the excitement possible out of crossing it. In a mass two hundred and fifty or three hundred sweating negroes churned up the mud of the Niger bank, yelling and shoving. It was stiflingly hot. Their goods rolled under foot. Their donkeys brayed and kicked. The ferry fleet consisted of only four little *pirogues*. Everyone wanted to go at once and nobody wanted to pay the price demanded. The donkeys disliked the *pirogues* and showed their distrust in the usual manner. Everybody yelled. And when a boatload, by Heaven's grace, got safe to the other side, its passengers shot off their guns in proof of joy, which increased the row and added to the nervous-ness of the donkeys.

Caillié, again sick with an attack of fever, stood for

several hours waiting his turn. "On the bank there was only one great bombax under which we could find shade, but there were so many crowded beneath it that I could not find a place. I saw a number of women and girls bathing in the river. They were all naked and seemed not to take much notice of the men who looked at them".

That these women should be unashamed was natural. Caillié had now entered into the land of the nearly nude. The sacred value of clothes had mercifully never been explained to these women. They felt nothing of the embarrassment or coyness or bravado inseparable from white nudism. This unselfconsciousness rather cheats travellers of an anticipated shock. It is a curious fact that even to those of us who are not altogether pure-minded the sight of naked African savages is not as a rule especially exciting. Perhaps, as the witty French saying goes, "*le noir habille*", black skin is a dress in itself.

Habitual complete nakedness on the part of adult natives of West Africa is not usual. I have never seen it. But the *cache-sexe* (which we translate by the Scriptural and not always accurate term of loin-cloth—since it may be made of all sorts of substances) is removed in public, when working alongside rivers, as nonchalantly as a white man might on occasion strip off his coat, or a working woman doff her overall. The *cache-sexe* of the women consists sometimes—as in the country where Caillié then was—of a cloth strip, usually blue, which forms a miniature apron about three inches wide at the waist and six inches wide at the bottom, and is attached by a string round the waist and by a string passing between the legs. In other districts both men and women wear leaves. On the coast not far from Kakandé, Caillié's starting-point, live a tribe whose men wear a basket-work shield similar to the receptable in which vintage wines are brought to table. Certain natives who are nearly naked feel amply clothed by reason of a multiplicity of small ornaments hung round waist and throat. Sometimes a negro wears flapping against his bare skin a complete "chatelaine" —tool-chest and toilet set, which includes a spatula for taking snuff and an iron hook to clean out his nose.

As René discovered, the river bank is the ideal place to observe negro dress styles and innocent nudity. The traveller may find himself disappointed of the naughty thrill, but he will enjoy many a friendly grin as he watches these men and women going about their business in their unadorned skins. The naked washerwoman dancing up and down on her dirty linen, the sober black man washing his neighbour's back with a pawful of sand, are pleasant pictures. Or the young maiden filling the family calabash, her voluptuous pointed bosom in the water, her rump in the air, her little round shaved head thrust forward and an alluring giggle on her face. Watch her walk up the bank in that flexible, catlike way. See her elder sister, full-breasted and carrying her nursling on her back. And the honourable old woman whose breasts are flat and V-shaped, hanging nearly to her waist: ugly to us, but in black Africa the mark of normal womanhood. An elderly woman with a firm bosom carries the open, humiliating proof of barrenness. These uncorseted, hard-working women must nurse their babies over prolonged periods, sometimes till the little boys and girls can join the family table, for animal's milk is a rarity. In Africa a tired bosom is the mark of matronly honour.

As for the children, their charm is beyond white rivalry, so winsome in their negro nudity that one almost wishes all the world's babies could be black! These nearly blue-black little girls, sleek-skinned as Damson plums, with a string of white beads at the base of their throats and another at the base of their stomachs, all smiles and infant coquetry, make one almost regret the old slave days.

For which of us could deny a momentary impulse to buy one of these delightful black dolls and stuff it with sweets?

Caillié, reeling with fever, waited and watched and at last got his chance amongst the crowd and was carried across to the other bank of the Niger, he being the first white ever to cross the great river in the ordinary way of ferry transit, and, as we have said, having done so on a free pass!

Scarce able to walk, he bade farewell reluctantly to the noble Joliba. It would be nine months before he would again see the Niger. It came near to being all eternity.

7

No white man had ever seen the country into which Caillié was now pushing his way. No white man would have the courage or the ability to follow him for generations to come.

From this point until he again saw the Niger his was a unique adventure, without white predecessors, and without white emulators until late in the nineteenth century. Caillié was now invading one of those great white patches on the map, which—marked "Unexplored Regions"— had so piqued him as a boy.

Anything was possible there. It was a fabulous stretch of country from which came only the gossip of black traders, told in shuddering whispers. Cannibals lived there, sharpening their teeth with bits of stone, making ready to drive them into men's flesh. Tribes lived there who ate their old people, the corpses of any traveller who chanced to meet death in their forests, even spiders and beetles. There, too, stood Kankan, a great negro city. Probably Caillié thought it fortunate that he would reach Kankan first and traverse later the fabled lands of terror. He did not guess the dangers which awaited him at Kankan.

Bad travel now—the heat was intense, and on top of stunning sunshine came chill storms of rain and lightning. Caillié was dazed with tropic fever. No shelter, no chance to stop and rest. On and on with the caravan, wading through streams, stumbling barefoot over coarse gravel and sharp pebbles, nourishing himself on uncouth messes. On the 16th of June they made twenty-two miles almost at a run, for they were impatient to get to Kankan, Caillié's fever by a miracle left him!

Kankan was the guide Lamfia's home-town. He had been absent for a long time and his entry was a local event. As soon as he led his caravan into the suburbs bands of excited negroes greeted him and followed him shouting into the city. Lamfia begged Caillié to raise his umbrella as he passed through the West Gate of Kankan—for the city possessed a city wall formed of a very thick and impenetrable hedge of prickles.

This was the first big inland African city Caillié had seen, having a population of 6,000, and numerous sub-urban villages clustering about—an orderly, well-governed place. The people of Kankan knew the world around them. Certain of them ventured on trading trips as far as the coast. Their market attracted customers from the adjoining pagan lands, men with self-scarred breasts and "very pointed teeth". Caillié met one man "who had his hair full of sheep droppings like the wool of a ram which has slept six months in the same straw". Kankan itself was clean and pretty, with date palms and pawpaws, little humped cattle, and townspeople neatly robed in white clothes of native cotton and wearing enormously wide straw hats.

Kankan today is still an important place, has twice as many inhabitants as in Caillié's time, and is the centre of an administrative "cercle". I was in Kankan in 1935.

The city is the terminus of the quaint little wood-burning railway to the coast, which in two days of jogging travel and an overnight rest in the mountains accomplishes a journey very nearly coinciding with that which took Caillié two months.

But the Kankan in which Caillié sojourned during a very troubled month in the summer of 1827 in no way survives in the Kankan of today.

Old Kankan was ravaged a half-century after Caillié's visit by the great conqueror Samori with his usual wanton thoroughness. This region of Africa—Kankan, Kouroussa where Samori held his infamous court under the historic baobab tree and filled the market-place with negro heads, and the lands to the east—was to be blood-soaked by Samori and his *sofas*—deceptively restful name for a band of tigerish warriors—before another white man should pass this way.

Samori was the ring-master of tropic Africa for more than twenty years. His infamous career is so typical of the savagery and cunning of the people of this stretch of Africa that some notion of his exploits is interesting. Better than anything else it illustrates what a terrible country Caillié was attempting to cross.

Samori was the pagan child of a poor kola pedlar and a mother who was captured into slavery, so that Samori served "seven years and seven months and seven days" to earn her freedom (or such was the claim of his black press agents!) Ambition boiled in him. He had "the mouth of an ogre", the heartless cruelty of a fiend. For policy, he turned Moslem and inaugurated what is so oddly called a "Holy War". Half a million square kilometres fell under his terror.

Slaves were his war chest. He swapped men and women—enemies or his own people—for guns and horses. He seized every grain of food in each helpless little village as he stormed by. The countryside was strewn with corpses and the bodies of the starving.

"Every small bush shelters a corpse, even on the path one finds a whitened skeleton alongside a dying man. It is hideous. Those who live seem like corpses on their legs, holding themselves upright by a cane, thin, their eyes expressing neither intelligence nor quite stupefaction. . . . They drag themselves along till they fall from inanition. Some . . . try to salute me, they have not the force to articulate a syllable—already the 'rictus' of death is on their faces."

(From the report of Captain Binger, who saw a corner of the land Samori had conquered).

Samori was one of the worst negroes in all history. And a really great man. The white world which he intimidated called him Black Alexander, or Napoleon, or Caesar. Even the Negro Charlemagne.

No one knew how many wives he had. Even in his old days he had three hundred at one time. Each wore big gold ear-rings. He decreed that his name should be terrible and that he who pronounced it should be killed. His diplomacy was superb. It being the moment of the "African Scramble" he played off the English and the French against one another, caused Sierra Leone to receive his representative with a twenty-one gun salute; told the French that England had sold him rapid-fire guns, and sent him the pretty present of a *canne-fusil* ; and permitted the French to think of his bloody empire as a "Protectorate", and to take his son, Karamoko, "Big Tooth", on a visit to Paris.

His attempt at English friendship came to an abrupt halt when his men massacred an English surveying party and captured its leader, Lieutenant Henderson, who was happily given up alive. And France also lost her temper with him.

So Samori came to the end of his fun. It was in 1898. Gouraud, then a captain, captured the mighty negro near the borders of Liberia with his 120,000 *sofas* and camp followers, the three hundred wives, three hundred and twenty children, much German ammunition, an English cannon, and 250,000 francs in money.

The pursuit of Samori to his last stand was terrible, forced marches through ankle-deep mud, sometimes through water stomach high, by villages where Samori had passed, "ruins encumbered with mummified corpses, corpses in putrefaction, dead and dying on top of one another, covered with worms and *magnans* (revolting fierce ants which devour everything, but seem to like corpses best). . . . Walking skeletons dragging themselves along, eating leaves".

(From a report of Major de Lartigue, who led the *colonne*.)

Samori, booty, and a reasonable number of wives were led to the railhead in French Guinea through rejoicing natives—as many of them as were left alive to rejoice.

"Samori!" cried out the French Colonel who announced his fate to this defeated warrior, "You are the most cruel man ever seen in the Sudan. You have not ceased for twenty years to massacre poor blacks. You have acted like a ferocious beast! . . . You shall be carried away to a part of Africa so remote that they will not know your name!" So Samori, once so powerful that his name was taboo, received an almost whimsical but very bitter punishment in being exiled to a land where his name was quite unknown, where he was just another negro.

He tried to commit suicide when he heard France's sentence. He died two years later in the Congo in obscurity. Twenty years later Gouraud, now a General, met Samori's son in Europe, a Senegalese officer, a tall handsome negro of distinguished manners, and learned that three other sons,[1] perhaps more than three, of the prolific Emperor

[1] Henry Bordeaux, *L'Epopée Noire*.

had died for France in what we still optimistically like
to describe as "*the* Great War!"

In Kankan Caillié met his first real danger. The
sophisticated and widely travelled people of Kankan
did not find that René resembled a Moor. A formal
meeting of the elders was called to examine him.

Caillié attended, terribly nervous. They all placed themselves upon tanned ox-skins and a prayer was offered up, in
which we may be sure the pseudo-Mussulman took care to
join with fervent piety. Then Lamfia was cross-questioned
as to how he had met Caillié, and told René's story.

What were the names of René's father and mother,
asked the shrewd city fathers, and were they still alive?
Caillié dodged that one. Alas, how could he know their
fate today, he sighed, when he had left home so young.

The elders listened soberly and said their decision would
be promulgated.

And so it was, with the greatest solemnity. The elders
called all Kankan together at the women's mosque, which
was used for public meetings, since the women—being
more frivolous than their men-folk—did not require it
frequently for religious purposes. Caillié, who had been
privately informed that the elders were favourable to
him, was invited to sit down in the midst of the throng
with Lamfia by his side. Lamfia retold the story of
Abdallahi, the pious exile who wanted to get back to his
fatherland, and a crier repeated his words after him in
a high voice, so that those outside who had not been
able to jam into the mosque might hear.

Then Caillié was invited to confirm it all, which he
did—speaking in Arabic.

It was a treat for the people of Kankan, drama on two
legs, a "travelogue". Their imaginations thrilled at the
thought of Egypt, of France, of Mecca, of that villainous

Monsieur Macaulay, the King of Sierra Leone, the would-be seducer of pious Mussulmans.

At the conclusion of the meeting Lamfia was praised for having aided this religious young man along his way and the population of Kankan was informed that Caillié was a person of merit, deserving of their best treatment.

It was another triumph of the well-told lie.

Having been received as a member in good standing of Kankan society, Caillié was now free to make his further plans. He decided that he would try to reach Jenné, the famous, rich and unknown city sometimes called by the natives "the sister of Timbuctoo"—albeit the sisters were a five-hundred-mile river journey apart. From what Caillié was told he hoped to get to Jenné in about three and a half months.

In preparation for his depature from Kankan, Caillié's first move was to lighten his *pacotille* by exchanging a little keg of powder and a piece of guinea cloth for Bouré gold. Not feeling himself as yet sufficiently master of the Mandingo idiom to undertake the bartering himself, Caillié entrusted the transaction to Lamfia.

Lamfia was an accomplished business man and knew all the technique of trade. He told his principal that the way to get the highest price for his goods was first to prepare a *gris-gris* by means of certain writing on a planchette (board on which school-children wrote their Koran lessons), to wash off the writing and to sprinkle with this water the objects for sale. Caillié submitted to his agent's whim, but suspected that the increase of price—if any—went to the profit of Lamfia. At any rate Caillié got his Bouré gold, and carried it with him to the other side of the Sahara, a precious and comforting nest-egg.

Caillié's departure with Lamfia was fixed to follow immediately after the fête—evidently Aid-el-Kebir, the feast of the sheep, which fell that year on the 5th of July, and was celebrated at Kankan with swagger magnificence.

Certain of the natives in the crowd were dressed in the old red coats of British soldiers, brought back from Sierra Leone by daring travellers and big spenders who had bought them at second, or third, or fourth hand, in exchange for Bouré gold. With these red coats—which may have seen Waterloo!—were worn the great local straw hats nearly a yard across, or else an imported European model from the coast. The Almamy himself was dressed in a garment of special interest to Caillié. This was a really handsome coat of scarlet cloth trimmed with gold fringes and braid. It had come to the Almamy from Major Peddie, who had sent rich preliminary gifts by messengers to various inland native chiefs to prepare the way for the journey he never lived to execute.

The Almamy's English coat was imitated by the Kankan elders, who wore short scarlet jackets trimmed with pieces of cotton stuff having a pattern of yellow flowers— the nearest they could get to gold fringe. Lamfia borrowed Caillié's umbrella for the festival, and wrapped himself in Caillié's wool shawl.

On the following day, René found himself in very grave trouble. He discovered that Lamfia was stealing his goods on a large scale. It was more than the usual "light fingeredness" of the native. It was almost open theft, insolent. Blackmail? What did Lamfia know? Had he somehow learned René's secret, or guessed it? From the beginning of their association Caillié had sensed that Lamfia was suspicious. Once he had overheard a conversation between the guide and his wife which suggested that they were spying upon him with a watchful eye.

Caillié saw that he was in great danger. Apart from a natural desire to protect his precious goods, he realized the threatening implication of this barefaced robbery.

It was not his razor and his bits of glass and cloth that were at stake, but his life itself.

He was in a cruel quandary. If he permitted Lamfia to continue to rob him unrebuked, the native would see that Caillié was afraid, would understand that his suspicions were well-founded, and would victimise him completely and then perhaps denounce him. Yet, if he attacked Lamfia openly, the native might round upon him and bring about his ruin. And this was the rascal who was to guide Caillié through the dangerous forests of Ouassoulou to the eastward!

What should he do? This was by far the most dangerous fix he had got into as yet.

Caillié had moral courage. He went to the chief of Kankan, the *dougou-tigui*, and accused Lamfia openly of theft. Lamfia, either from fear of being involved in Caillié's downfall, or from lack of real proof, made no attempt to betray Caillié's secret.

He did, however, claim his traditional right, as accused person, to the hot-iron test, whereby the accused and the accuser submit to the application of hot irons on the tongue, he who flinches being counted to be in the wrong. Caillié by the vigour of his attack dodged this horror. But the mention of such a thing must have been a gruesome indication to him of the harshness of local laws, and must have suggested what might have happened to him had Lamfia dared to turn informer. Swift, grisly visions of the severed hand, of stumbling blindness. Native law was hard. In the Kankan region the law of retaliation prevailed. He who assassinated was killed. Who hurt another lost limb or eye to match his victim's injury. For theft, the punishment was amputation at the wrist of the right hand. (From a study of native laws in the *cercle* of Kankan made by Lieutenant Pinchon and quoted in *Notre Colonie de la Côte d'Ivoire* by Villamur and Richaud.) Binger witnessed the punishment of three men who had stolen cowries—the values of a cowry being only a fraction of a centime. The chief of the village cut off the right hand of each man. The hands were hung upon a post and exposed for several days. The three thieves went off without aid or sympathy. One died next day. The other two lived.

Caillié's fault in tricking Kankan's religion was a novel crime for which some novel punishment would have had to be designed, and this no doubt would have been seen to with savage enthusiasm.

Although Caillié was the victor in his public dispute with Lamfia, and protection and a new lodging place were provided for him, his position was now very unhealthy.

Lamfia had wriggled out of punishment, but felt very bitter and, as soon as he got back his nerve, began to drop dangerous hints about Caillié, whose position from the start had not been secure at Kankan.

Caillié hurried out of the city by the first caravan he could discover going in his direction, luckily one led by a certain Arafanba, described by René as "the best, gentlest and kindest Mandingo I ever saw".

8

THE FIRST NIGHT out of Kankan the caravan came to the dreaded Forest of Ouassoulou. In the hope of dodging the notorious wandering bandits Caillié and his thirteen companions plunged into the woods after dark, sneaking along in dead silence, afraid to whisper or cough or even slap at the clouds of teasing mosquitoes. A terrible rainstorm fell upon them. Going was very hard.

Safe out of the bandit zone, they paused to eat and rest, and Caillié, who because of the rain had been unable to keep on his sandals, nursed a badly wounded foot. Black thoughts came to him while the caravan snored.

He listened to the night birds crying. A savage wilderness was round him. It was a land of strange wild things, of monstrous insects—great flat spiders, deadly scorpions, loathsome centipedes, and of ferocious animals—*bonirou*, the hyena, with its lugubrious cry, sniffing the wind and sending back upon the breeze its own stench, ready to attack and mutilate a sleeping man with those jaws that are capable of crunching a gun barrel—the dark-skinned panther hunting and hungry, the lion, the elephant even, and the coiling cold snake. Caillié heard only the night birds and the croaking of frogs, but the forest might well have concealed the rest, and—for just that one night—Caillié had had enough of adventure!

It was not like him to be down-hearted. Probably it was nature's warning of sickness to come. He considered gloomily the hardships before him, with the approaching rainy season. Another reflection passed through his head. He thought to himself and sets down in his *Journal* that if he had gone with Lamfia through these woods according to the original programme, Lamfia could have robbed him without pity.

Seemingly the idea of self-defence did not occur to René. It is an extraordinary circumstance that never during all his travels does René Caillié record having struck a blow. Once, years before his great journey, he tells of wrestling with a robber. Apart from this, I have found no reference in his *Journal* to his ever fighting with anyone. So far as I know he never owned a gun nor fired off a shot in his life. René was certainly not the typical adventurer. Perhaps real adventurers never are! But a man who had the courage to go quite alone into unknown Africa, as Caillié did, scarcely needs to prove his manhood by a readiness to exchange punches, or an ability to handle firearms.

After the forest they came to pleasant country, threaded with brooklets. Sometimes, far off, Caillié saw what must have seemed like the castle of France—termite castles, *hiwi* by name, edifices ten, even twenty feet high, strong as rock, grouped together like a miniature medieval city, each edifice a chateau tower, or a spired cathedral. They were the work of termites, vulgarly white ants, yet more vulgarly "bug-a-bugs", called in this region *mouri*—those inoffensive-looking, squashy, blind little demons, a band of which have been known to destroy a half-dozen wooden telegraph poles in a single night, leaving only a paper thin shell.

Sometimes he saw the mushroom nests of the termites— a field of giant clay mushrooms, a foot high, a yard high, some double or treble, on top of one another.

Where *mouri* comes with his spires or his mushrooms, the native farmer moves out. But when *mouri* deserts his castles, the native is recompensed, for the earth which the termites have used for their building is valued for hut making and the construction of grain containers, and—when powdered and toasted—is eaten by pregnant negresses, as a bone builder for the baby-to-come, I presume.

Presently they came to the fertile farming country of Ouassoulou and Caillié forgot his depression. His peasant soul rejoiced, and contentedly he pronounced the natives to be as good farmers as in France. They were practically without religion, so far as Caillié could discover, and they were very dirty. Yet, having neither godliness nor cleanliness, the Ouassoulous were kind, and Nature had blessed them. Caillié, who was accustomed to set down what illnesses prevailed in each native land he passed through, says of these people: "I did not notice in this country a single case of illness; they are all robust and healthy."

By night they danced to the music of strange instruments, as many as twenty performers in the band and children augmenting the noise by beating in time on pieces of iron. Gay folk, and Caillié sets it down with pleasure that, though they nearly danced the night through, "their dance had no indecency".

Ouassoulou's satisfaction with Caillié was as great as his in them. "We have never seen a man like him!" they cried, and ran along by his side expressing the opinion that he was both "good and handsome". Was his whiteness natural, they asked his guide.

There was no need here for his usual fiction, for, in their childlike simplicity, they had no fear of strangers, no horror of Christians. Caillié always got on better with pagans—naturally enough, for with them there was not so great a strain of constant play-acting.

Of an evening, the good folk of the various Ouassoulou villages would cluster round him, lighting handfuls of straw so as to see and admire him, chuckling with delight and amazement. Surely this white man had no skin at all, since the glow of his blood showed through so clearly! When he walked through their villages carrying his miraculous umbrella, putting it up and furling it at will, their joy was boundless. Probably men talked about that umbrella amongst the Ouassoulous years after its owner had gone to his rest.

At Ségala, the capital, Caillié was received with cordiality by the chief, a gallant monarch wearing a single gold ear-ring in his left ear. He possessed so many wives, each in her separate *case* with her babies, that they made a little village round the royal thatched clay hut. He entertained Caillié to a supper which the Frenchman described as "not too bad" (*assez bon*) being rice with sour milk to which "he had added as a treat a little salt".

Salt ! It was Africa's constant cry now, always in Caillié's ears; a constant longing with him and with those around him. Caillié had reached the saltless belt, far from the sea, far from the salt mines of the Sahara.

In these lands where the usual food—gruel-like or porridge-like preparations of various grains—was outstandingly unpalatable without salt, by peculiar bad luck, salt was an article of the highest luxury. It was cruel. To us who take our salt ungratefully for granted it would require a huge effort of imagination to understand how almost unbearable life would be in lands where salt did not exist. In 1936 the *Lancet* reported an experiment in absolutely saltless living over a period of days, and told of the resultant listlessness, nausea, cramps, strange thirst, and so on. A man's salt consumption is said to be normally ten to twelve pounds per year.

To import salt from the Sahara—the only place where it existed in exportable quantities—meant a trek across blazing desert and roadless wastes and might mean death or capture into slavery. Every pound of salt was figuratively dyed with blood.

The profits matched the danger. A slab of salt which at the mines was worth only a little more than the labour of extracting it, had a value of five francs or more at Timbuctoo, fifty-five francs at Bamako, and as much as two-hundred and forty francs in Southern Sudan. In some remote lands the transporting of salt would have been so expensive that the inhabitants had literally none at all. It has been suggested that this was one of the incentives to cannibalism.

Caillié was now in country where salt was money, actually used as coinage—a few grains at a time—and lick your hand while bargaining! Caillié tells of salt prices in terms of human life. The regular established price of a slave at Sambatikila (Samatiguila on the modern map) was thirty small "bricks" of salt. From what Caillié says I would estimate that the average "brick" would have weighed about five pounds. Roughly, a man sold for his weight in salt! It being peace time, the salt

price which Caillié recorded was cheap. When the negroes
went to war, salt became extra dear, and slaves—being
war prisoners—extra cheap. Then a man's value in salt
might be but one-fifth his weight. As recently as 1901
Delafosse was offered a whole cow in exchange for two
pounds of salt (a kilogramme).

Salt was for festivals and holidays. Caillié perforce
shared the flavourless, unwholesome diet of the natives. No
more golden oranges, nor *caura* with their plumlike savour.
No bananas at three beads a dozen. Caillié's stomach
longed for palatable food.

9

AT SAMATIGUILA, WHERE Caillié passed five
days at the end of July, there was not only a shortage of
salt, but a shortage of everything. Samatiguila was a
pitiful place. It was almost foodless. Caillié arrived at the
thinnest time of the year. Natives, to whom economy is
unknown, eat their food when the crops come in and
go without when their food is finished, a habit so common
that the month in their primitive lunar calendar which
approximately coincides with Caillié's arrival at Samatiguila had the title of "Starvation Month", or "Month
of Privation". Despite bad times, the Almamy welcomed
Caillié with enthusiasm, promised to find him a new
guide, for the excellent Arafanba could accompany him
no further, and expressed his delight at receiving in his
kingdom a man who came from near Mecca and was
actually on his way back to the holy spot. He furthermore
asked that his compliments should be given "to the
old men of Mecca", and presented Caillié with a silver
bracelet of the value of three francs "as a reminder".
This message—the sending of regards to the old folks of
a foreign place—was, as a matter of fact, quite in accord

with local etiquette, and occurred frequently in official communications between native rulers.

But despite the Almamy's distinguished courtesy, his entertainment was meagre. Days passed without the customary offer of food to the visiting caravan. And when a stray portion of saltless rice or a dish of boiled herbs did come Caillié's way he had the embarrassing knowledge that he was depriving the residents of the place of their own scant share.

He should have controlled both appetite and pride, and rested at Samatiguila until his injured foot was healed.

Here it was that René made the first great mistake of his journey. Every day since Kankan he had walked with pain. An abrasion on his left heel became a wound, which grew worse as he ploughed through gravelly soil and stubble or waded through swollen streams. He wrapped his foot as best he could in a bandage of rags, but this would not remain in place while walking. How often in the months to come he must have regretted the impatience which caused him to hurry forward.

But the approaching rainy season frightened him. The countryside was already awash, and the worst of the rains yet to come. Every brooklet had become a little river, every little river had grown big. The ground was soaked and slippery. Frail bridges had been swept away. There was no shelter. He must push forward or risk being bogged for months.

So Caillié made an almost fatally unwise decision.

On the second of August he left Samatiguila and limped along for a further twenty-four miles, always in pouring rain. He was suffering agony. On the afternoon of the second day the party arrived at a small place which he had the courage to describe as "a pretty little village" This was Timé (correctly spelt Tiémé). In this "pretty little village" René Caillié was to pass through hell.

10

TIÉMÉ IS IN the far interior of the Ivory Coast Colony not far from Odienné. Although Caillié had been three and a half months on the road—travelling about half the time and half the time waiting upon the vagaries of guides reluctant to leave home—and although he had tramped, according to his own estimate, $529\frac{1}{4}$ miles, he was still a long, long way from Timbuctoo. Tiémé is at the lowest, the most southerly point of that S-on-its-side, which was the general form of Caillié's route. Before he would get to Timbuctoo he would have to walk nearly five hundred miles more, and ride another five hundred miles in a Niger *pirogue*. Roughly he had struggled over about one-third of the distance which he had to cover from the sea to the secret city.

Tiémé was one of those almost invisible villages of savage Africa. It scarcely seemed to rise above the ground —a group of poor little huts, a few trees, a bit of scanty cultivation, a bunch of naked black children, their mothers and grandmothers in vague flapping drapery and bare bosoms, some yapping dogs.

Tiémé sheltered Caillié—or, more properly speaking, refrained from hurting him. Tiémé indifferently watched him as he nearly died and fought his way back to strength, and Tiémé immediately forgot all about him.

The Commandant of Odienné, the administrator in control of this region, very kindly made on my behalf an inquiry amongst the population of modern Tiémé (now 1,471 negroes) and discovered that there is no old man there today who recalls ever hearing when he was young a tradition about a white man or Arab who came there to live in the long ago.

But that after all merely proves the cleverness with which Caillié, even in dire stress, handled himself and maintained his masquerade of insignificance.

The blacks of Tiémé must have been flabbergasted by the erection in the middle of their little village a few months ago of a monument to the undetected *toubab* (white man)—a ten-foot column bearing Caillié's name.

Caillié limped into Tiémé on August 3, 1827. He had fever as well as a bad foot. His guide led him to the home of his brother, Baba. Baba was temporarily absent but his mother welcomed Caillié with fine courtesy. She was Manman, and if it had not been for her Caillié would never have got to Timbuctoo.

Manman was a wrinkled old lady, a very old lady indeed for Africa. She was, Caillié thought, sixty years old. Viewed with a critical eye Manman was a queer figure, thin and leathery, with puckered face, sparse grey wool, sagging breasts half wrapped in her tattered *pagne*, bare feet cracked like the hooves of an aged horse, big work-worn palms salmon-tinted as are the insides of negroes' hands and with sensitive movements like the paws of animals; a big motherly smile unhampered by teeth. But who could look at Manman with a critical eye? She was as kind as a bitch to her pups, or a hen to her chickens, instinctively kind.

Manman received the strange new-comer with unhesitating hospitality. He was prostrated with fatigue and pain and weakness. She made him rest upon an ox-skin rug and offered him some stewed-up herbs, to which she generously added a little of her store of salt. But Caillié was too feverish to eat. So Manman laid him down upon the straw mat which was her own bed.

Baba returned. He led Caillié to present his respects to the chief of the village, a venerable Mohammedan who was Baba's father, but who did not reside with Baba's mother.

Manman had a hut of her own with her children. This was according to custom and did not suggest a rift in the family. Flimsy local architecture which restricted the size of buildings, and natural human preference, both opposed the lodging of all of a man's wives and offspring in one house.

The old chief made a *beau geste* to the stranger. He gave René a lump of raw meat. Also his consent that René should remain in the village until the departure of his caravan which was stopping to load up with kola nuts, Tiémé being a clearing-house for kola. Caillié confidently expected that he would be fit to travel along with them. A few days' rest was all he required, he thought.

The Mussulman's gift of welcome was, oddly enough, wild pig meat. René tasted it, suspected a trap, and pushed it away indignantly, hungry though he was. This was the act of a hero, for *kossé-beli*, the wild pig's meat must have been almost irresistibly succulent to a famished man. African wild pig, *potamochère* or *phacochère*, is an ugly fellow to look at but splendid to eat.

"Eat it! It's good! We don't think *this* is pig! cried the guide, and René let himself be persuaded with difficulty, tasting the pork hesitatingly and suspiciously, as if tempted into a new sin. It was one of those bits of comedy which René always enjoyed.

The caravan busily prepared for the next stage of their journey. They packed their kola nuts in baskets with wrapping of fresh leaves of a special sort, dark green leaves with a yet darker green border, which centuries of native experimenting had proved to be the one sort of packing which, provided fresh leaves were applied from time to time, would enable them to travel the nuts to the northern markets unspoilt and unshrivelled.

Kolas were their life. These details were vitally important. The nuts were packed three thousand five hundred to a basket, a terrific weight which would be borne on the head—heads of men and women alike—and carried day after day across country as far as the Niger, five hundred miles away. Caillié says he could barely lift one of the baskets.

Kolas were exchanged for salt. Salt was then brought back here to the saltless country. It was another crushing struggle, each man staggering under two and a half salt bars, big as tombstones, and each woman carrying two bars *and* the cooking pots! Home at last and the salt exchanged for slaves.

If a man and his wife earned one slave by the return trading trip—7,000 kolas carried one way and four and a half salt bars brought back—they were jubilant. Travel expenses were high: food, dues, custom charges. As much as twenty kola nuts per load might be exacted as toll at some villages on the route. However slaves, purchased one by one, meant wealth. If a man had ten slaves he was rich, he could retire and let the slaves work for him. So in his prime he put his strong woolly head under his huge bundle, and made his wife do the same. Thus did the folk of Tiémé provide for their old age.

Caillié watched the caravan make its preparations, watched at first with interest, then with foreboding, at last with bitter envy.

For as the days passed he saw that his foot was not getting any better.

With dismay he recognized that his luck had changed. He asked himself if he dared attempt to go with the caravan. In roadless Africa men walked, or they stayed behind. Horses and donkeys were rare, beyond Caillié's purse and outside the possibilities of his masquerade. Mile after mile of walking with the caravan across country would be impossible for a cripple. If he fell behind, these ambitious business men and their wives would not wait for him.

He must stay at Tiémé until his foot was cured. Disgust swept through him as he watched the strong black backs, the striding black legs of the caravan plunging off through the bush, while he remained behind.

Caillié does not put a name to the foot trouble which afflicted him. In tropic Africa, infested by vermin and where travellers went barefoot on narrow beaten paths so that they intercommunicated whatever was wrong with them, foot and leg troubles were common and various.

A person who discovered that his feet or legs gave him trouble had a wide choice of possible maladies to worry about. For instance, he might say, "Jiggers!" (or chigoes, or learnedly, *sarcopsila penetrans*).

The jigger is a sort of sand flea, very small but affectionate. She has a flattering desire to raise her family on human feet. She burrows under the skin or toe-nails, fattens with her unborn brood, and—if not removed with disinfected needle and her infants destroyed—turns her human victim into a mass of painful small abscesses. West African residents have their native servants examine their feet and perform the necessary extermination at least once a week, and if wise they avoid going barefoot, or leaving their footware about on the bare floor.

Another possible diagnosis would be guinea worm. Guinea worms are one of the scare stories of the tropics. The native name for this agonizing complaint is translatable as "*the* Misery". It is said that this humble admirer of the human race pushes her way into our bodies with drinking water. She is no fatter than a horse-hair. Once she gets in, she wants to get out again, and makes for the open air through the skin, often the skin of legs or feet. This produces a sore so tender that sufferers howl with the pain of it. Should the guinea worm break on her slow crawl to freedom, that part of her which remains in the body will seek a new escape and form a new abscess, so it is the custom to reel her upon a twig or bit of straw, three or four turns per day. Sometimes she is two yards long. So the sufferer has a long time to howl! Severe cases leave permanent bone injury and a bad scar. There were, and may still be, villages where guinea worms were so common an affliction that everybody had them every year.

There is also the grotesque and tragic elephantiasis, and Africa's army of lepers is vast. All in all, when a traveller who has gone barefoot—as Caillié did—over native paths and shared native lodgings, first perceives foot troubles, a nightmare procession of possibilities crosses his mind.

Caillié's lameness, it has been suggested, was a bad case of kraw-kraw (or cro-cro). This is the local name for a form of ulcer, said to be produced by a parasite which occurs in certain streams and lakes.

However he may have diagnosed his sickness, Caillié saw that it would prevent his travelling until, at least, the end of the month of August. It meant loss of time, waste of resources, increased danger of detection as a white man, for the people of Tiémé would have ample opportunity to study his looks and his ways. He called on patience and prudence, and he asked Baba to rent him a hut for his exclusive use.

Baba agreed. The rent was a pair of scissors, "an article which was very rare at Tiémé and of very high price".

On the 7th of August René moved in. It was probably the first time in his life that he had a home all of his own, and he was destined to be very miserable in it.

I I

HIS HOUSE WAS unpretentious. Pressed earthen walls five inches thick, roof of straw. Just high enough for a small man like Caillié to stand upright. No escape for smoke, and—the rains being on—a fire had to be kept burning night and day. Some smoke filtered out through the door and the chinks in the straw roof, the rest remained inside, choking fumes and greasy soot. It was rather like living inside a chimney.

There was no furniture, but simply a mat on the damp ground—chair by day, bed by night.

There were other inconveniences too. These earthen village houses were built of mud dug up alongside the village, mud full of trash and garbage. Toast up that mud inside a hut and smell it. Watch the grubs and little white worms come wriggling down your walls. Wash it in vain with the native disinfectant—cow-dung mixed with water.

Such a place might serve as a white man's shelter between two days of exciting effort, when fatigue and interest in the route dulled squeamish sensibility. Up to this point Caillié had accepted such lodgings cheerfully. But as a home over a period of inactivity and invalidism, it took bearing.

Manman did her best. On market-day Caillié turned over the shopping money to her—glass beads in suitable quantity—and the old body would go out and buy his week's supply of rice or of "Hungry Rice" *foigné* (or *fonio* or *fundi*—it is a spell-as-you-like word), which is a little grain-like grass seed, swift ripening, and so a delight to negro improvidence.

Twice a day Manman would bring him his food, a wooden dish filled with rice or with *tau*. *Tau*, from René's description, tasted somewhat as it sounds. It was a thick mess of *foigné* flour, greenish-grey, flavourless and saltless.

With the big wooden dish came a little earthen dish in which was a stew of herbs or cooked peanuts. For all her good qualities, it must be admitted that Manman was no *cordon bleu*. From the store which he kept by his side Caillié would permit himself to add the luxury of a very little salt. An extravagance, but as he says, "without it it would have been impossible for me to eat at all". Sometimes he would also stir into his food a bit of shea butter, the vegetable grease so popular with African negroes and usually so nauseating to white palates and noses.

Caillié ate shea butter uncomplainingly and described the shea trees carefully: how they looked like pear trees and how the leaves grew smaller as the tree grew older. The fruit was big as the egg of a guinea hen, the nut within—this was the butter—big as a pigeon's egg. The nut was dried, squashed, boiled, moulded into balls like pale green wax, packed in leaves. There it was, ready for market, butter and ointment both. Experimentally I have bought a lump, price five centimes, but I have not tried it either externally or internally.

In René's housekeeping budget shea butter figured at a price in beads equal to four sous a pound.

And that was his menu: twice a day rice or *tau*. *Tau* or rice. Another wooden dish of *tau*. Another wooden dish of rice. There was practically no meat. There was no fruit. No vegetables except an occasional yam. Dried fish was available—fish caught in the nearby streams and brought to market after being permitted to go bad in the natural fashion of fish. Anyone who has smelt native dried fish will sympathize with Caillié for not receiving any of it into his home. No wonder Caillié pronounced the diet of Tiémé "detestable".

Fever fell on him. He dosed himself with what he called "*kinine*". His landlord, Baba, recommended a competing remedy. He brought to Caillié's hut a piece of old paper on which there had been written a passage from the Koran, a very good medicine passage for fevers. He told René to copy the words on a writing-board, wash them off, and drink the water. René thanked Baba, followed his instructions to the letter, except that he did not drink the water. Next day he was better, and Baba, who did not know of this slight divergence from his prescription, was delighted with the efficacy of his remedy.

Early days at Tiémé were not so bad. Caillié even enjoyed himself. The women of Tiémé found him a novelty. They laughed at his long nose and cooed with amazement at his white skin. He gave away a few gallant presents of beads. I suspect that the girls of Tiémé flirted with him.

And then Caillié, who was hoping that he was getting better, discovered a new sore—another sore on the same foot. It was a tragedy, a relapse just when he dared hope he was getting better. Caillié's new sore was worse than the first. He must have studied it with sick horror.

Manman and he talked it over. Manman procured some baobab leaves. Boiled baobab leaves made a splendid poultice. It was sure to reduce swellings. Manman boiled the baobab leaves.

Having no cloth to hold the poultice, Caillié proposed to use his turban which was a pathetic indication of the man's absolute lack of resources. Manman protested against such male extravagance. What was this reckless young guest of hers doing? His turban! All dirtied up with a baobab compress! Better no compress, she scolded, than sacrifice this handsome piece of cloth. Cloth was so very rare in Tiémé.

The swelling was reduced but there still remained the sore "twice as big as an *écu* of six francs"—an *écu* was a silver coin, big as a crown or a dollar.

Baba again intervened, and this time with a cure which was practical. He sent one of his slaves to seek a certain root which had caustic properties, boiled it to a pulp, and crushed it with a rock until it was a sort of pomade. With the water in which the root had been cooked he washed René's wound. He applied then the mashed root, and, having no linen for a bandage, he covered the

dressing with a "big leaf having a strong aromatic odour"
—just a leaf on an open sore!

The complete lack of surgical cleanliness in native
medicine shocks us today, but would not have seemed so
barbaric to René a century ago. It is an astonishing fact
that the natives often were cured under such treatment
and that Caillié lived and got well. A usual dressing in
primitive surgery was to put dust on the wound, as for
instance, in Timbuctoo after the circumcision operation.
Native doses, the result of centuries of traditional experience, were made from the materials which were always
at hand. There was no room for a medicine cupboard in
the native hut. Had a man fever, his friends ran out and
fetched tamarind leaves. Pawpaw leaves were a laxative.

Poison, the ugly sister of curative medicine, gave native
cunning a fine chance. Scratch a bad negro and you found
a Borgia. The habit of concealing poison in kolas—the
sacred token of friendship, the symbol of mutual forgive-
ness—was especially mean. *Kouna* was the poison used on
arrows. If fresh, *kouna* was mortal, but when stale caused
a wound from which a man might recover if a secret
antidote were taken, for which the wounded man must
pay through the nose. A cheaper antidote was to put a
pinch of powder in the wound and set it off! There was
another poison, *doung-kono*, "which is prepared in the
following fashion" according to Captain Binger. "The
stem of the millet plant is introduced into the *anus* of
a corpse and left there three weeks. Then dried and
crushed. The resulting powder mixed with powdered
flavouring matters used in the sauce which is served with
tau is not noticeable in taste and it is impossible to observe
that one is ill. It is only after several days that the stomach
begins to swell slightly. At the end of a month plumpness
is manifest, one realizes that it is unnatural fat. And in

eight or ten days one dies. Even the science of a European doctor could not save the poisoned person. *Doung-kono* may be detected if a pinch of the contaminated flavouring be thrown into milk. It makes the milk bubble up."

The triumph of native villainy was *korti*—poison and magic combined. Thrown in a man's face it would kill him. Or a secret poisoner could slip a little under his thumb-nail and nonchalantly dip the thumb into the calabash when he served his victim a drink. But the unique feature of *korti* was that it could in certain cases —according to native belief—kill its victim at a distance, at hundreds of miles.

12

MANMAN BECAME RENÉ'S nurse. She had observed with respect her son's method of dressing René's foot and subsequently, as Caillié records gratefully, "it was the good old woman who undertook to give me the treatment night and morning. Often she consoled me by the hope of a rapid cure".

There is no question from whose lips it was that Caillié learned the simple word of encouragement which he included in the little Mandingo vocabulary in his *Journal* —the simple, soft word "*Adiba*" which means, he says, "You will be cured!"

"In gratitude for her care," writes Caillié, "I made her the present of a fine piece of coloured cloth which gave her great pleasure, for probably she had never had so beautiful a thing in her possession. An instant after-wards her son came to thank me and asked me with a really serious air who had put the flowers onto the cloth. I laughed at his simplicity and told him it was the white people. He went on, still serious, saying he believed only God could make a thing so beautiful."

So Caillié dragged through a whole month of inactivity, lying on the damp ground of his hut unable to walk, but not suffering great pain.

Caillié, like all sick men, became conscious of women in a new way. To sick men women turn to something more than irritants and objects of joy. She who tends him, and by association all her sex, takes on a serious importance which they never had to him before. Most men think about women soberly for the first time when they are ill. Thus Caillié, lying on his mat, or crawling to the low doorway of his hut for an airing, noted and observed the women of Tiémé and their ways.

Women were, at any rate, the sex more available just then for observation. It was the time of the rains, and during the rains the men refused to go outdoors. All day the men of Tiémé remained in their huts round a big fire, sewing *coussabes* "as a pastime"—to quote Caillié. If obliged to go out they protected themselves against the wet and mud by putting on a sort of wooden *sabot* with a sole two and a half inches thick.

The women were more hardy. They had to be. Barefoot they plunged round in the slush, seeing to everything. They fetched the water and the wood, often from long distances, and attended to all other outdoor matters during the rainy season. As a matter of fact, rain or shine, it was the women of Tiémé who made the wheels of primitive life go round. They were the strong sex. They did most of the farming, they carried the heavier load—sometimes walking laden while their husbands rode blandly on horse or donkey. Theirs was the long work of sunning and threshing and washing the *foigné*, and of crushing it into coarse flour in a mortar.

René Caillié—young, gallant and Gallic—was scandalized to observe a state of society where women were used as servants, and glamour and romance were utterly lacking. The cynical summing up of a negro women's life, "beast of burden by day, instrument of pleasure by night", distressed the young Frenchman, who was able to record only one piece of chivalry on the part of the men of Tiémé—they killed the chickens!

Caillié was astounded that there were never any pleasantries between man and wife. Probably he observed that a wife did not even call her husband by name, but referred to him as "the father of little So-and-So".

Once he asked Baba why he never joked with the women of his family. Said Baba, "because if I did they would begin to make fun of me, and would not do my bidding any longer!"

Certainly woman's lot in black Africa was hard. And certainly if the joy was to the idle, it was very much a man's world. Maybe, however, there was another kind of joy in belonging to the half of the community on which the main responsibilities of life rested—provider, as well as sweetheart and mother. Perhaps the women of Tiémé and all the other hard-driven negresses rejoiced in their strength and courage, banged the pestle up and down with pride, carried the heavier load haughtily, and took grave satisfaction in their bravery at childbirth.

René tells with pity and admiration of the woman he observed on his route who was big with child yet carried her porter's load. She was taken ill and had her baby in a cottonfield by the way, catching up with the caravan a few hours later. To this he adds, as a postscript, that the babies were born "white, just a little yellow, and that they blacken progressively up to the tenth day, when they are quite black".

The humane system of polygamy luckily distributed the work amongst several matrons. In Tiémé—the population being of mixed religions—some men had the four traditional wives of Islam; others, who were pagans, had as many as they could feed. Polygamy did not hurt female pride. It did not threaten the security of the women and their children, nor carry any social obliquy. If the women were jealous of their fellow wives at times, this, after all, was but the fate of woman the world over!

But polygamy naturally offended Caillié. It has offended many travellers and missionaries who have followed him. It is notable that it did not shock that other heroic and eccentric African traveller, Mary Kingsley, who approved of polygamy though she lived in the prim Victorian age and was by her own admission a sexless woman. (She said in a letter to her biographer, Mr. Gwynn: "I make the confession humbly quite as I would make the confession of being deaf or blind, I know nothing myself of love. I have read about it . . . but I have never been in love, nor has anyone ever been in love with me.")

The native woman herself, if she ever questioned her state at all, liked polygamy. It spread the endlessly complex housework and farm labour amongst several women and it shifted the entertainment of her husband from her during the early period of her baby's life.

Another advantage—there were no black old maids, despite the unbalanced population in lands where vast numbers of men were dragged off to slavery and the women often left behind. Every girl, plain or pretty, lived a complete woman's life. There were no superfluous women. An old maid was an abnormality, an obvious freak of nature, *gwana-muso*, the unsellable woman. No normal girl ever dreamed of such a fate. Nor need she ever dream of becoming a prostitute, for prostitution in the civilized sense was unknown and unneeded. Impure girls there were and bastard babies spoken of contemptuously as *iri-la-do* (wood-louse) or *n'a-ma-de* (the dung child). Adulterous wives were common enough, but that a woman should pass her life in the gloom of formal prostitution would have been absurd and unthinkable. In short, a woman had the satisfaction of knowing that she was an article with a real market value.

Contrary to what then, and still, maintains openly in many white lands and indirectly in most of the white world, it was the man who paid the *dot*. A woman had no need to bring money or the prospect of money to her husband.

In Tiémé in Caillié's day the price of a first-class wife was as much as the value of three or four slaves.[1] This meant tramping back and forth over hundreds of miles under many heavy loads of kola and salt. It must have been rather pleasing to the maidens of Tiémé to roll over on their mats inside snug huts of a night and think of all this hard work being done to save up their purchase money!

To these maidens came before marriage a curious ritual experience—both symbolical and physical, like the circumcision obligatory upon their brothers. A cruel operation, it was to them a matter of pride and delight; a whole series of complex ceremonials attended its performance, and festivals followed. The maidens went from door to door carrying wands of honour and accompanied by a chaperoning old woman to receive felicitations and gifts. It was the gayest time of their whole lives: no work to do till they were cured, and a constant series of rejoicings and feasts. This lasted for six weeks till the girls were well again, banquet following banquet—and "always with

[1] Today there are no bargains in wives either. In fact at Saint-Louis in 1930 the price and expenses of marriage were so exorbitant that marriage seemed about to become a luxury for the rich only, and the native population met formally on the 17th of August and fixed the *dot* of young girls at a maximum of 1,000 francs, widows at 500, and the same figure for unmarried mothers. Also (Article VII) the tam-tam was forbidden at weddings, fifty francs and no more might be spent on griots (Article VIII), and (Article IX) the coiffing of the bride must not cost over forty francs. (From *Les Pêcheurs de Guet N'Dar* by N. Leca.) Previous to the passing of these rules, *dot* and wedding expenses could easily amount up to the extent of a tax upon the groom of 3,000 or 4,000 francs.

The cost of a wife today in French West Africa as a whole runs from thirty to a thousand francs, or more. (Georges Hardy, *L'Afrique Occidentale Française*.)

salt"! Everybody profited, for the great plates of *tau* and rice which were offered to the maidens were passed about to friends and neighbours. "On these occasions", says Caillié, "I was never forgotten. The good negress, my housekeeper, always giving me my part."

In due time, when the aspect of her young bosom proved she had come to marriageable age, when she was *kogo-fa*, or full-breasted, each black maiden was sought in marriage, and her marriage price paid in advance. Again she was the heroine of a feast, paid for by the bridegroom. Then she settled down to her life-work of keeping her husband in idleness.

And yet she was not altogether downtrodden. Says René gloomily—for he subsequently had a rough time at the hands of the Tiémé ladies—"the women of this part of the world are very difficult to manage".

13

WITH SEPTEMBER CAME the deceptive hope that the rains were about to cease. It was a disappointment. The rain was now not absolutely continuous, but it still rained every day. Then came the period of violent storms prophesying the end of the rains. As the rains petered off, although the heat increased, the air became fresher.

Through the weeks Caillié lolled about in his hut, with smoke in his eyes and damp beneath him, eating interminable wooden dishes of *tau* and trying to keep his heart up. Hours passed so slowly—the four parts of the day by which time was counted at Tiémé, *Sogo-ma*, the morning, *Tile*, the full day, named after the sun, *Ula*, the late afternoon, and *Susuma*, the night.

Like all sick people he noticed small things. He was entertained by the local custom which prescribed that after meals everyone thanked his table mates and then thanked any persons whom he might encounter in the village paths—a sort of Grace in its savage way. Said Caillié shrewdly:

"One could easily judge of the quality of the meal they had eaten by the more or less gay way in which they would pronounce the words 'Thank-you!' Sometimes they would even come to my door and thank me."

He observed the unexpected gentleness and orderly life of these savages. There were no beggars. Each home took care of its own old folk. Crimes of violence were rare. A murder in a village near Tiémé created an immense hullabaloo in the whole countryside—much more of a scandal than a similar crime in Europe. But black fingers were light. The people of Tiémé were not thieves by deliberate intention, but they often took things they fancied. Even amongst near relatives, etiquette permitted one to count or measure carefully any goods confided to another. Tiémé folk habitually accused members of their family of stealing and no feelings would be hurt. Superstition protected the farmer. Upon ripe crops was placed a *gris-gris*, a bit of paper specially prepared, and none ventured near, despite the low standard of honesty.

Another local fault was a complete lack of hospitality. During all of René's long stay at Tiémé only the old chief, who gave him a piece of wild pig meat, ever made him a present. This coldness toward strangers was comprehensible. Tiémé was on a trade route and would have been the victim of every caravan, had it not steeled its heart against the ravenous traveller.

So Caillié whiled away his imprisonment. As the weather improved he found that his foot was improving too. He told himself that he would be able to leave toward the end of October.

"I looked forward to this happy moment with impatience, as may be imagined, for despite the care of the good old woman and all her kindness to me, I desired ardently to bid her good-bye."

The rains ceased altogether. It was early November: *Ka-ule*, "The Red Sky", the intermediate period between the rainy season and the cold weather. Caillié began to make inquiries about a caravan going in the direction of Timbuctoo. He took on successive days two observations with string and cane to determine as best he could the position of the little village which he hoped soon to leave. He was the explorer again.

But instead of getting better, Caillié had been getting worse. He was a very sick man and did not know it. The languor which had been upon him during the past weeks marked the first stages of one of the most distressing illnesses known to man, now happily very uncommon. Caillié was a victim of scurvy. On November 10 he became aware of the fact, sickeningly and shrinkingly aware that but for a miracle he was a doomed man. It was the blackest moment in all his hard life.

Scurvy was a disease so dreadful and once so common that the word itself had the evil distinction of coming to mean contemptible. It was the nightmare sickness of sailors, soldiers, explorers and those in beleaguered cities, the disease of adventurous men, the intrepid, the gallant and the unyielding—a poor reward for courage!

Scurvy was the result of poor diet, the usual belief being that it was caused by the absence of vegetables and fruit. Thus it was especially associated with sailors in the days before refrigeration, and before steam, when voyages were long and becalmings frequent.

In a world where there is much to complain about, we can at least be thankful that we have practically stamped out scurvy. The Merchant Shipping Act of 1867 required ten ounces of lemon juice to be carried per man per day, except for boats going where lemons already existed. Incidentally, scurvy indirectly gave the British navy that name which has now become American slang for Englishmen—"Limeys".

Says, Caillié: "I experienced this hideous malady in all its horrors." And its horrors are considerable: haggard face and general weakness, ulcerated gums, loosened teeth, livid purplish spots beneath the skin, ulcers on the legs, paralysis of the knees, awful prostration and depression and a condition of such weakness that complications often cause death.

Caillié, son of his times, knew just what to expect. And, cruellest knowledge of all, he knew how easily he might have been cured by simple treatment—good diet, astringents for local use (mere vinegar would have served), and decent comfort. These ordinary things were as far from him as the moon. He could only lie on the bare ground of his wretched hut and watch the progress of his sickness. Tempestuous longings swept through him for green juicy feeds. In delirium he tasted again the flavour of *caura*, the sweet wild plum, and of the *cobai* which the natives adore, and the cool pulp of the *néoe*, which is shaped like a potato.

But at Tiémé at this time of the year there was absolutely nothing to help him. The tropic sun beat down on a brown earth. There was nothing but dried-up grass, dried-up trees. The very look of them, the rustling sound of them, the dusty dry smell of them tortured him. Everything that meant cure and safety and success was absent. He was helpless in this dried-up world.

Manman forced him twice a day to drink rice water. He could not eat. Poor old Manman: all the beauty had gone out of her piece of flowered cloth. She looked in pity

at her strange protégé, and taught him lovingly another
phrase for his Mandingo vocabulary. It was "*Amaukou!*"
Do not cry!

14

Tropic africa was a land of famine. The negro
was always ravenous. "The greatest pleasure you can give
a black", said an oldtime colonial officer, "is to feed him,
and his happiest moment is when he is belching contentedly after a huge meal," when—as the native saying
puts it—"his belly is sweet".

In the old days hunger was pitiful. One might see
starving blacks robbing the giant ant nests of their grain,
or even foraging among the horse droppings. And it was
not altogether a matter of native improvidence or slothful
farming either.

Nature did not in the first instance lay out a generous
African garden. Before the whites and the Arabs arrived
most of the food we think of as typically African had never
been seen, and these new plants were slow in penetrating
the interior. For instance, maize corn, yams, oranges,
lemons, manioc, rice, sugar-cane, peanuts, onions, and pineapples were all importations. One wonders what the primitive
negro could have found to eat during the centuries before
explorers and invaders and colonists came to his lands. Certainly he did not find much, either in quantity or variety.

One who eats with natives must put his prejudices in his
pocket. Many a shocking ingredient is slipped into the stew.

Caillié tells about one such surprise which befell him
not far from Tiémé:

"I had not yet had any lunch so I sought out a Bambara
woman who was mashing cooked yams and bought some from
her for some glass beads. She gave me in a separate dish a

little gumbo sauce and when I dipped my yams into this sauce I found—to my great regret—little feet and I realized that she had served me mouse sauce."

Mouse sauce—or rather, stewed mice—was, and still is, a usual dish amongst the Bambaras. And for the information of those who may be interested I will give the authentic directions for preparing the dish, as I myself obtained them while at Ségou on the Niger, Ségou whose walls, so runs the story, "rested on the blood of 60,000 massacred slaves". The proud city which refused Mungo Park admission, is now a peaceable place which actually possesses a little hotel. (Hotels are rare in tropic West Africa. Usually travellers sleep in "campements", providing their own food and bedding.) Madame of the Hotel du Niger summoned a Bambara youth and invited him to tell me how to make the dish. The boy, in a fine new *boubou*—one shoulder printed "10 metres" and the other shoulder "Nana Bolo"—obliged as follows: Clean your mice, add salt and pepper. Prepare a *soumbala* sauce. (*Soumbala* is a basic flavouring used in native cookery, sweetish and not pleasing to our palates. It is made with the golden flour got from crushing and fermenting the fruits of the *nété*.) Combine your seasoned mice, your *soumbala* and water. Cook till the mice are tender and serve hot.

He said affably to Madame, who interpreted, "Mice are good. They eat very clean food". And this, after all, is true. Mice eat as we do ourselves, and a visitor from another planet might marvel at our distinctions and repugnances.

Caillié, who had grown somewhat hardened, seemed most disturbed because the mice used in the stews were not always fresh killed. Caught in honey jars by the children, they would be gutted and singed and laid aside in a corner till needed. Sometimes they might wait a week. Mouse was one thing: high mouse was another!

Africa could offer some very queer dishes to the traveller. Here are a few striking items from the native menu, some as Caillié reported them, some which I have seen—but not eaten—myself, some recorded by other travellers, but all of the regions Caillié visited:

Little Dogs—classed as butcher's meat and carefully fattened. Roasted whole in their skins. The cooked meat has a reddish appearance, and Caillié said it was better than camel.

Flying Ants—a delicacy fried. When the moment of their flight arrived it was a real festival—the ant season had opened! Everybody hunted. The ants were fried in shea butter. It was a treat, an orgy.

Betti—a dish made with flies called *betti* and millet flour. Sampled by Mollien in Futa Jalon.

Caterpillars—in the Sudan were dried and added to the sauce served with *tau*. Only such caterpillars were acceptable as had fed on shea butter trees.

Grass-hopper Pâté—a Tuareg dish eaten in the Sahara.

Locusts (which fly in such dense clouds that they obscure the sun and have been known, when settling, to break the boughs of trees)—caught and preserved, formed the main meat item in certain regions.

Rats—such a *bonne-bouche* on the Guinea coast that children were forbidden to eat them. Rats were to be reserved for fighting men! The giant Gambia rat, big as a rabbit, is another favourite food item.

The hen's egg, the one article of food which to a white man's taste would have seemed unspoilable by native cooking, was unfortunately forbidden to Caillié. There was in tropic Africa a religious or traditional antipathy to hens' eggs, though there were armies of chickens and guinea chickens. Egg eating in the native mind was associated with Christianity. The hope of seeing Mungo Park eat an egg—raw, whole, shell and all, which they believed was the white custom—attracted native crowds to whom such a spectacle had all the interest of the performance of a sword-swallower.

Africa is a home of food prejudices. The killing of this or that animal is forbidden to certain groups and families by a command so frightening that a native might die from a sort of self-hypnotism if he found that unwittingly he had transgressed. This notion of respectful kinship between certain humans and certain animals still further restricts the already so limited menu.

Take snakes, for instance—they are usually an esteemed item of food but are absolutely forbidden in certain black kitchens. One origin of the snake taboo can be found in the following story, reported by Paul Guebhard:

One day a Timbonké mother left her baby alone in the hut. When it abruptly ceased crying, she became alarmed and returned to find that a horned viper was beside her child. She dared not make a move. Her baby resumed the consoling occupation which had caused him to cease his crying. He reached for the viper's tail and sucked at it, as if it were his mother's nipple.

Thereafter Timbonké men and women, though they did not entrust their babies to viper wet-nurses, regarded the viper with reverence. Never would they kill it. If they find a dead viper, it must be interred piously under a little heap of stones.

It is not in any spirit of frivolity that I have left René agonizing in his hut at Tiémé to digress into an account of the savage *cuisine*. I have wanted to make clear how awful was the diet in the old days of a traveller who ate the same as the local natives. Today every white traveller has preserved foods of some kind. There was no such thing available for Caillié.

15

As CAILLIÉ LAY ill and almost starving he grew poorer and poorer. His trade goods were going fast. He saw that, if his sickness continued, he would find himself absolutely destitute.

Tiémé suspected his plight. Baba frowned on him. The gay black wenches who had flirted and giggled when he had beads to give away, peeked contemptuously into the tent where he lay, with his fevered head tight against the pack which held all that was between him and beggary.

When it was all over, and Tiémé a nightmare memory, he wrote: "I feared that my brain would be affected by the force of the pains which I suffered in my cranium. I was fifteen days without an instant's sleep. To put a crown on my misfortunes, the wound in my foot reopened, and I saw all hope of getting away vanish. Imagine my situation! Alone in the interior of a savage country, stretched out ill on the wet ground, having no pillow but the bag which held my goods, without medicines, with no one to care for me but the old mother of Baba who twice a day brought me a little rice water which she obliged me to drink, for I could not eat. I became an actual skeleton. Finally I was in so sad a state as to inspire pity even in those who were the least inclined to sympathize with me.

"I had lost all my energy. Suffering absorbed all my thoughts. There remained only one idea—that of death. I desired it and begged God for it, God in whom alone I put all my trust, not in the hopes of a cure, for I had this hope no longer, but in the hope of another life which would be happier. It was the only true consolation I had during this long illness, and I owed this consolation to the religious convictions which I have acquired during the numerous adversities of my wandering life. For we are so made that it is often in misfortune and when abandoned by all our friends that we turn toward the Divinity to seek consolations which are never refused."

Caillié's twenty-eighth birthday fell during this period of his great sorrow. The only greeting he heard was "*I ni ségè*", the local salutation specially reserved for the sick and miserable. Probably Manman was the only one who took even that much daily notice of him.

What a dramatic contrast there is between René's hideous twenty-eighth birthday and the splendid honours which came to him at the moment of his twenty-ninth. Caillié was to turn twenty-nine in Paris, a young hero, a marvel, the proud recipient of prizes and a Chevalier of the Legion of Honour.

16

RENÉ CAILLIÉ'S RECOVERY from scurvy was a miracle. It was a triumph of self cure. He cured himself by bitter disgust at the interruption of his great plans, by frenzied determination to get well and get on.

The only tangible help he received was from an old negress introduced by Baba. Baba was naturally dissatisfied with his tenant guest of the many ailments. Caillié had been with him since the beginning of August, always ill. And though Caillié was as generous as his means permitted, Baba knew that the stranger's store of goods was not large, and that if Caillié's bad luck continued, the traveller would sooner or later become a public charge, or a private charge upon himself, Baba.

Seeing that René did not get well, he came to visit him. Baba was evidently a capable person. He sent for an old woman of the country who knew a supposed secret cure for Caillié's disease.

The old lady arrived and gave her orders. No salt, no meat, even in the form of *bouillon*. The same evening she returned with a piece of "red wood" wrapped in the corner of her *pagne*. She boiled the wood. It was probably *diala*, a pseudo-mahogany, used by natives as an astringent, either boiled or crushed in powder. But it being the old woman's secret cure, she did not, of course, divulge its name to

Caillié. She instructed him to use the exceedingly bitter brew as a mouth wash.

Says Caillié, "the relief it brought me was very slight". But slowly, very slowly, he began to get better. Convalescence commenced about mid-December. The boiled "red wood" may have helped. No doubt a little kindness and attention helped too. But what really saved Caillié was his courage and his dream.

His self-confidence, except for the one brief moment of agonized despair which I have quoted, never weakened. He writes:

"Notwithstanding the ghastly state in which I found myself, I did not renounce continuing. I would have preferred to die on the road than to turn back on my tracks without having made greater discoveries. Alone in my hut I gave myself up to thought, and I sought the means which I should employ to get to the Niger, where I hoped to embark to go to Timbuctoo, and so to arrive one day at this mysterious city, object of my search. I never regretted for a single instant the resolution which brought me to these wilds, where I seemed to have come only to suffer a thousand ills."

It was a splendid statement of intention. It showed a fine ability to face the music unflinchingly. I have not had the heart to set down the details of Caillié's hideous sufferings and of his mutilations and disfigurements. Suffice to say that, when he expressed this determination to go on and win, his condition was literally what he called it—affreux.

There is a native proverb which runs: "*Neddo na wara nîwa, so hattâ watta duhol.*" Its general meaning is that one who has been able to kill an elephant needs give no ocular proof of his manhood. (Into French the Fula words may be rendered verbatim without offence: "*Un homme tue un éléphant, mais cela ne l'empêchera pas de remettre sa culotte.*")

Like the elephant killer, Caillié proved himself when by

sheer will-power he recovered from a deadly disease and gathered himself together for a fresh and terrific effort.

But Caillié never saw an elephant! This caused "many persons to express amazement", according to Jomard, for the popular notion of Africa in those days was that it was alive with monstrous beasts. It was the home of the elephant "which some call an Oliphant—the biggest of all foure footed beasts. His forelegs are longer than his hinder, he hath ancles in the lower part of his hinder legges . . . his snout or tronke is so long and in such forme that it is to him in the stead of a hand", in the words of the sixteenth-century traveller quoted by Hakluyt. The search for "Elephants' teeth" was one of the motives for the very early African voyages. The first guinea coins, made from gold from the Guinea coast, were stamped with elephants. Probably when René after his return from his great African adventure told people that the nearest he had come to an elephant was to see its traces, they laughed, but such was a fact.

Probably René saw no elephants because—always hurrying toward his goal—he did not stray from main paths and villages. He was often in elephant country both during his main journey and in his earlier African adventures. He might have met elephants even in Senegal. In Futa Jalon they were so familiar that the local name for the Great Bear constellation was "The Elephant". Near Freetown René's chances of meeting elephants would have been less good. That the elephant was not indigenous near Freetown is indicated by a quaint offer made by the Governor and Council of Sierra Leone in 1808 as follows:— "To the person who shall first introduce into the colony a living elephant, a gold medal value £10–10–0, or in money £10–10–0."

At Tiémé Caillié was in the hinterland of the old Coste des Dents, the Ivory Coast, which was the very home of "morfil", elephants' tusks. In the region between Tiémé and Timbuctoo elephants were a pest. A later traveller (Captain Binger in 1887) found the countryside "torn to pieces by elephants" and saw "boys in the forks of trees playing on a flute called *fabrésoro* to keep away the birds and especially the elephants which destroy everything". Timbuctoo had, and still has, elephant neighbours— horizontal-backed beasts, relatively small, who live in the lake country near the city. And one old-time elephant made himself famous by getting all the way to Morocco.[1]

But René—one of the greatest African travellers of them all—went to his grave with his longing to see an elephant unrealized.

Caillié was better and the fine season had begun, the good days before the annual grass burning. The weather was fresh and relatively healthy. The crops were in. It was the time called the Month of Threshing.

His foot was improving, the worst symptoms of scurvy were passing away. Leaning on a cane he went out joyfully to see the world again, limping as far as the "*Banancoro*", the village meeting-place where men loafed by day and young folk danced by night. Most villages had a *Banancoro;* the word merely meant under (*coro*) the cotton tree (*banan*).

During the day the *Banancoro* was the local tavern. There the old men of Tiémé squatted, took snuff, munched grated kola, and talked "of trade and their old travels", great yarns for Caillié to hear.

To the old men of Tiémé trade and travel both meant just one thing, and that was kola. Kola was the commercial life of the countryside. The very name given to the country

[1] An Arab historian, El-Oufrani, tells of the arrival of an elephant in Morocco in the year 1592. This beast was brought from the Sudan, some determined person having induced the great creature to cross the Sahara. "The day when this animal entered into Morocco was a great event. All the population of the first town (Elmansour) came out of their homes—men, women, children, very old people. In the month of Ramadan, 1599, the elephant was led to Fez." With this elephant tobacco was introduced into Morocco, the negroes who led him having brought it. (From the *History of the Saadian Dynasty* translated into French by M. C. Houdas.)

to the south was Ourou-kolu, Land of the Kolas. All
Tiémé's gossip was about the high spots and adventures of
the trade. They told one another marvels and listened with
fine negro credulity. There was one favourite yarn to the
effect that at Timbuctoo a single kola nut would fetch
more than enough salt to flavour twenty holiday meals for
a family. There was a story that on the far coasts, near the
mouth of the great river where the white men lived, kolas
were so rare and so precious that a kola addict would give
you a slave for just one nut.[1]

They whispered with awe of the mysterious land whence
the kolas came. Fifteen days' journey south of Tiémé were
two little towns, Teute and Cani, where the caravans went
to get their supplies of nuts. But these were not where
the kolas actually grew. These places were secret and
forbidden, farther yet to the south. Caillié says the kolas
grew in the lands of a tribe with the incredible name of the
Kissi-Kissi. (The Kissi-Kissi country lay somewhat to the
north of Freetown.)

The home of the Kissi tribes will seem to any English
reader a very appropriate spot in which to grow a tree
whose fruit is so popular as an aphrodisiac. A primitive
negro, even if he understood English, would see no point
in the jest, for negroes had to be taught to kiss, and
originally regarded the amorous white practice, which
they described scornfully as "sucking the mouth", as both
dangerous and mad.

The caravans which went from Tiémé to get kolas were
stopped at Teute and Cani. The situation of the lands
beyond was known only to a fraternity of kola brokers.
These intermediaries wrapped their business in mystery.
They bargained with the trader from the north, took his

[1] Both these rumours would have been justified. At Timbuctoo in the short season
a kola cost 80 to 100 shells and a pound of salt the same, says Barth. The swapping of
a slave for a kola is mentioned by Captain G. F. Lyon, R.N., in *A Narrative of Travels
in Northern Africa*, (1821).

salt and bade him wait. Then in the dead of night—so the whisper came back to Tiémé—a band of trusted local women would be despatched to some unknown spot to the south, a few men accompanying them as guards. Two days later, again by dark, they returned with the agreed quantity of kola nuts.

A trader who tried to follow and see where the women went would have been killed without more talk. And furthermore, the old men told one another, speaking from behind their hands, the people down there where the kola trees grew were *mokhodomo*, eaters of men; one of the thrills of travel to the negro imagination was that the inhabitants of far countries were always suspected—rightly or wrongly —of being cannibals.

The kola was more than a luxury, more than a prop for polygamy. The kola was a restorative for those under great physical strain. It was a tonic and a help against fever. It could keep you awake and it could make you sleep. It was said to take the place of food at a pinch, and after you had the taste of a kola in your mouth, the vilest water tasted like wine or sweet syrup.

To whites the bitter flavour of this nut—which is either magenta tinted or white and looks rather like a peeled Brazil nut—is at first disagreeable. The kola is definitely an acquired taste. Some white colonists form the kola habit, though the average European in Africa would indignantly repudiate the idea of practising this negro vice. Proof is that in France kolas are often peddled in market-places—four nuts for five francs. The modern black African still adores kolas and blesses modern civilization because it transports them fresh to him. I was told that the ship on which I rode up the Guinea coast to Dakar brought a cargo of 75,000 francs' worth for distribution inland from that port. To the native Mussulman, to whom alcoholic stimulant is forbidden, kolas are a treasure.

In Caillié's day the kola had importance both as a drug and as a sacred symbol. Breaking and sharing a kola meant a pledge of friendship, and "eating the kola" together was an official act between chiefs, marking the end of a war. Public policy was indicated in terms of kolas: two red signified war, one white nut broken meant peace.

There was magic in kolas. If a man with kola juice in his mouth were to spit upon a centipede both insect and wasteful spitter would die suddenly in a flash of flame! Kolas formed part of the paraphernalia of the sand diviner. Kolas had power to foretell the future by the manner of their falling when thrown in the air: their shape, more pointed at one end than at the other, naturally adapted them to a complex code in fortune telling.

Caillié, squatting beside the old men at the *Banancoro*, here and there slipped in a question. Jenné was two months off, they told him, and the folk along the road were poor and pagans who ate anything and everything, "dogs, cats, rats, mice, snakes and lizards!" They were always fighting amongst themselves with bows and arrows, and they went about nearly naked.

And how far beyond Jenné lay Timbuctoo, he asked. Up went scrawny black hands in ignorance, pink palms in the sun. No one could give the answer, except that the distance was immense. No man from Tiémé had ever dreamed of going so far. Geography was nothing to them. They only sought to get to a given market with kolas, ignoring even the names of the places they passed through on the route. "I shall find out!" thought Caillié. He could scarcely wait to get strong. He treated himself to a great luxury, buying a few chickens which good old Manman cooked for him with rice. His appetite came back. His strength increased. He threw away his cane and began to hope that before very long he would feel able to travel.

It was all the more needful for him to get away because things were becoming additionally awkward for him at Tiémé. Baba had turned very rapacious, and saw to it that everything which Caillié bought was got from his relatives and paid for at excessive prices. Even Manman went the way of all housekeepers and, when she shopped on Caillié's behalf, bought with Caillié's glass beads enough grain for her own family as well. Baba committed the unforgivable sin of stealing Caillié's salt to give to his horse! It was the culminating affront, but economically sound. Pampering should be for the horse, for a horse— when imported into that part of Africa—was worth fifteen or even twenty times as much as a man.

Caillié saw that he must get out of Tiémé before he was ruined. To prove to Baba that he had little left to give away he invited him to inspect the goods bag. Caillié adds, "but before this mark of confidence I took care to hide away anything which might rouse his cupidity".

It was hard to find a guide. Round the *Banancoro* loafed a number of idle negroes but none of them wanted work. One man agreed to lead him for some ten days' journey along the beginning of the way, but when the day fixed for departure arrived, the negro decided to remain at home, despite the handsome offer of an iron pot to which he had taken a fancy—Caillié's washing-basin—a pair of scissors, one and a half *aunes* (an *aune* was an ancient measure, being about forty-five inches) of fine coloured cloth, and two sheets of paper.

Now Baba took charge of Caillié's problem with efficiency and found him a guide. Baba's young brother, Karamo-osla, the same with whom Caillié had hoped to go forward toward Jenné in August, had come back, and had now gone south for fresh kola supplies. He would soon be at Tiémé again with the kolas, and then off again to Jenné. Baba would arrange for Caillié to accompany him north.

On January 1, 1828, Caillié saw with joy the arrival of Karamo-osla in Tiémé; or, more properly, heard him, for it was after nightfall when the caravan bustled into the village, its little bells tinkling.

Everybody rushed out of doors. Friends of the caravan members received gifts of new kolas, and offered in return great calabashes of *tau* and rice. The travellers were ravenous, and like camels they ate hugely. They would remain eight days at Tiémé, and planned to stow away five or six meals every day—and did so! They sometimes even got up in the middle of the night to eat.

The last day before the departure of the caravan was "a great fête day": I quote Caillié's words. It was the funeral of the mother of one of the caravan members, a festival of the first order, where everybody had a good time. There was feasting, the firing off of guns, dancing, speeches, music: great drums, flutes, and cymbals, bands of children "neatly dressed in leaves with ostrich plumes on their heads holding a round basket half filled with bits of iron and rocks which they shook in time to the music"; a group of the male relatives of the defunct all dressed in white and carrying each a flat piece of iron against which he beat out a tune with a smaller piece.

The bereaved son did not, according to Caillié, appear to be grief-stricken. Probably he was too busy acting as master of ceremonies. There was something to be said for the negro funeral custom whereby clamour and excitement diverted the childish minds of the survivors from their grief. A funeral in a non-Mussulman family would have been even more circus-like. At pagan funerals foaming brown *dolo*, the native beer, flowed and the dancing had a way of becoming rather rough, youths and girls leaping and whirling in frenzy, the favourite step for the girls being a jump in the air as high as possible with their feet together and touching their buttocks with their heels. Amongst some negro tribes the intoxication was a crazy affair. Fasting commenced at the moment of a relative's death; so did drinking. The result is easily imagined. Other negroes celebrated their funeral rites with gruesome savagery and strewed the graves of dead friends with the slain bodies of men. Loyal towns sent from ten to a hundred slaves to be killed at royal obsequies. Amongst these tribes the wise slave skipped into the jungle when the master or a local notable fell ill. It is said that at the death of a certain Ashanti queen in about 1816 more than 3,500 slaves were slaughtered, their severed heads lining the grave like blossoms!

In comparison with such orgies of beer and blood, the funeral which Caillié attended on his last day in Tiémé was a demure affair. Says Caillié: "I remarked the orderliness which never ceased to reign, though the fête was very gay!" The younger set danced almost all night, while Caillié's friend withdrew from the odd supper he had given in his mother's honour and ate his meal with Caillié.

Next day, the 9th of January 1828, he bade Manman good-bye and set off again, after a cruel delay of five months.

A monument has lately been raised at Tiémé in Caillie's honour. It bears the inscription:

Août 1827 à Janvier 1828
RENÉ CAILLIÉ
se rendant à Tombouctou séjourna à Tiémé
(1936)

It was erected by the initiative of the Commandant of Odienné, whom I have already mentioned as having kindly made at my request inquiries amongst the Tiémé natives as to whether there was any tradition of Caillié's stay amongst them. It pleases me to think that in directing attention to this village as the setting of a tragic period in the career of a French hero, Caillié's first English bio-grapher may have played a part, and that my request for information may have been—quite without intention on my part—a sort of corner-stone for René Caillié's monument at Tiémé.

17

WHEN RENÉ SET off with the jingling, hurrying caravan toward Jenné he deserved his name. He really was *re-né*, reborn, a new man. He had met and beaten the worst Africa could do. He knew now that he was sure of victory.

The throb and pound and bustle of primitive travel was in the brisk dry air, eager negroes swinging along toward a rich market under their loads of kolas.

The caravan grew. Soon there were some fifty men, thirty-five women, eight chiefs and a group of slaves, also fifteen asses. Heel to toe they clattered along, every man with bells on, the chiefs and their wives in the lead. It must have been gay going as they streamed across the country, all tinkle and chatter and laughter, negroes and negresses jostling and joking and playing tricks. Their loads were heavy but their hopes were big, and none bigger than René's.

It was cheerful pagan country with lively, dancing, near-naked people—pleasanter and safer people to Caillié than watchful Mussulmans. They adored his umbrella, called it a trick hat-*libri*. They admired his pale skin, and listened with amazement to the story of Abdallahi's pious pilgrimage. When occasionally his appearance startled them they were quickly won to friendliness.

The women wore almost no clothes; a belt embroidered with cowry shells encircled their waists and passed between their legs, fastening in the front, and from this belt fluttered a few short wisps of cotton. Caillié deplored the local custom of feminine facial decoration which consisted of wearing a slender piece of stick thrust into a hole pierced in the lower lip. He inquired, always eager for information, how they held the wood in place and found out that it was bolted in by a second scrap of wood worn inside the lip. He also informed himself on the native method of piercing the aperture, starting in childhood with a tiny hole and a tiny sliver of wood and gradually increasing wood and hole until the desired effect was obtained. Said he, "I was really stupefied"; but the maidens of Mauzé might have confided an almost equally painful story of corsets! Later he came to a section where nose rings, made of glass, copper or even gold, were fashionable.

René, always gallant and sympathetic with the troubles of women, was less solicitous about the sufferings which the men of this region also underwent in acquiring their tribal scars on face and body. There was no need for the initiated to ask a travelling negro whence he came. He carried his address carved on his person.

It was the happiest season of the negro year, the "Time of Rejoicing". The rains were over, the crops were in. The villagers fished and hunted and danced.

Caillié delighted in watching their fun. Round a big bonfire they danced nearly the whole night, thumping the ground rhythmically, clapping and leaping and wriggling, lusty black bucks and pretty wenches, all to the noise of the local orchestra, drums augmented by bits of iron and bells and flutes. The dances he pronounced to be in no way indecent. Sometimes the women sang savage airs in a manner which he found sonorous and pleasing, whilst they jumped gracefully up and down in time to their singing and shook little tambourines. These villages seemed always *en fête*, and a tired traveller could repose himself in their happiness. The natives were "gentle and human, lived contentedly and did not bother about the future".

Presently the caravan, now three hundred strong, reached the considerable town of Tangrera (now spelt Tengréla), a very important market centre and a walled city, a little African Carcassonne with walls and towers of clay.

René had been especially recommended to the chief of Tengréla by the chief of Tiémé. The two chiefs were brothers, the ruler of Tangréla being so aged that he could not speak, which is perhaps one reason for the town's prosperity! With feeble signs of senile approval he listened to Caillié's oft-told tale.

Inspired by the local interest in his story, René, while at Tengréla, baptized those imaginary parents in Egypt. He told listening admirers that his father had the name of Mohammed Abdoulkerim and that his mother was called Miriam.

Caillié was lodged at Tengréla in a large mud house possessing two doors and a window: quite a palace. His host and some friends sat that evening round a vat of hydromel (honey-beer) from which in turn and without pause they dipped and drank by the aid of a little calabash. They were all drunk beyond talking. Caillié, faithful to the religious scruples of his masquerade, could not join the fun.

The fact that Caillié omitted to sample native intoxicants—honey-beer, made of fermented millet and honey, and *dolo*, made of large red millet—annoyed Jomard, and must have been a hard deprivation to the young traveller in a thirsty land. Ample were his temptations. Among some tribes every woman knew how to make beer. The customary toast as the calabash passed from male hand to male hand was " *Mousso, kabancoro oussi*", which meant: "Women—to the sweat of your armpits!" —a tribute to the effort of the brewers. Mungo Park's heart was gladdened, far from his native Scotland, by the spectacle of an outdoor tavern where eighty to a hundred calabashes of beer were displayed, and consumed, each calabash containing two gallons!

Pagan Africa, where men spent their "youth in debauchery, their middle age in idleness and their old days without remorse"—to quote the shocked comment of a very early missionary—was at times a light-hearted land. But it also showed another side to Caillié. Filth, poor food—the usual almost equine diet of unsalted mush—horribly dirty drinking water, drawn from slimy pools on whose brinks villages threw their garbage. And worse dangers yet. He mentions quite casually, for instance, that at Badiarana, a prosperous big village into which the caravan bustled on January 28th, he found in the chief's hut that his trusted man—the man who collected the kolas which were paid as travellers' tax—*was a leper!* He had his hands and his feet covered with hideous sores, but in this saw no reason for retiring from his office of counting the kolas which the chief and others would subsequently be chewing, nor presumably to abandon the solaces of matrimony.

In savage Africa leprosy—an unspeakable horror to the white world—is regarded with toleration. The stumped arm and disfigured face, and the blanched patches on black skins, which also are said to be leprous, are all so common that even whites learn not to shudder. It is fiction that every contact with a leper brings inevitable death. A leper is a deadly danger only at a certain time.

An article in the *Revue des Deux Mondes* (January 15th, 1936) by Pasteur Vallery-Radot says, with regard to French West Africa, that it is to be estimated that leprosy attacks 1 to 2 per cent of the black population. On the outskirts of Bamako one may see a great establishment to which lepers of many tribes are brought. To make their misery less cruel, they are encouraged to build themselves huts, according to the various shapes and models to which they have been accustomed, and a mosque rises amongst gardens which they may cultivate for their own feeding according to the habitual menus of their several homelands.

The primitive native did not shrink from his leprous fellows. Lepers married and bred children and might drink from the common calabash except where they had actually a sore on the lips. But certain unexplainable restrictions were put upon them. Amongst some tribes, for instance, they were forbidden to eat special food items —goats, eels, chicken. Or the usual funeral fete was omitted and a leper's burial took place at night, sometimes upon an ant-hill—this last a piece of savage wisdom, for by morning no corpse would remain to infect or offend. In the ancient desert city of Sajilmasa the work of removing the town's filth by night was imposed upon lepers.

To finish this hideous subject on a note less grim, let us quote from an early Niger traveller who learned the native belief that leprosy was not a matter of contagion at all. Leprosy, it seemed, was contracted when a man ate a Niger mud-fish in the full of the moon, then drank sweet milk, slept all night under a white blanket, and drank water in the morning.

At a neighbouring village to that in which Caillié found the leper chief he encountered a peculiar social manifestation.

"Do not stay outdoors after dark, or the *Lous* will get you and beat you pitilessly!" a negro friend warned him. In the night Caillié heard a great roaring and slipped from his hut to watch the *Lous* ramp through the village. —a gang of men and boys hung with bells and scraps of metal, screaming savage defiance. They were the members of the local branch of one of the great African secret societies. All women and non-members hid at their approach.

Black Africa had many such powerful secret orders—
the famous Poro, Simo, Komo, and many more. Also
the women's Bundi. To the casual white observer they
seemed a mere excuse for oppression and violence and sex
exaltation, an opportunity to dress in grotesque disguises,
to wear masks and to make wild riot by night. But it
seems that they had real value to their savage members,
were an important social, political and economic force.
Their members helped the brother in trouble far from
home. They lent money to their embarrassed fellows.
And they joined together to kill a bad debtor! A shop-
worn anecdote on the West Coast attempts to establish
a family resemblance between these negro secret societies
and Free Masonry, telling how a shipwrecked British
officer was helped by the Simo society who welcomed
him instantly as a brother in distress.

Be that as it may, there was no question that young
blacks learned courage and self-control from the preliminary initiation procedure. Very horrifying and uncomfortable was this preparation for manhood and
membership.

First came circumcision. Then a period of startling
invalidhood and minor torture (as, for instance, that they
might not attend to nature's requirements during a day).
Finally a night made awful by artfully calculated horrors,
the approach of the monster, a colossal animal able to
knock over the tallest trees, whose giant feet could shake
the earth—(adult members let fall trees ready cut and
held in place with ropes, other members pounded barrels
to imitate the mighty footsteps!).[1]

Boys who kept their heads, healths and tempers during
this period of strain became members. Some, I think,
must have perished under the physical and nervous strain.

[1] The details I have instanced are from a work, *Les Mandingues*, by Henri Labouret,
Director of the Institut International d'Études Africaines, and are of the region
where Caillié watched the *Lous*.

In the old days the ceremonies of these societies were so desperately secret that women and non-initiates who ventured near were killed, and all the village shivered in their huts while the great "roarer"—a "lion drum"—made the night hideous.

The so-called simple savage was full of complexities. Some of his queer superstitions masked tact and kindness. Deformed babies were blamed to the unseen possession of the mother by a bad spirit. A man having hernia might explain his weakness by the fact that his wife had touched the tail of a palm civet, and skin complaints could be attributed to having broken a crane's eggs.

The reason behind other superstitions was less clear. A puzzle, for instance, was the invisible devil who invaded huts in outsize human form, walking with his feet in the air and head down, drank up the family beer reserve and did no other harm, but—failing free beer—caused the householder to break out in a rash all over his body.

Another devil (also introduced to our notice by Père Mangin of the White Fathers in his book on the Mossi and Sudan) was a tiny creature, an inch or two high, shaped like a man, or a woman, and coloured sometimes black and sometimes bright red. When they mated they always had twins. "Kikirsi" was their name and they loved honey and hated pepper. Shrewd housewives put a sprinkling of the latter on their honey-pots.

A real conundrum was the superstition which forbade making any use of the piece of cloth cut out to make the neck opening of a shirt. If used, the wearer would have his head slashed open.

Implied warnings to housewives lay in certain beliefs. For instance, that recently deceased persons returned and consumed the real force of the food left about at night, so that next day, though the food looked the same, it would give no strength to those who ate it. Sometimes supernatural little dish-lickers visited huts after dark and poisoned the calabashes with their tongues—another lesson to slatternly matrons inclined to "stack" the dirty dishes. Another warning to women was the belief that a dead husband could return and kill her if she loved again before the flesh had gone off his skeleton—estimated at about four months in that climate.

Every day Caillié's caravan saw new places. Only once in the whole two months' journey from Tiémé to Jenné did they pause for a single day's rest in their rush northward with their fresh kolas. There were frequent additions to the band, till they numbered over five hundred.

Some days they pushed forward in a fog of dust, or suffocated by the dry grass that rustled high above their heads. Some days they found themselves to the windward of a belt where grass was being burnt off. Then everybody choked and wept, and the donkeys heaved off their packs. At swaying bridges the donkeys balked. At fords they swam cantankerously and reluctantly, and the black men and women stripped naked.

As they neared the village where they planned to sleep the night, one man was sent ahead to arrange for quarters, and the women scampered after him so as to get the cooking started and water heated for the men to sponge themselves off.

Beside fires in the open air they ate, clawing ravenously at the big calabash—the average cost per meal and per person was, by the way, five cowries, or half of a French *sou !*

Then, having inspected and repacked their kolas and rubbed down their tired muscles with shea butter, the men fell into dreamless sleep on the bare earthen floor, while bats squeaked and flapped in the straw roof, spiders crawled over their legs and rats sniffed at their toes.

And the women—oh, those tireless negresses!—sat up a little while to spin cotton by the light of shea butter lamps, this being their little private perquisite, the equivalent of the "egg-money" enjoyed by the farmer's wife. With their tiny cotton profits they would buy themselves beads at Jenné.

Then up again and off next day on to the North toward the kola markets. Caillié, just off a sick bed, carried on with the brittle energy of convalescence. His malady was still with him. He ate apart because the condition of his chewing humiliated him and made him an unsightly companion. Once, he says with cold bravery, "I went away from the others at a halting place, not wishing to make them witness my sufferings and the painful operation which I was obliged to perform upon myself, having none capable of aiding me. I extracted a piece of bone, part of my palate."

He suffered constantly from colds, for he could not sleep in the smoky draughty huts, and outdoors the night winter chill bit into his frail, sparsely-clad body—his clothes being now in rags. He coughed and spat blood.

Yet there is happiness and joy of living in almost every page of this part of his narrative. He felt sure of victory.

18

CAILLIÉ WAS MAKING maps. No white man had ever passed this way.

Suddenly he had a great stroke of luck. He chanced upon a Mandingo trader able to furnish definite information about Kong, the geographic mystery. This clashing syllable (correctly pronounced Pon, with a sort of kissing noise) was a puzzle. What was Kong? City, country, mountain range? A few years before Caillié's time the white world had begun to hear glowing rumours in which the name figured.

Thanks to his Mandingo friend Caillié was able to clear up the Kong mystery. Kong, Caillié learned, was the name of a great negro metropolis, rich and remote, forty-five days' journey toward the Equator. The *Encyclopædia Britannica* pays René the compliment of calling him "the first European to visit Kong". But this is not true. René did not go to Kong. He could not turn off southward. He was hurrying toward a mystery more exciting even than Kong, and his road went north. He did, however, by a jab of his hand set Kong on the map, and gave a meaning and a definite geographical position to the word.

This is how Caillié fixed the position of Kong. He was familiar with that sixth sense which native travellers possess for knowing instinctively the exact direction in which lies any place they have visited. Caillié watched his Mandingo acquaintance as he pointed repeatedly toward the city they were gossiping about. Of course René did not dare pull out his compass and identify the direction before the negroes, but he noted exactly where the man was sitting and chose a mark in a line with his pointing hand. Next morning secretly René fixed the direction as "S.S.E. or S.1/4 S.E." The approximate distance was indicated by the time—forty-five days—of caravan travel.

Kong today is relatively insignificant. Great Kong was for the white world like one of those flowers that blooms for a single night. A bare swift glimpse of the city in its old splendour—then Kong was ravished by Samori.

The Kong which Binger saw in 1888 was a unique negro capital, tolerant and gentle and wise, where almost every man could read, and the streets were full of song and contentment. A city of quaint delights was Kong. Little girls sold kolas and honey in the streets, crying in their baby voices, "*Li douna, douna é!*" (Here is sweet, sweet honey!) and "*Ourou baba é!*" (Very big kolas!). At night, even indoors, rude loud talk was forbidden, and the police who kept order emphasized their authority and amused the populace by disguising themselves as wild animals.

It is one of history's tragedies that this gracious ebony capital, which according to the calculations of its learned men had remained for eight hundred and fifty years a closed and contented secret from all the world except its immediate negro neighbours, should have been trampled down by Samori. To Binger, their first miraculous white visitor, on the eve of the cataclysm, they confided, like people in a fairy-story, the artless list of their six wishes, the six things needed to make Kong perfectly happy. This list ran:

1. A remedy for guinea worm.
2. A remedy for goitre.
3. A method of cutting through rock so as to sink wells easily.
4. A red dye.
5. A charm to ensure intelligence to children.
6. A safe and short route to some European trading-post.

At Tamero on February 29th, Caillié had an encounter which gave him pleasure, meeting there a Moor from Tafilalet, the oasis in North Sahara. In himself the stranger was not an enticing person, being miserably poor and ill and occupied in de-lousing himself at the moment when a local woman, believing he and Caillié-Abdallahi were fellow-countrymen, made an introduction. But it must have sent a thrill through Caillié's tired body to realize that he had at last reached a point in his tremendous journey where he met a traveller coming from North Africa. It was a ray of promise, promise that some day he would finish this awful ordeal.

A few days later he saw for sale a clasp-knife of Moroccan manufacture. It was like the green leaf which came to Noah!

The caravan pushed on toward Jenné in a buzz of war talk, war being in progress between Jenné and Ségou, then the Bambaran capital. The caravan marched in formation, a party of men armed with bows and arrows in advance, then the women, then more armed men, and in the rear the aged traders and chiefs with their donkeys. Caillié dropped out of the file to let them tramp by him. It took a full quarter of an hour and was "really imposing". Jenné and the river country were very near. Aquatic birds stood one-legged in the marshes. On the 6th of March René ate a slice of fresh fish which he was told had been caught in the Niger. "I found it delicious," he says. "You would not eat better in Europe!"

On the evening of March 10th he saw a glorious sight, a big *pirogue* going down river. "Where to?" he asked, breathless, not daring to hope what the answer would be. "*To Timbuctoo!*" they told him. Next night he slept in Jenné, the handsome island city, the Mont St. Michel of the Sudan.

19

FOR A FEW days Caillié paused, waiting to arrange for his passage by *pirogue* toward Timbuctoo. It was a luxurious rest.

He was well lodged in a house which actually boasted stairs—something René had not seen for more than a year. Also there were interior toilet facilities, for Jenné had a city sewerage system, and had possessed this amenity when many great towns of Europe still poured their filth into the open street. René's house was proudly beautiful on the usual Jenné architectural model, with a dignified windowless front, and leaning slightly inward and back from the street, like a haughty nobleman who avoids contaminating contacts. Within was an open court for air and light.

Above was a terrace where, in the cool of the evening, supper was served. He ate palatable meals again—sometimes rice with fresh meat and charming little Jenné onions, sometimes a *cous-cous* made with fresh fish, and always plenty of salt.

And when supper was over and he was alone, he would look out across wide flat land beyond the city of Jenné, out over the meandering rivers and the plains beyond, and would search the north-eastern horizon. Over there —*two hundred and fifty miles away*, as the crow flies— was *Timbuctoo !*

Jenné (so spelt by some English and by Caillié himself, on all French maps with a D—Djenné or Dienné— pronounced by the inhabitants Dhi-enné) was, and still is, one of the marvels of Africa. Its situation, protected by a gigantic natural moat, kept it safe from attackers. Native history tells us that Jenné, which was supposedly founded about the year 800, was able to resist ninety-nine sieges and to hold off its only conqueror, the terrible Sonni Ali, for seven years, seven months and seven days. For once he was merciful; the city was not battered and crushed like other negro places and is intact even today, a living picture of black medieval power, a place almost Egyptian in general appearance.

Its name, garbled by native traders, was imputed to the Guinea coast and so—imported into England with the gold of Africa—was used to designate the honoured English *guinea*. Yet Jenné, so powerful and prosperous, by one of the mysteries of fame attained a merely local prominence, while Timbuctoo, the black football of history, spells wild Africa to every child in the world. Timbuctoo was Cleopatra, possessing some odd power to capture the imagination. Jenné was Cleopatra's sober, worthy, hard-working sister—a happy city without a history.

Until René Caillié's visit in 1828 no white man had been to the closed city of Jenné. René, who had read Mungo Park's book, had the Scot's horrifying assurance that a white traveller going there would "sacrifice his life to no purpose". Subsequent to Caillié's visit no whites saw the inside of Jenné until the French took the town in 1893.

René, the pseudo-Egyptian, became something of a "lion" at Jenné! He was lodged free and entertained with cordial enthusiasm by the local gentry, for these were no dull black savages, but a sophisticated community with a taste for unusual gossip.

They listened with bated delight—as might a European gathering to an account of primitive perversion and savagery—to Caillié's stories of how he had been obliged whilst with the Christians to eat pork and drink strong liquor. They snubbed a listener who inquired whether it was true that the Christians ate their slaves: only an out-of-town boor could be so silly as to think that, they apologized. And then they angled for more shocking details about how René had been forcibly stuffed with pork, and obliged to swill down *eau-de-vie*.

The Jenné people were intelligent. Most of them could read. They had tidy ways. Here at last René enjoyed a simple satisfaction long forbidden him. He could use his pocket handkerchief without rousing dangerous amazement!

All the inhabitants were fully clothed in white costumes. Even the children wore clothes, and everyone had pretty multi-coloured slippers. The men wore red bonnets surmounted by muslin turbans. The women gleamed with beads of coloured glass, with amber and coral and gold nose- and ear-rings, and clanked silver bracelets and wide anklets.

In the midst of the well-dressed crowd, slave dealers drove flocks of naked slaves for sale, crying their prices. A fine young slave cost up to 40,000 cowries. Naturally the purchaser wanted to see just what he was getting, but the brutal and humiliating display of fellow humans offended Caillié.

The glorious mosque of Jenné, built in the eleventh century and reputedly more wonderful even than that of Mecca, was still standing in Caillié's time. He was the only white who ever saw it in its original form, for two years later it was destroyed by Ahmadu, the great leader of the Fula conquests, whose name, Sekou Ahmadu Lobbo, was in Caillié's time on every lip in the land, and which Caillié misunderstood comically, taking the prefix Sekou or Cheikou, which is merely a corruption of Sheik of "Venerable", to be Ségou, the city.

Fanatical "Segou" Ahmadu was the last man one would have thought to find destroying a Muslim holy edifice, but it was because of his very godliness that Ahmadu demolished the mosque. In the very shadow of the sacred building was Jenné's "red light" district. Even through the mosque itself there skipped sometimes by night lewd dancing girls and their admirers. He vowed a vow, as a youth, that when he realized his ambitions and became great he would punish these walls for the debauchery they had sheltered and shaded. Or such was the story confided to Felix Dubois when first the French occupied the city.

At Jenné Caillié met and accepted cheerfully a great bereavement. He parted from his umbrella—a wrench indeed, for it was of enormous practical value in this land of sun-stroke, his one luxury, and his solitary fun-producer. It went as a gift to the Cherif who befriended him, Oulad Marmou, whose gaze from the first had rested hungrily upon the English-made novelty.

But in exchange Caillié got a splendid return. The Cherif agreed to arrange for René's passage by *pirogue* to Timbuctoo.

To this great service he added minor kindnesses. One day he gave a dinner-party in René's honour, a truly elegant and cosmopolitan affair. There were present, besides René, the mock Egyptian, seven Moors and a negro —all business men of Jenné, sitting on cushions round a squat table with legs three inches high. They were served by a young and beautiful slave girl, and the best of the Cherif's trays and imported cups and dishes were used, but of course no knives nor forks.

René, though he had now been eating with his fingers for nearly a year, had not acquired real native grace in tossing food by balls into his mouth, and was embarrassed before these gentlemen of Jenné, whose private opinion was that his Christian ex-master had sadly neglected this poor young man's training in the matter of table-manners.

Suddenly out of the blue sky—and no sky could be bluer than the March sky of Jenné—there came to Caillié a most thrilling piece of news, news that rocked him with mixed emotions.

In casual talk with one Hassan, a young Moorish friend in the Jenné market-place, he learned that, "there had arrived at Timbuctoo a Christian, after having been attacked and terribly beaten on his way there, that he had remained some time in the city to get his health back, *but that he had died*, Hassan knew not how".

It was clear to René that this tragic figure must be Laing. "Why did the Christian go to Timbuctoo?" he inquired with pretended indifference. "To write the country," answered Hassan, meaning as an explorer.

Caillié must have wondered daily and hourly how Laing was faring. He must often have said to himself that if ever he did himself get to Timbuctoo it might be only to learn that Laing had been there already and returned to the white world triumphant, that whatever secrets

Timbuctoo held were already discovered and made public, that all his own bitter months of martyrdom had been an absurd waste. It would be only human that he should feel relief to be rid of a rival who seemed to have every advantage in the Timbuctoo race.

But his only comment was: "I deplored the sad fate of the intrepid traveller and I reflected sadly that if those about me should guess at my masquerade, my fate would be like his."

Caillié's *pacotille* from Sierra Leone went with him no longer. It was useless to carry European goods and trinkets to Timbuctoo, where such things, coming across the Sahara by caravan, were more common and cheaper than at Jenné. He sold everything, aided—or, to be frank, cheated—by his amiable host, Haggi-Mohammed.

The trading was masked in the usual process of bargaining, bluffing and incidental exchange of gifts in which Caillié had now become very expert. Haggi-Mohammed gave Caillié, on the side, a *coussabe* and some dates. René gave him an *aune* of very fine *indienne* cloth, and so on. Some African races have a single word with the meaning: "to-give-a-little-present-to-catch-a-bigger-one". The wise trader seems to be he who stops first in the ritual gift-swapping.

With the cowry money realized—30,000 cowries—Caillié bought his outfit of trade goods for Timbuctoo: Jenné specialities, items not specified, but presumably made-up clothing—the tailoring of Jenné being locally famous—and native cloth and bits of ivory. He also procured articles for his personal use on the river trip: candles of yellow wax to see by on the *pirogue*, some dry bread (price, his last pair of English scissors), and a supply of a mixed drink made with millet water and honey.

On the afternoon of March 22nd the Cherif earned his umbrella. He completed his arrangements for René's passage. Caillié, he announced, should hold himself in readiness to embark for Timbuctoo next morning. "Hold himself in readiness"—Caillié had been poised on one foot to embark for Timbuctoo ever since he was a little lad in Mauzé! There was no need to fear that Caillié would miss the Timbuctoo *pirogue*.

20

THE PIROGUES WHICH carried men and women and goods to and from Timbuctoo were colossal things, huge beyond any white notion of river canoes. Some, Caillié says, were a hundred feet long and could carry eighty tons. There are no such canoes on the Niger now.

Caillié's boat, on which he embarked for the first stage of his voyage amid the farewell cries of "*Salam alékoum, Abdallahi!*" of his Jenné friends, was smaller—about twelve tons—for in the immediate neighbourhood of Jenné there was low water to navigate.

At two in the afternoon of the same day, having pushed and shoved their way through the shallows, they attained, so Caillié tells us, "the majestic Joliba"—the name Niger was in Caillié's day regarded as a vulgarism. He was wrong. It would be several days before he would see the Niger, and the big river into which they pushed their way on that first afternoon was the Bani. Jenné is not on one of the arms of the Joliba, as Caillié believed and as the natives evidently thought—for they called the city "One of the Five Pearls of the Niger". Jenné's river, the Bani, is a mighty, independent stream, the Niger's mate. The two rivers lie in twin beds side by side and lovingly communicate by a system of streams and brooks and marshland. Say the natives nowadays, the Bani is the Niger's secret lover who constantly fathers children upon the great mother river and finally at Mopti, meets her openly, marries her, makes an honest river of her, and dies in her arms.

René's mistake and that of his contemporaries is easy to understand. On large-scale maps the Jenné region is shown as one wide sweep of water, mingled brooks and marsh. To differentiate between the lovers was almost impossible.

At Couna, about fifty miles below Jenné, the goods and slaves and passengers of the Jenné *pirogue* were transhipped with heaving and sweating and splashing into one of the river leviathans.

Caillié was now in the vessel that was destined to carry him to his journey's end, to the port of Timbuctoo.

She was a sixty-tonner: Columbus, by the way, reached America in a ship presumed to be of only about a hundred tons. Caillié's boat was some ninety feet long and twelve across, drawing six feet, and had a partial covering of mats. She was literally tied together with bits of string, and seemed as frail and flimsy a craft as ever attempted to carry a valuable cargo down a vast river. The cargo was treasure, life itself to Timbuctoo; food-stuffs and raw material for this desert capital which could produce nothing, and man power, slaves in irons. In Caillié's boat there were nearly fifty slaves. Yet, with a confidence in their assorted gods which seems on the whole to have been justified, these happy-go-lucky mariners entrusted thousands of lives and billions of cowries' worth of property every year to boats that were a mere patchwork. For lack of proper wood they were made of small planks sewn together with fibre or palm-leaf rope, the cracks and holes filled with straw and clay and embroidered over with more sewing, a marvellous and laughable mosaic.

These boats always leaked. Two men worked continuously in six-hour shifts baling amidships with calabashes. In the deep slimy puddle squatted women passengers cooking rice in big earthen pots raised on little feet.

Fore and aft the goods were stored, at the bottom stuff which could stand wetting, blocks of shea butter, earthen jars and so on, then the more delicate goods, kola nuts, rice and millet in sacks, honey, peanuts, cotton, shipments of the famous Jenné onions, certain made-up goods. On top of this rode the human cargo, the chained-up slaves, some bare-headed under the cruel sun, some bent double, or lying in a heap like worms, under the low matting roof. A tangled mess it was indeed, smelling of dirt and the variegated sweat of every tribe in mid-Africa.

Slowly, very slowly, they travelled toward Timbuctoo. Their rate, Caillié estimated, was two miles per hour! The Niger is a most dawdling, leisurely river. A drop of her water takes, it is said, just a year and a half from source to sea, and along the flat Saharan stretch she is especially slow.

Where the bank was suitable her crew dragged the boat along with ropes. Otherwise poles were used, and—in deep water—paddles. There were sixteen in the crew, fine, almost naked Bosos of the caste of Niger fishermen and sailors, a group with a language of their own and a system of handling the Niger trade by mutual effort and benefit which seems like that of an idealized Trade Union.[1] Two men were at the helm, and, moon permitting, they travelled night and day. The captain was purser and steward as well, and Caillié hated him thoroughly.

The fare Jenné to Timbuctoo, tourist class, was 1,500 cowries, Felix Dubois tells us. That was in Caillié's day about seven and a half francs, certainly cheap enough for a four weeks' journey on the most mysterious of rivers

---

[1] *Le Plateau Central Nigérien* by Lt. Louis Desplagnes.

to the most sought-for city in the world. The distance covered Caillié estimated as 524 miles. It was a trip the like of which no white man had ever made, nor has ever made since. René himself does not mention the matter of fare; he seems to have travelled on a free pass, arranged by the Cherif in Jenné for the famous umbrella. The Cherif paid 300 cowries to the captain to cover Caillié's food *en route*. In Caillié's opinion this sum was excessive by at least 299 shells![1]

The captain-steward and René started disputing on the first evening out of Jenné. So much for informal friendly arrangements made by distinguished third parties. Caillié had reason to feel that a fool and his umbrella had been soon parted. The negro made angry demands, threatened to throw René off the boat, obliged him to sleep out on the open deck—victim of mosquitoes and river damp— and fed him as he did the slaves.

It was a constant fight down the river till René "lent" the cantankerous negro a thousand cowries, whereupon he became docile. Caillié then gave him a scrap of coloured cloth to make himself a bonnet and saw his enemy transformed into an affectionate chum, who shared with him the poor best that the ship's larder had to offer. Caillié had learnt, as all travellers must, that it pays to tip the steward.

The Niger was a river too generous to measure her waters between set banks. Sometimes she filled the whole horizon. At some times and seasons she was twenty-five miles wide. She ran free and wide, a pale blue sash carelessly draped across the belly of Africa. She was more

---

[1] When I rode on the Niger from Gao to Mopti in 1934 and 1935 the average cost per mile was just over two francs, without food. Over the part covered by Caillié the cost ran about three francs a mile, because we occupied what was alleged to be "the *Cabine de Luxe*". On the section Gao to Timbuctoo (port Kabara), the boat being small and poor, the cost was less.

than a river, more than an inland sea. She was a whole world of water. And what calm strength she had—the only thing in Nature that dared oppose the terrible Sahara. Riding on her waters that split the Saharan red sand-dunes from the green plains of the Sudan, René —as every traveller must—marvelled at her godlike power.

Listen and hear the grateful whispers of all her family —the clapping fins of a million fish, the barking of crocodiles, the contented pig-like grunting of hippos, the nickering of young colts, noses just over the tall sugary *borgou*, the placid gratitude of humped cattle slavering sweet *borgou* juice, the ecstatic squawk of river birds. Even the little termites in their huge cone-shaped nests bless her. The Niger is mother of the Sudan.

René saw the Niger like a highroad, strung with villages. Yet by the time of René's voyage the prosperity of this stretch of the Niger valley had already waned and it was not densely populous as in the old great days of negro empire. In those old days if the chief of Jenné had an order to transmit he had no need to send a messenger, but had only to cause the city crier to call out his command from the Jenné gates, and, village to village, men repeated it so that in an hour's time his wishes were known two hundred miles away.[1]

Sometimes the *pirogue* paused at a market village. Naked girls of twelve or fourteen ran along the bank by the canoe's side, offering such things as dried fish, sour milk, butter and a sweet drink made from *borgou*.

Caillié dared not buy, it being the season of the Ramadan fast. As a traveller he might automatically benefit by a sort of dispensation from the fast, but it was not safe for him to risk the slightest critical comment, so he declined. All travellers will agree it is very easy to deny oneself

---

[1] Felix Dubois, *Tombouctou la Mystérieuse.*

Niger dried fish. It was no sacrifice to refuse *borgou*, for the beverage, to persons unaccustomed to its use, is a vigorous purgative.

At one stopping place where they had stuck on a sand-bank, the pagan slaves involved the *pirogue* in a scandal with the Ramadan-conscious locality. Freed of their irons for a brief moment's exercise, the unhappy creatures were so stiff and bruised that at first they could scarcely walk, but soon, negro-like, forgot their troubles and fell to dancing, men and women together, leaping and laughing. At this came running the village elders, thirty strong, armed with bows and arrows, screaming that their respectable neighbourhood was being desecrated, and demanding payment of a 5,000-cowry fine. The captain, a slick fellow, compromised by agreeing that each slave should receive five lashes. Says Caillié consolingly, they were not whacked hard, and the instant the fanatics had departed, resumed their dancing. It was impossible indeed, even under slavery, to take *all* the joy out of black life.

Villages almost lived in the river. Babies cunningly caught fish with millet flour sprinkled on the water. Women washed clothes and calabashes, their single garment tucked high as a brassière. Young negro bucks and belles did their courting in the water. René watched them dancing and jumping and splashing in couples—"swimming out together" perhaps they called it.

At a certain village pretty and confiding Fula women clustered round Caillié, let him look into their little round huts made of woven matting, which he found very neat and clean, and, before he left them to get aboard the *pirogue*, begged him to bless handfuls of sand as pious souvenirs of his visit. This he did, murmuring Koranic words above their slim black palms, and saw them fold away the sacred grains in a knot at the end of their single garment.

Crocodiles were busy; it was their laying season, each enthusiastic mother laying scores of eggs. It is said that these small eggs taste like duck's eggs. Shy hippos Caillié saw from afar, only heads above water, square heads like boxes, dangerous fellow travellers in the Niger, for, natives told him, "if they passed near a canoe they could shatter it with a mere push". Again he saw them playing together clumsily, saw, too, the gigantic pits dug by the feet of elephants that had come to drink, but alas, got no glimpse of the animals themselves, though that night the roars of mighty wild beasts echoed back and forth across the Niger.

Sometimes the bank showed the little delicate triangles of gazelles' hooves, the print of monkeys' hands, the trail of crawling things, the authoritative paw marks of lions. In the branches of trees trimmed with great crimson and orange flowers were clouds of snowy aigrettes and glorious birds which dared to wear bright colours in this still almost gun-less land. Eels were six feet long. Fish were enormous; all but one—the *borou*—edible. Even the insects were gigantic; there were spiders that measured two inches across the stomach.

It was the womb of the world.

On April 2nd, after eleven days' river travel, they reached Lake Débo where the Niger swelled into so wide a sweep of water that Caillié saw the sun set on a horizon like the sea and was reminded of the far Atlantic.

Lake Débo was mystery and terror to these inland negroes. To them it was the "Dark Lake". There, so they whispered in awe, "canoes lose sight of land for one whole day!" When the *pirogue* entered Débo all those aboard cried at the top of their lungs, "*Salam! Salam!*" and fear was in every heart. Mungo Park had passed this way on his last unrecorded voyage; but no white man had ever seen Débo and lived.

To Caillié Débo brought a gay thrill, for as they paddled into the lake he thought himself justified (to use his own modest phrase) in naming an island. It was a sugar-loaf of rock, singular contrast with the rest of the landscape. In the native belief, there was golden treasure hidden there. René called it Isle Saint-Charles, and later named two other little islands Henri and Marie-Thérèse after H.R.H. the Duc de Bordeaux and Madame la Dauphine.

It was a boy's dream come true: exploring virgin country and christening its landmarks. Men in years to come, he may have thought, would say; "That is Isle Saint-Charles. It was René Caillié who named it!" But on the map today Isle Saint-Charles bears its native name of Sorba or Sariba. However, Caillié had the satisfaction of informing the royal family of France about their exotic namesakes.

Caillié loved the Saharan Niger. Simply worded tributes to its grandeur and majesty fill his pages. His Niger story was a revelation to the white world and his enthusiasm was the original cornerstone on which his country based its African colonial ambitions, its occupation of French Sudan and the lands south and north. Caillié's victory over Timbuctoo was spectacular. His Niger story was inspiring. Timbuctoo may have been a disappointment, the Niger was a call to conquest.

At Sa, the walled village and busy river port (probably Caillié means what is now spelt Saféré or Saréféré), René's *pirogue* joined company with thirty or forty other big canoes. From this point the Niger was a River of Fear, terrorized by the piratical Tuareg. No richly laden *pirogue* dared travel alone, and even in a group they were not safe.

At almost every mile Tuareg accosted them, approaching in small boats and demanding tribute. The negro traders paid. They were frightened by the cruel prestige of the Tuareg name, by their odd and sinister appearance —they were veiled to the eyes in the ritual *litham*—and by what Caillié shrewdly describes as their mysterious "talent for inspiring fear".

Not only did the cringing traders pay them tribute, giving each Taureg pillager some part of the cargo, but also they entertained him, feeding him and trying to placate him with calabashes of sweet drink, *jenné-hari* (honey water from Jenné) for which these bad men of the Niger had a comically inappropriate passion.

With this new development René's troubles increased. The Tuareg, he was told, considered all pale-skinned Moors rich. As one indignant Moor complained to Caillié; "Folk believe we were made by Allah with a layer of gold between our skin and our flesh". So René, poor as he was, would be in especial danger, and a danger to his fellows.

He was ordered to hide, and day after day he crouched, chin on knees, in a far corner of the covered portion of the *pirogue*, in stifling heat and able to see out only by means of a chink in the matting.

Caillié was but too glad to avoid the notice of the Tuareg. They might, he thought, have killed Mungo Park. Rumour ran that it was they who murdered Laing. The gunmen of the Sahara have never been hospitable to explorers.

21

AT EIGHT O'CLOCK on the morning of April 18, 1828, the *pirogue* sighted the palms of Kabara, principal port of Timbuctoo.

By rights this should have been the most splendid day in Caillié's life. But the *pirogue* swarmed with threatening

Tuareg and Caillié dared not show his pale, eager face. It was in a swaddling blanket, his head covered up while he pretended to be a sleeping negro slave, that he approached the spot of his dreams.

"Never did a day seem so long to me, nor so tiring," he says pitifully. What torture it must have been to lie motionless and hidden at such a moment, the culminating victory of his life.

René says that he prayed that day to God to protect him at the city of fatal repute. What other thoughts were his during the smothering hours? Probably as he lay there under the blanket he consolidated his notions about Timbuctoo and arrived at a very true idea of what was before him. To imagine the weird strangeness of the desert capital was impossible. But Caillié could guess that materially Timbuctoo would not be splendid. By now what he had heard and observed and deduced suggested this.

The peasant boy in him regretted that there would be no golden roofs and gorgeous palaces. But, as an explorer, he longed not for a fairy-story but to see what Timbuctoo really would be like. The more Timbuctoo differed from the hyperbole of native travellers—all that the white world had to go upon—the greater would be Caillié's satisfaction as a discoverer, the greater the value of his exploit. There was no need for him to come so far, at the daily risk of his life, in order to repeat to the world a familiar story of golden glamour.

Caillié had struggled across a wild continent to find out the truth; the more unexpected it was, the better.

When the night fell he threw off the blanket and strained his eyes toward the shore. He was safe now from Tuareg danger: at night in negroland, all men are black!

At sun-up next day, the 19th of April, he watched the

pirogue edging toward Kabara. At one in the afternoon they were in port and Caillié went ashore in a small boat. It was the day of the festival that marks the end of the Ramadan period of fasting and sacrifice, a happy day, and everyone was in gay dress and holiday mood.

For René Caillié it was the happy day that ended a Ramadan just one year long.

For, by a really extraordinary coincidence, it was exactly a year, day for day, since he had started on his great journey.

From Kabara to Timbuctoo is a hard tramp into the desert. It was impossible to go forward that night. Caillié slept at Kabara under the stars. Next day, April 20th, 1828, to his delight he was greeted by slaves sent by Sidi-Abdallahi-Chebir, the friend of the Jenné Cherif, who had received advance news of the Egyptian pilgrim, and who bade René to come at once to his house in Timbuctoo.

Delighted by this affectionate welcome to the dread city, René set off with the slaves across the wastes—a five-mile tramp, in soft sand, up mid-leg at every step.

Wheeling round them as they struggled was a villainous old Tuareg on a curvetting horse. He threatened to grab one of the young slaves, but was bought off by the promise of gifts when the party reached Timbuctoo. He stared at René greedily. "Who is the pale-face, the man with red ears (quaint descriptive phrase used by Saharans of whites)? Is he rich?"

Hurriedly René denied the dangerous charge. He was poorest of the poor, he cried.

But truly he was richest of the rich. He was about to realize a lifetime's unswerving ambition.

As the sun touched the horizon he climbed up the last great sand-dune and saw before him the secret city of the desert. He was at last in Timbuctoo.

BOOK III

THE AMAZING CITY of Timbuctoo was all around him, but René Caillié could not see it. The slaves of his new protector hurried him forward, the sudden African night came down. Timbuctoo was all black shadows, the dim forms of houses, mysterious openings and twisting lanes, flickering lights, women's voices laughing softly at eventide, the smell of strange foods cooking, and beyond, great blank spaces stretching to infinity. To René nothing was real except his triumph.

They came to the house of good Abdallahi-Chebir. There were excited greetings, questions, explanations, supper, the chatter of many men. Caillié playing his part with automatic skill.

Then it was bedtime. He could be alone at last and hug his joy.

Parade of peacocks, crack of pennants, blare of strident brass, rain of rose leaves. "I've won!" whispered René. His *Journal*: "Never had I felt like this! . . . I confided my transports to the breast of God. With ardour I thanked Him . . . for His protection in the midst of so many obstacles and perils."

His mind darted back, played leap-frog over the series of remembered obstacles. He saw his poverty-stricken youth, heard the jeers of Mauzé, the snubs of Baron Roger. He dragged himself over mountains, bruised his limbs against the rocks of swollen rivers. He saw a thousand suspicious black faces, winced at the torture of past pain, felt the rasp of thirst and the pale, sick wrench of hunger. What a road it had been—Mauzé to Timbuctoo!

He wondered if he was sane. The heat was breathless, stifling, like air inside a feather pillow. He could not sleep. He was shaken with amazement at himself, mad with pride and delight.

And he was oppressed by a nameless grief, the grief for a lost ambition.

Caillié was lonely. He tossed and turned on the ground of Timbuctoo like a man amorous and bereaved of a dear sweetheart. All his life he had slept with longing, but tonight, victorious, he lay sleepless and alone.

2

ON APRIL 21ST, the day after his arrival, Caillié walked out into the streets of Timbuctoo. Affecting the sober preoccupation of a pious young man on a pilgrimage, he made his way from his lodgings to the home of Sidi-Abdallahi-Chebir. It was his duty to pay his respects to his host, and vital to his safety to keep in close touch with his protector.

Sidi-Abdallahi took an immediate fancy to René, welcomed him to Timbuctoo like a son come home. It was the oddest of friendships, sincere affection on both sides. René Caillié, Christian explorer at the zenith of his accomplishment and the most dangerous point in his masquerade, concealing his real self like a criminal, attracted Sidi-Abdallahi, the dignified, ardent Mussulman, the prosperous, bored business man. And Caillié not only desperately needed the courtly little broker, but honestly liked him, called him a man "gentle, calm, very reserved, with a face inspiring respect and a grave demeanour that had in it something imposing"—all this although he was but five feet high and pitted with smallpox.

Sidi-Abdallahi delighted in Caillié's talk. He could barely restrain his curiosity about this romantic religious

Egyptian and his adventures in search of the God of his childhood. Caillié was a delight to him, a private entertainment. He blessed the Jenné Cherif. He could not do too much for this stranger. Caillié's English umbrella, cast upon the waters, was not lost after all.

One of the little broker's houses should be Caillié's free of cost. It was that little clay house near the Great Mosque, which is now a shrine.

Sidi-Abdallahi's protection was precious in this fanatical city. Caillié thanked Heaven for his confiding kindness and dared to hope that he might stay at Timbuctoo in safety, and get away unharmed. For him only to play his part, and this he did with all his heart and energy. It was the best performance of his life. Caillié became a tradition in Timbuctoo. Not the Caillié we honour, but the young Egyptian who had spurned the Christians and risked his life across Africa to regain a Mussulman home. A manuscript account of Caillié's life, dwelling on the detestable habits of Christians and the pious longings of Abdallahi, the Egyptian, to go home, was written and preserved in the archives of the city. What a fitting final chapter to this *exposé* of Christian ways had the chronicler discovered that the very hero of his tale was an example of Christian trickery![1]

And now, friendship cemented with his protector, Caillié went for his first stroll round Timbuctoo, a pleasure that no man ever worked so hard to earn.

It was a city of sand. Everything was uni-coloured, a yellowy white. Not a blade of grass, nor a green leaf. Not a bird, not a single dog. Nothing but sand. Only the men and women broke the beige monotony. But oh, the women of Timbuctoo, famous in all Africa: even the demure pencil

---

[1] Félix Dubois was told about the manuscript when in Timbuctoo just after the French occupation (*Tombouctou la Mystérieuse*).

of Abdallahi, the pious Egyptian, admitted they were "very pretty".

They were women who had bathed in love through the centuries, whose mothers and grandmothers had loved strangers at the culminating moment of their desert escape, or the shivering pinnacle of their desert dread. How many men had died caressing the memory of their image! How many staggered into Timbuctoo hot with longing for their beauty! The women of Timbuctoo carried in their blood and bones the gratitude of men. Generations of brave travellers had sobbed out relief at deliverance, or horror of the ordeal to come, in the arms of the consoling women of Timbuctoo. Chastity would have been a niggardly vice where so many tortured men needed tenderness.

Caillié, walking through the streets of the city, understood that Timbuctoo, lure of travellers, was a golden city in symbolism only. Its gold was not tangible; there were no golden roofs. It was symbol of opportunity, of joy, of remoteness and mystery. He saw that it was the strangest city in the world, far stranger than he had pictured it. He sought for a place where he might observe safely and make his notes.

He picked for his purpose the tower of the Great Mosque, the Ghinghéréber, relic from the days of mighty Kankan-Moussa, gorgeous negro king who departed for Mecca in 1324, the Pilgrim Magnificent, with a caravan of 60,000. Before His Majesty there plunged across the Sahara five hundred picked young slaves each bearing a six-pound solid gold staff. Eighty camels carried Kankan-Moussa's money for the voyage, three hundred pounds of gold-dust to each camel. These are facts "preserved by more than one contemporary witness".

Ghinghéréber still bore Kankan-Moussa's glorious name

over the main gate. From its minaret René Caillié looked out over Timbuctoo. Here he might study the city as he liked. Here he might write, his papers masked in the leaves of his Koran—his seemingly pious meditations a delight to all Timbuctoo.

Caillié saw an unwalled triangle of big low sand-tinted houses where lived the rich, and the round humpies of their slaves . . . a wedge thrust into the desert. This was no comely city comforted by a green oasis. The desert reached up to the very doors of the houses. To have placed a city here seemed the maddest work of man.

It was a city without water, food, proper building material, fire-wood. Most of the year it was intolerably hot and on winter nights almost freezingly cold. It was in the constant danger of being starved out by an enemy who stopped the road to the waterway—some twelve miles off in the dry season.

Yet Timbuctoo had been boundlessly rich and was still, is still, one of few very famous cities in the world.

The Timbuctoo which Caillié saw from his tower had diminished. The days were no more when men spent 600,000 cowries on a single banquet, or made to the girls of their passing fancy the princely offering of five hundred bars of precious salt, price of slaves' torture and camels' bones. In those golden days the mosque where Caillié stood, the greatest of the city's seven places of prayer, was the centre of the population. Now it stood on the south-western outskirts.

But Timbuctoo was not like other cities in old age, disfigured by ruins. She had shrunk back into the sand whence she came, grown old gracefully.

From the street came up to Caillié the droning call of the water-seller, *"Hari-koy! Tye fo hari!"* The price was a cowry for a single pint. It came from a dug-out puddle far beyond the city to the westward. Its taste was horrid and it was almost boiling.

Inside dim houses brokers and traders counted and argued and pawed at great heaps of merchandise brought from the north and from the south: tusks of elephants sewed up in skin bags, ostrich feathers, leather, wax, incense, musk, indigo, gum arabic, gold-dust, dates, bars of rock salt, sacks of grain, tea, sugar, and European manufactured goods. Not a single object in their store-houses was produced in Timbuctoo itself. The city was completely parasitical, nothing but a great clearing-house where shrewd men made fortunes under hard conditions. Caillié compared its appeal to that of the colonies to Europeans. A fortune, René said, could be made by a Moor in four years' trading, and then, Allah permitting, he would struggle back across the desert to a land where water was free and cool.

Timbuctoo began her hectic career about 1100, a mere nomad camp on the Sahara's rim. Its name, legend tells us, means "the-Old-Woman-With-a-Big-Navel"— surely no very definite identification for the old lady, in this land where crude midwifery disfigures so many and scant drapery leaves their misfortune evident. Perhaps the name meant womb or hole, the first settlement having been in a depression between sandhills. Perhaps it meant a well.

Almost instantly, and mysteriously, Timbuctoo became a great African market centre. This delighted the Tuareg. They bit at its heels, oppressed it, persecuted it, black-mailed it. Timbuctoo was for them a trap which attracted from all over Africa rich men whom they might despoil, men who were merchants not warriors, soft men who submitted and paid.

Timbuctoo called for help to Kankan-Moussa the Magnificent, hero of that black and gold pilgrimage which stunned Mecca. Kankan-Moussa, ruler of one of the vastest kingdoms in the world, and his successors after him, held Timbuctoo under their protection. Of his line was the luxurious Souleiman, whose guardsmen had gold-tipped spears and whose orchestra had golden bells.

Again the Tuareg persecuted the city, and again Timbuctoo appealed for help, this time to another great black emperor, the tyrant Sonni Ali, the Songhai. Sonni Ali, suckled on the wicked milk of an idolatress, was lascivious and cruel, a great soldier, a terrible ruler in peace, who executed men thoughtlessly and without emotion. He carved a bloody autograph across the face of Timbuctoo. When he took the city he slaughtered three hundred virgins because, having been dragged across the sands to his camp, they complained of being tired.[1] His adultery, in fact, was notable even for an ungodly tropic negro. Ali was pagan at heart and Mohammedan in name only; it was his habit to dispose of the five daily ritual prayers in a lump by merely saying to Allah: "You know all these prayers already, take your pick!"

Yet Sonni Ali had in death that which to the negro fancy might have made dying sweet, for his sons caused him to be stuffed with honey to prevent putrefaction.

On the heels of Sonni Ali came a noble negro ruler who wore a term of obloquy for his chosen title. He had been Ali's right-hand man, and stole the power from Ali's sons. Accusingly they called him "*askia*", meaning usurper, and Mohammed, the interloper, took Askia for the name of his dynasty. There were Askias in the

[1] Félix Dubois's translation of the *Tarikh-es-Soudan*. Houdas's translation of this seventeenth-century Arabic History of Negroland gives the number as thirty, and adds that the place of their martyrdom was known for hundreds of years by a name whose equivalent is "The Place of the Virgins' Sacrifice".

Sudan for a hundred years. Askia the Great was king of all the wide belt of Africa from Chad to the Atlantic and from mid-Sahara to Dahomey. It took six months to cross his kingdom. He went with dignified pomp to Mecca and hobnobbed with the Caliph of Egypt. Yet in the end Askia reaped the bitter crop of the usurper, being deposed by the eldest of his one hundred sons.

These years—roughly the century which followed Columbus's voyage—were the great days of Timbuctoo. The city, it is said, was so large that it stretched to the banks of the Niger, its merchants were the richest, its wise men the wisest in the land. No city had saints more ascetic, nor women more lovely. No city anywhere ever received so varied an assortment of races, saw so many tints and shapes of face, heard of so many ways of life, so many faiths and moral codes. The men and women of Timbuctoo were indeed people of the world.

Timbuctoo held African commerce in her fist. She was at the crossroads where Saharan trade from Morocco and the salt mines of the desert met and exchanged with the exotic goods of Negroland. Camels could go no further, for the juicy fodder of the humid grass-lands was death to their sensitive stomachs. *Pirogues* obviously could go no further. On every camel load and every *pirogue* cargo the brokers, merchants, food sellers, baggage handlers, entertainers, prostitutes, hairdressers, and landlords of Timbuctoo took profit.

Morocco, whose traders frequented Timbuctoo, observed this gay prosperity and was tempted. In the reign of El Mansour-d'ed Dehebi (meaning The-Victorious-and-the-Golden), who gained the latter part of his name by reason of his Timbuctoo plunder, Morocco procured guns and cannon. It was the moment to pounce on the rich neighbour over the desert. Salt was the pretext for Morocco's attack, jealousy for the ownership of the Saharan salt mines, hideous torture chambers where slaves laboured in conditions of unthinkable horror.

A hundred and thirty days it took Morocco's army to march in misery across the Sahara. To have sent an army on such an expedition seems greed gone mad, but El Mansour ordered it and his general obeyed. It was in the winter of 1590–91. Eight thousand camels, guns by thousands, gunners on foot and mounted, an army of 4,000—of them all hardly more than a tenth lived to scream their joy at the sight of the Niger—"El Oued el Kebir!"—the Great Waters at last! They had drunk the boiling blood from their own gnawed fingers, burning their vitals like sea water.

Not very far from Timbuctoo they met the negro army of the Great Askia's descendant, Askia Ishak II, forty thousand brave fellows, but armed only with spears and javelins. The smell of gun smoke and the mysterious death from afar, was a vile miracle to them. It broke their resistance. They sat down upon the sands and waited to be slain.

Timbuctoo was taken. The Moroccan musketeers avenged themselves for their desert sufferings. Their ferocity was without control. Eighty-three members of the royal family were destroyed with cunning cruelty, some being crucified. Disorder and sorrow fell on the land. There was famine. Men ate corpses. There was pestilence.

Out of Morocco's conquest and subsequent abandonment of Timbuctoo to her fate came fresh chances for the Tuareg, always ready to fall on Timbuctoo in her weakness.

During the year before Caillié's arrival in Timbuctoo the Tuareg were momentarily checked in their desert piracy by Ahmadu, the Fula leader. But Fula policing was inadequate.

The Tuareg took a tax from every desert caravan and every *pirogue*, and Timbuctoo, the city, paid them tribute. But this did not satisfy the pirates, who sought also to collect informal individual contributions at odd times. These they sardonically called "presents". If a Tuareg was in town, he picked a prosperous-looking house and demanded entry. Some of the house doors of Timbuctoo still bear the scars of Tuareg lances. None dared refuse the visit. The visiting Tuareg strode in, pushed the family aside, and established himself in the master's bedroom, enjoyed the best food and drink and in departing took what he fancied. Bands of Tuareg prowled about the suburbs, so that rich merchants never dared leave the city limits and forbade even their slaves to go outside the town after nightfall.

Caillié thought it astonishing that Timbuctoo and the nearby villages and towns submitted to "the humiliating and ruinous yoke of the Tuareg". It amazed him that the appearance of "two or three Tuareg could throw horror into a group of villages". It does seem astounding. But far better fighters than the fat merchants of Timbuctoo found the Tuareg hard to handle. Sixty-six years after Caillié's visit, his countrymen were destined to have tragic proof of the extraordinary cunning and savagery of the Tuareg.

But what made Caillié particularly indignant was that the people of Timbuctoo assured him that the only creature whom they loathed as bitterly as they did the Tuareg was the Christian!

3

René, coming down from the mosque tower, found himself a popular local celebrity. To put it into terms of the modern white world, he must have seemed like a cross between a student preparing to take holy orders and a crank touring round the world in a wheelbarrow, an entertaining mixture of the meritorious and the eccentric. The people of Timbuctoo offered him little gifts and petted him. It is indeed astonishing that the first of the hated Christians to give the white world news of this place should have been practically a guest of the city.

From the Ghinghéréber Mosque to the house assigned to him by Sidi-Abdallahi-Chebir was but a short distance. After the sunset prayer the streets, "broad enough for three horsemen to ride abreast", were filled with the movement of those who during the torrid hours of the day had dozed in their homes, for Caillié had come to Timbuctoo at its hottest period called *Koron*, "the heat". The east wind blew continuously, burning and laden with sand. The air was thick with sand, stinging and inconceivably dry. Lips cracked, noses bled, human hair when touched gave out little electric storms. It was so dry that perspiration failed.

"*Hari koy!*" cried the water sellers. Persons of substance gave themselves the luxury of a drink, straining the warm sandy liquid through their teeth. Timbuctoo's one Doum palm tree bent and crackled before the east wind. On the house roofs the bales of grass brought from the far-off Niger marshes, precious fodder for the unlucky town goats, turned to tinder.

And yet how strange and how beautiful was this city on the edge of the world, with its vast horizon—giving man the illusion of immortality. The stars were huge, warm, and very real. They seemed but a few miles away, the lights of another city. The universe seemed tangible: stretch out a hand and stroke the Southern Cross, run the Milky Way through your fingers.

The women of Timbuctoo, unveiled and draped with the conscious grace of women who know they are charming, stared at the stranger and smiled at him from under their twinkling coiffures, triumphs of the city's famous hairdressers. Multiple little balls of hair nodded archly, little rat-tails thrust out into his face like horns, each tipped at the end with an openwork gold or silver bauble, or with a trinket of coral or cornelian. Their eyes were ravishing from the artful use of antimony. Their glances were full of curiosity.

Slave women passed to and fro, selling delicacies. Rice cakes cooked in shea butter; "*Dyi-dyi dungo !*" they cried —"Our cakes are greasy and hot!" They offered spice cakes too, *nemti*, said to give the young folk dreams of love. "*Idye kayne hollondi !*" they warned customers with sly enticement, "Cakes that will drive boys mad!"

On the *timtims* (earthen benches built before the houses) sat groups of women swathed in soft robes of white and tender hues, beautiful native weaving or silken gauze. Their feet rested on the sand, encased in soft leather slippers gay as bonbon boxes, trimmed with embroidered *motifs* in silk or inlays of vividly contrasting leathers, pale green, water-melon pink, garnet, lemon, violet. Some had soles of supple leather which was tinted a splendid imperial indigo.

The waning light picked out the gleams of their ornaments: delicate coral or gold rings clipped on fine nostrils, heavy throat pendants of amber and gold, anklets on slim dark insteps, gracious silver plaques called *kakaw* clasped cunningly to the curve above salmon-red heels.

The day had been long and lonely inside dim shady houses. Now was the best hour of all, the swift hour of tropic twilight, the sudden coming of the stars, and the women of Timbuctoo, sweet with the scent of musk and cloves, bloomed in all their smiling finery. Their gaze rested in momentary appraisal—frank yet innocent— upon each unfamiliar male face, for from mother to daughter they inherited a love of strangers.

That young René, strolling homewards amidst so much beauty, maintained a sober mien is probable. His conduct would have perforce been exemplary to accord with his pious pretence.

René did, however, gossip with them, to the extent of learning that "they have the habit of greasing their heads and body with butter—though less profusely than do the Bambara and Mandingo women—the great heat augmented by the burning east wind making this necessary".

In the streets of Timbuctoo Caillié had an encounter with two women which embarrassed him very much, though the others took it as a matter of course. He met a couple of women who had been his travelling companions on the Niger *pirogue*, women to whom he had probably rendered little services during the long trip, with whom he may even have flirted; and found that they were being driven along the city streets for sale like animals.

Caillié, always tender and chivalrous in his attitude toward black women, was distressed, and did not know where to look. But the two women smiled gaily. They accepted their slavery as a natural state, and, provided they found purchasers in Timbuctoo, were quite content. They dreaded taking the fancy of some buyer from over-desert.

The Sahara crossing was a hideous ordeal to slaves. Their black faces turned a sickly grey—which is the negro's way of paling—when folk spoke of the desert. They knew that in the great sands there were certain wells, wells of fluctuating water supply, around which one might see heaped up skeletons of men and women, each skeleton festooned in the chains of slavery. If a mate was unlucky enough to be bought for the northern market, his friends bade him farewell as to a doomed man.

Domestic slavery, for the slave who worked for one master, offered living conditions which were said to be "preferable to those of the European artisan and farm hand" and "better than that of the agricultural labourer in England", to quote two men, one French, one English, who knew Africa (Georges Hardy and A. B. Ellis). We modern white people, to whom liberty is something which we talk about but rarely experience, have no reason to commiserate with a black slave merely because he was not free.

But the ceremonial sacrifice of human beings is utterly shocking. For horror I find it hard to beat a simple passage in Captain Mockler-Ferryman's account of a Niger mission, wherein he tells of the scene witnessed after the death of a native king. A group of slaves "listened outside, their faces distorted with excitement though they dared not utter a sound" while the Commissioner and a local chief discussed whether or not they would now start the enforcement of a new English rule forbidding the sacrifice of slaves at funerals. Those listening outside were the problematical sacrifice!

At Timbuctoo a dreadful festival was annually celebrated for a period of two hundred years up to the very year before Caillié's visit. It commemorated the Moroccan victory in the Sudan. A great wax doll was placed on the shoulders of a slave at a spot half-way across the sands to Kabara and he was told that if he could run with it back to town he would be set free.

A group of sportsmen on horseback chased him with lances and swords. Few blacks, even if they reached the city with the doll, lived to enjoy their freedom, but it was regarded as a joyous entertainment by the onlookers, and pieces of the doll were distributed as souvenirs to the crowd.

4

THE HOUSE IN which Caillié took his airless ease and savoured his triumph was a very queer little building. When I looked at it in the winter of 1934–35 I thought that, more than anything else, it looked like the big brother of a child's sand-castle at the sea-side, something a giant child might have moulded with wet sand out of a huge square biscuit tin. This is the usual Timbuctoo architecture, imposed by local conditions. Timbuctoo's clay is of poor quality. There is no stone except a substance called *alhor* which is found under the surface in the folds between the sand-dunes[1] and which turns firm when exposed to the air. Wood, of course, is a great luxury. Metal is altogether lacking: even keys in René's day were made of wood. Houses face north or south, for "bad spirits"—and much sand—come in with the prevailing wind, which is east in winter and spring and west in the summer.

Caillié's house was identified after the French occupation, Félix Dubois having got in touch with those who had known Sidi-Abdallahi-Chebir's surviving wife and son.

René saw the house built; it was still in process of construction when he was installed in it. The interior arrangements presumably suited local demands and conditions,

[1]Dupuis-Yakouba, *Industries et Principales Professions des Habitants de la Région de Tombouctou.*

but in no way suited Caillié, for into the long, narrow, windowless room light and air came only from the court-yard, and he smothered miserably during hot nights.

It was with joy that he sought the windswept tower of the Mosque, or even the baked and sandy streets.

Sidi-Abdallahi one day escorted his protégé on a formal visit to the King of Timbuctoo, that potentate about whom Europe had heard such extravagant stories. René found him a courteous person and affable, dressed like any other notable of the city and, so René says, "of a very dark black".

Osman was his name and he held the governing power under the remote control of the Fula Ahmadu and the immediate thumb of the Tuareg. When the Tuareg chief came to Timbuctoo, King Osman sang very small, Caillié tells us.

It is said that Osman, under the instructions of the Fula, gave the actual order for Laing to be killed. At any rate, when Osman turned Laing out of the city, the King and the Englishman must both have guessed what his fate was going to be.

There was one place which possessed a horrid fascina-tion for Caillié. He could not keep away from it, although he knew that, both for the sake of his own nerves and because of the suspicions which his interest might create, his notice of the place was a mistake. This was that little clay house in which Laing had lived during the days of his stay at Timbuctoo.

Caillié sought the friendship of the owner of Laing's lodging-place and found him "a humane man" who offered Caillié dates, a *bonne-bouche* at Timbuctoo, and who made him a farewell present of a blue cotton *culotte* (a pair of full trousers or drawers in the native style). From this generous person and others Caillié gradually and imperceptibly wormed the story of Laing's last days.

How often Caillié must have speculated anxiously as to what it was in Laing's behaviour which produced such suspicion and anger that he was pushed out of the city into the hands of murderers. How often he must have searched into his own conduct, wondering if he too was distrusted.

He knew that some accident or slip might betray him at any moment. His masquerade, like all successful performances, seems easy. Only Caillié knew how difficult it was. Someone might see him writing, or making sketches, or taking observations—for Caillié found courage to do his trick with the cane and cord even at Timbuctoo. His bag might be searched by a thief and suspicious objects found. There was even a chance in this metropolis, where so many natives came trading, that some black from Senegal or Sierra Leone might recognize him.

And yet curiosity, pity, fear masking as courage, made him seek for every detail about Laing. Let us follow René along the sandy path to Laing's house and hear, as he did, what befell Major Laing in Timbuctoo.

5

MAJOR LAING, CAILLIÉ was told, made his first appearance in Timbuctoo in a state of such pitiable weakness that his native companions had been obliged to tie him to his camel. He had been brutally handled by Tuareg or other nomads on his way over the desert from Tripoli.

This we know also from Laing's own letter to his father-in-law, the British Consul, Colonel Warrington of Tripoli, whose daughter Emma married the dashing Englishman on the eve of his adventure, only two days before he set off. Laing wrote Warrington that he had received twenty-four wounds: there was "one cut on my left cheek which fractured the jawbone and has divided the ear . . . and a dreadful gash on the back of the neck which slightly scratched the windpipe".

Laing, they told Caillié, was cured of his wounds thanks to "an ointment known to the white men": a fine fairy-tale touch this, an ointment capable of curing twenty-four wounds and a broken jaw. Laing ate little, which seems but natural: mostly eggs and chickens. When he appeared in public he was tormented by demands that he should repeat that "there is but one God and Mohammed is his prophet"; to which Laing invariably answered "there is but one God", and then closed his mouth. But so far as Caillié could ascertain he was not actually maltreated while in Timbuctoo. Once by night he went secretly to the Niger. Laing in an earlier expedition just failed to attain the Niger's source, and his longing to see the mysterious river in its mature grandeur is comprehensible, even though the excursion across hostile Tuareg country was made at the risk of his life.

After this excursion, the Englishman, so Caillié was told, showed a desire to return to Europe by way of the Niger route to Ségou and overland to Senegal. This was forbidden and he decided to go into the desert, hoping to strike back to the Niger later. But almost as soon as he left Timbuctoo he was murdered.

Striking items of the Laing story, as revealed to Caillié, were that Laing had drawn plans of the town before the eyes of everyone, that he had "written the city and all that it contained", and that he was believed to have stated that he had been "sent by the King of England, his master, to find out all about Timbuctoo and the marvels it contained".

It is doubtful whether Laing actually went so far as to make this almost threatening remark to a city which had never had luck with invaders, was already paying tribute to the Tuaregs, knew it would soon have to pay a second master in the conquering Fulas, and certainly had no desire to have still a third yoke thrust upon its long-suffering neck by a mysterious unknown called "The King of England".

But, whatever he may have said, Laing's very presence gave offence, special personal offence in addition to the natural objection to him because he was a Christian. Various explanations for this have been suggested. Dubois was told years afterward that his unpopularity and eventual murder could be attributed to his reserved behaviour in the city. This mysterious stranger in his odd clothing (Laing, according to Caillié's informant, never quitted his European dress) puzzled them. His business-like preoccupation with notebooks and papers as he hurried about the streets of their town suggested that he had come not in good fellowship or for trade but as a spy.

Binger heard long-surviving native gossip to the effect that Laing, having good-heartedly offered medicine to an old sick woman, was suspected when she died of having poisoned her. Barth thought that Laing was detestable to the natives because of the cruel behaviour of his predecessor, Mungo Park; Laing himself is said to have blamed Park bitterly, saying that he made the way hard for whites who followed him.

Whatever was the combination of reasons, Laing left Timbuctoo to go to a swift death, and a death made yet more painful by the fact that in dying he must have realized that all his work and suffering had been in vain, that his report about Timbuctoo would die with him. This is indeed what happened. His papers have never been found. His sacrifice was completely wasted. He was like a man seeking news of the moon and heroically volunteering to be shot through space. Caillié came back and told what the moon was like. That was the difference.

Caillié was informed that five days out of Timbuctoo (probably it was less than two days, not five) a certain nomad chief arrested Laing, ordered him to forswear Christianity and turn Moslem on the spot. Laing proudly refused, and two of the chief's slaves at his orders choked Laing with a knot made in an uncoiled turban, one slave pulling at each end. His body was left where it fell, and his goods divided amongst the assassins and passed on from hand to hand. To Caillié later, when he was not far from the northern rim of the Sahara at a spot over a thousand miles from where Laing was murdered, there was shown a brass-bound pocket compass made in England, Laing's without doubt. Says Caillié: "If it had not been for the precautions I was obliged to observe . . . I should have thought this a treasure, but I could not without compromising myself show that I attached the slightest value to the instrument, of whose uses I was even obliged to pretend I was quite ignorant."

In 1910 a French official mission attempted to find out something more definite about Laing, and Bonnel de Mézières, an accomplished explorer, went to Araouane in the desert, saw the old written records of the place, and found an old man of eighty-two who had known the assassins and said that he could lead the investigator to the actual spot. In 1912 Bonnel de Mézières published a book, *Le Major A. Gordon Laing*, telling how under an *athilé* (or *ethel*) tree—a poor bit of scrub not twelve feet high, but a desert landmark—situated at a spot named Sahab, about thirty miles north of Timbuctoo, he found, four feet below ground, bones, bits of skull, some fragments of wooden boxes and a piece of a sock.

Laing's body, it was said, had been buried by a passing nomad, this man afterwards apologizing that he "never would have done the pious act had he known it was a Christian"!

These remains Bonnel de Mézières transported to Timbuctoo.[1] A gruesome photograph is printed in the book which shows three officials examining the bones. A paper under the stamp of the French Republic states that they "apparently belonged to an adult human being". They were suitably buried.

Laing is not forgotten by the English. In 1931 an English party was, I think, seeking for his traces. English colonial officials came especially to Timbuctoo recently to pay tribute to his memory, and his house bears a plaque which reads: "To Major Alexander Gordon Laing, 2nd West India Regiment, First European to Reach Timbuctoo, Fell Here in 1826. Erected in his honour and memory by the African Society London 1930."

At the time of my visit the house was closed and locked. It is somewhat smaller than Caillié's house but of similar style. It has two floors and in one of the rooms upstairs, alone and far from his sweet English bride, Laing recovered from his fever and his twenty-four wounds and found courage to study this city which hated his presence and punished him so cruelly for his curiosity.

6

THE ISOLATION OF Timbuctoo and its ferocity toward non-believers cannot be better realized than in

---

[1] Later exploration suggests that perhaps an error was made. Doctor Théodore Monod says that his explorations in 1934–5 make him think "it is not absolutely certain that the tree near which M. Bonnel de Mézières searched is that beneath which the English traveller was assassinated". From *Le Monde Colonial Illustré*, November 1935.

the fact that it remembered angrily over a period of seventy-five years the only three whites of whom it had knowledge, and sincerely believed them to be inter-related, the members of one odious family coming to annoy and harm their city. Laing in 1826 was hated because of the behaviour along the Niger of Mungo Park, a "Fighting Christian" indeed, who in 1805 gave the Sudan its first and very odd notion of the gentle faith of Jesus. Barth, who came to Timbuctoo in 1853, was popularly believed to be Laing's son, and Laing's murderers bound themselves by an oath to kill Barth too. Very luckily for the great explorer-mercenary—Barth was a German working for England—the son of Laing's murderer died suddenly, which to the superstitious natives seemed a warning to leave Barth alone.

These three men, of whom Park was known in the city merely by hearsay, were the only avowed Christians who were able to approach Timbuctoo for three-quarters of a century. Even today Timbuctoo does not see many Christians. The official and military white population is small. There are a few whites in charge of the local branches of big West African trading houses. Visitors are very rare, for Timbuctoo is still one of the most difficult cities in the world to reach.

Barth, the next explorer after Caillié to give the world news of Timbuctoo, reached there twenty-five years after René's visit. Barth's stay at Timbuctoo was a miserable affair; it was the most dangerous time of his whole five years of African exploration. He scarcely dared venture outdoors. So his account of Timbuctoo, though infinitely more detailed and pedantic than Caillié's, is less interesting.

At Timbuctoo Barth was ever mindful of what he called "*our nation*", meaning England. He made a gallant attempt to secure a presentation golden diadem as an offering for Queen Victoria, and he joined himself to the local movement of protest against the French advances into the Sahara, which advised the French "not to enter the desert under any pretext whatsoever, except as single travellers". Barth, though so unhappy at Timbuctoo, had confidence in the great possibilities of the place if opened to white trade. This he believed would be done by England, never by France.

The house where Barth lodged, virtually a prisoner, is said to be preserved, but although I asked about it, I did not see it. Barth must have left the Timbuctoo region gladly to proceed down the Niger banks toward Gao, where he rejoiced the populace by appearing at a native ceremony in his evening clothes, which, so black and shiny, were mistaken for a coat of mail.

After Barth's visit Timbuctoo limped through history unseen by whites, and in great internal disorder. The desert was unsafe for caravans. Tuareg pillage had gone beyond itself. The pirates had so maimed the goose that her golden eggs were small as millet seeds.

Such prosperous merchants as survived in the city pretended poverty, let their houses go to ruin, and dressed in rags. They even took to grinding grain for *couscous* as silently as possible instead of pounding it in a proud mortar as of old. By such subterfuges alone could they avoid Tuareg depredations.

In 1880 an Austrian, Lenz, was in Timbuctoo for a few days, meeting no opposition. The house of Lenz, last of the four whites to see the city prior to the French occupation, is marked with his name. A man with many wives and a cat with white kittens were living in it when I saw it. I was kindly permitted to go upstairs.

During the latter half of the last century, when the city, though still closed against white exploitation, was known to be broken and impoverished by bad government, the world, because its greedy expectations had been disappointed, began to make fun of Timbuctoo. A comic verse that rhymed the city's name with "*Hymn Book too*" did far more to advertise the city to the public than did young Tennyson's university prize poem. To it were added a variety of less polite limericks. "Go to Timbuctoo!" became a catchword. In short, Timbuctoo was the best known city in all Africa, although only four white men had ever seen it.

In the winter of 1893–4 the French came. The first group arrived by the Niger, and the population, always merchants and never warriors, sent a message of submission. "We are women," they said, "we do not fight." But this message was unintentionally deceptive. Timbuctoo was no kitten waiting to be picked up and caressed. The French approached the city and established themselves, leaving the boats in which they had come down the Niger at Kabara in charge of the young officer Aube. Pursuing an attacking party of Tuareg, Aube was trapped and killed with one white man and eighteen natives who were under his command. It was at that tragic place midway between Kabara and Timbuctoo, whose native name, Ourou Maira, means "Nobody Hears". Ourou Maira was a locality designed expressly by Satan as an ambush for the Tuareg, his favourite race.

A second French party arrived a few days later. Its leader, Lieutenant-Colonel Bonnier, undertook to avenge Aube, marched cross country in pursuit of the Tuareg, took prisoners and cattle. Bonnier and his men camped at a place called Tacoubao, happy and victorious. That night Bonnier, ten other European officers and two non-commissioned officers were killed, and also some sixty native *tirailleurs*. Three whites got away. It was a fine night for the Tuareg.

In Timbuctoo years afterwards one of these same Tuareg, now a pacified friend of France, told the story of that night to the leaders of the Haardt Mission, a group of Frenchmen who first crossed the Sahara by automobile, using caterpillar cars, in 1923.

This, according to the old Tuareg chief, Cheboum, is how the Tuareg fooled a French Colonel. The French made camp. To the eastward of the camp were the captured herds. The French posted sentinels, felicitated one another, and slept. The Tuareg skulked near unseen, to the west of the camp. Just before the dawn they called out to their captured animals. The cattle were trained, as was then the Tuareg custom, to such a point that they knew their masters' voices like so many good dogs. They came joyously galloping to the familiar call, knocking over tents, men and stacked arms. There was helpless disorder. "We had only", said Cheboum simply, "to poignard the survivors!"

It was a trick typical of Tuareg battle cunning, and is one of the many incidents which show that Caillié guessed wrong when he spoke slightingly of the Tuareg and suggested that the Sudan had merely to make an effort to rid itself of their oppression.

Now a third French party came to Timbuctoo. It arrived on February 12, 1894. Then Aube and Bonnier were avenged. Timbuctoo was French. The leader of this third party, the next Frenchman after René Caillié to distinguish himself in Timbuctoo, was Joffre. Sixty-six years had passed since Caillié's discovery.

Like Caillié, Joffre wrote a book about Timbuctoo. "My March to Timbuctoo" is its title in the English translation.

7

ON OR ABOUT May Day, 1828, Caillié rented the camel which, God willing, would carry him across the Sahara. It was to Caillié a transaction full of gloom and foreboding. He dreaded the desert. He was very, very tired of hardship, and the Sahara would be the worst hardship of all.

The bargain was no doubt consummated at a place called Abaradiou, a little distance into the desert where it was the custom to park the camels when caravans arrived. At Abaradiou were straw huts for the camel men and big puddles where the camels could take in their great cargo of water—a camel can store a hundred quarts of water in his cavernous and elastic inside. Here were stretches of the mean and sparse pasturage in which this perverse animal delights. A camel has a very peculiar digestion. He literally screams when ample good fodder of a variety he does not fancy is pressed upon him[1] and finds his health in lapping up steely-pointed thorns and tough juiceless twigs with his big leather lips, pausing between mouthfuls like a morose connoisseur eating the first asparagus of the season.

Abaradiou, when the most important salt caravan arrived in mid-winter, was a riot. All Timbuctoo came running at the news of its approach. The *azalai* was near! The eyes of all Timbuctoo looked north, over the shimmering sand, straining and squinting, looking for that great cloud of golden dust. The salt army came, many hundreds, sometimes many thousands, of camels loaded with great "tombstones" of marble salt. It was an emotional moment in the life of the city, almost a sacrament. Life itself had come to Timbuctoo.

Women, sleek and elegant, hair newly garnished,

[1] E. F. Gautier, *La Conquête du Sahara*.

bangles ashine, glowed with excitement. The heartfree beauties clapped the caravan as it passed, and picked out the handsomer strangers with coquettish glances. The others, the wives and mistresses of travellers, carried a burning dread in their hearts. Would he come back safe, or had the desert taken him?

Salt was a cruel master. The *azalai fête* was mask for tragedy and terror: slaves burnt to the bone in salt mines, dying camels abandoned as the caravan marched on, men perishing of thirst, a dreadful, maddening death.

But from the death of the few came life for all mid-Africa. Listen to the chant of the proud *azalai* bringing salt:

" ' Salt is the flower of the earth! He who brings it to you cannot know trouble or poverty. Salt is as strong as gold.

' Eat it and your blood will not turn to water. Flower of the earth, it makes the body strong.

' Bring out your yellow gold-dust and your slaves that we may trade. Bring out the young camels. Make ready the beautiful women.

' We are the masters of your stomachs, we bring salt. Our salt bars are more than can be counted!' "[1]

Caillié paid for the rental of his camel and the right to join a north-bound caravan with the goods brought from Jenné, 30,000 cowries' worth. Sidi-Abdallahi-Chebir took the goods and paid the camel owner in money, giving him ten mitkhals of gold. The mitkhal was a weight used for gold-dust, equal to "twenty-four grains of the kharub tree, or ninety-six grains of wheat".

The price of Caillié's ride on the Niger was 1,500 cowries, seven and a half francs. The Saharan trip cost 150 francs—twenty times as much. It threatened to be at least twenty times as hard for the poor traveller.

Never did Caillié feel so far from home and so completely alone in Africa as when he looked out across

[1] From *Le Pacha de Tombouctou*, by André Demaison (Grasset).

this great dry sea which no man had ever traversed without hellish torture.

And yet he chose this route deliberately and of free will. He might have gone to Europe by an easier way. His alleged final destination was of course Egypt, but his glib tongue could easily have found a way to persuade Sidi-Abdallahi that it would be better for him not to attempt the desert crossing after all. The sympathetic little broker would have arranged for Caillié's journey toward Egypt by some round-about but less terrible route.

Says Caillié: "I confess that the Saharan crossing in midsummer frightened me very much. I feared I might not survive . . . but after long reflection I decided. . . . I thought that if I went via Ségou and Sansanding to our posts at Gallam (Gallam was up the Senegal, from there he could have proceeded easily to the Senegal coast) jealous people . . . would doubt my arrival at Timbuctoo, whilst by returning via the Barbary States, the very point of my arrival would impose conviction on the envious."

So Caillié, merely that his accomplishment should finish in a manner that would be exactly right, just to prove his feat beyond a shadow of question, decided to attack the Sahara.

At sunrise on May 4th, René and his kind old friend parted, exchanging little gifts and breakfasting together— tea, fresh bread and butter. Sidi-Abdallahi made a last-minute attempt to keep Caillié in Timbuctoo. He would set him up in business and Caillié would make a fortune. Their farewell was so prolonged that René missed the departure of the caravan and had to run across the sands for a mile in its pursuit, arriving so breathless that he fell fainting to the ground. They picked him up and put him on a camel's back.

And so René Caillié, first European who ever got safely away from Timbuctoo the Mysterious, set off to carry the news of his discovery back to the white world.

BOOK IV

RENÉ CAILLIÉ, HIGH upon his camel, looked out over a new battlefield. Now he must conquer the Sahara. Eleven hundred miles to the north was normal land, desert's end, Moroccan green. Beyond was the ear of France waiting to hear his story.

René rode packed round with ostrich plumes, for he had rented merely a seat on a camel, not its exclusive use. A camel could carry five hundred pounds across the desert, rim to rim. It would be impossible to waste his power upon the transportation of one slim young man, unless this young man were very rich. Some camels carried goods only, the heavy loads. Others carried light stuff and passengers, or water. In the caravan there were about six hundred camels, with them Moorish trader-masters, camel-hands, and black slaves.

Caillié was the only passenger. This western route was not the choice of Mecca pilgrims, and such were the only people reckless enough to undertake the journey except for gain.

He was the first white man ever to join his fortunes to a trans-Saharan trader's caravan. He was the first white man ever to see the interior of the Western Sahara. He thought himself to be the first white man who had ever crossed the Sahara from the south. In this last matter he was mistaken. Clapperton had crossed the Sahara three years before from the south, and I wonder Caillié did not know this. Clapperton's companion during part of his exploration was the spectacular adventurer, Dixon Denham, and this man and Caillié were at Freetown at the same moment and engaged in a similar kind of work. Denham during the last months of Caillié's stay at Sierra Leone was General Superintendent of Liberated Africans, whose "duties were to instruct settlers in agriculture". (*The Handbook of Sierra Leone*.) Presumably Denham, who later became Lieutenant-Governor, was not in the same set as the queer little Frenchman, and the two never gossiped about travel.

There would be just twenty-two wells along Caillié's route from one rim of the desert to the other. But, alas, not at regularly spaced intervals. Many gaps would be four and five days long. Once the caravan would struggle for eight days from well to well. Always—it being the hottest time of the year—they would have the fear of finding that the wells had dried up. There would be the constant dread of Tuareg attack, pillage, and capture into slavery. There was the danger of overwhelming sandstorms. Sometimes whole caravans were lost in one way or another. In 1805 a caravan of 2,000 camels had disappeared without a trace on this same Timbuctoo to Morocco route. Did they die of thirst, were they killed by pillagers, did sand bury them? It was a favourite subject of speculation in tropic Africa in Caillié's time. But no one, we may be sure, brought up the subject on that first day, as Caillié's caravan plunged into the desert. It was better not to remember.

Yet Caillié set out joyously. His mood was exhilarated. He imagined that he dreaded the desert, but in this he lied to himself. He would never have been content to go back to the white world without experiencing the ultimate thrill of Africa, without matching himself against the hardest test of all. Caillié *had* to cross the Sahara, had to do it not to prove the truth of his exploration, but to satisfy himself.

The Sahara on that first day out of Timbuctoo showed herself in her characteristic aspect. The ground was sandy. The Sahara, despite popular notion, is not always sandy, and only about one-tenth of her area is made up of those rolling dunes shown in pictures. She has nearly as many varieties of bad ground as other parts of the earth —rocks, gorges and mountains, and wide pebbly stretches that look like dead prairies covered with fine coal and are called *reg*.

René's camel dawdled, munching the last bits of dried vegetation on the desert's rim. The water in his distended stomach gurgled at every step. He was full to bursting point, but still had room in his elastic inside to stow an odd mouthful of spiked thistle, or a knife-like scrap of *hâd* bush.

The camel—Gageba was his name—knew what was before him. His life and the lives of his ancestors had been a shuttle of wretchedness, back and forth across the Sahara on big slow feet, carrying five hundred-pound loads. His life and the very existence of the caravan depended upon his keeping his strength up. He knew that he must never pass a thistle by. So he combed the sands with his patient pop-eyes, and ambled from nibble to nibble. At all times Gageba's pace was slow. Caillié estimated that the caravan plodded across the Sahara at a speed of two miles an hour. On exceptionally bad ground they made only a mile an hour.

The first day they went eighteen miles and camped at five in the afternoon in a ravine of yellow sand where there was shade. They supped, a calabash of water, some *dokhnou*, the familiar mixture of honey and flour, diluted as required to a paste-like food. It was the handiest form of sustenance where no fuel existed for cooking, and was easy to transport. That first night there was a little bread left from Caillié's Timbuctoo breakfast, already dried stiff as a brick in the desert air so that it had first to be soaked in water.

The second day at dawn they were off, the six hundred camels spread out seemingly in aimless fashion, but every nose headed north, for the beasts knew where the next well was, five days off at Araouane.

The country became worse. It was, Caillié thought, as if they were walking along the bottom of a dried-up ocean. To place bare flesh upon the ground caused insupportable pain as if one had touched a hot stove. There were no living things except a few gazelles, lovely animals which almost never drink but moisten their insides with the sparse juice of dry desert plants, and vultures flying high.

Then suddenly, far off, they saw something moving, saw it many miles away. In the nothingness of the Sahara, the slightest object is noticed at a great distance.

The caravan paused, quaked to a man. It was a solitary camel approaching. Bleakly they admitted the worst. It probably carried a scout for a band of Tuareg marauders.

The camel came nearer, no clumsy pack camel but a proud *mehari*, a riding camel, fast moving, superbly arched and as graceful as one of these queer animals is capable of being. On his back were two men of extraordinary appearance, the first of whom directed his mount by pinching its neck according to a recognized code with skilled movements of his limber bare toes. The *mehari* slowed its pace, walking now with the high steps of an ostrich.

The caravan studied its two riders. They were a pair of Tuareg in all the magnificence of their desert panoply. They were lean men, rangy and strong as plaited leather. Their faces were so closely veiled that there showed only their cynical eyes and a bare inch of nose bridge. They carried nothing at all but weapons. To the *mehari's* saddle hung their great oryx-hide shields, five feet long and garnished with a design like the Cross. Each man had a barbed spear, tall as himself, his beloved *allagh*; it was a puny Tuareg who could not make a bull's-eye with his spear at fifteen yards. Each man wore at his waist a sheath-knife, and bound along his forearm the typical Tuareg weapon, a dagger, point caressing his elbow, hilt ever ready to his hand. Each man had also a sword, surmounted by a handle in the shape of the Cross, and a stone ring on his left arm above the elbow, called *ahabeg*, a useful implement in close fighting. They were indeed a very ungenial pair of ruffians.

Caillié trembled with the rest. He was now so poor that he had no goods to worry about. "A thousand thieves cannot despoil a naked man", says the Arab. But Caillié knew that he lived or died with the caravan.

The Tuareg spoke in their harsh Tamajegh, each syllable hard as a hammer-stroke. A sigh of relief came from the whole caravan. They understood that these men were not scouts for a band of desert pirates but isolated travellers, singing the familiar Tuareg refrain of "*Ikfai !*" which means "Give me something!"

These two warriors had left home with all their weapons and no provisions, knowing that a caravan was coming northward and that, meeting it in the desert, they could enjoy free drink and food. Unwelcome guests they would be, so long as it suited their convenience, drinking deep at the precious water-bags, enjoying the sweetest *dokhnou*. But, Allah be praised, they were not the forerunners of a band of pirates.

2

On the sixth day after leaving Timbuctoo they reached Araouane, a place till Caillié's time quite unknown except as a name, and believed to be merely a watering place for caravans.

René was astonished by Araouane, astonished and disgusted. It was a town of 3,000 crouching like a lone idiot alongside sand-dunes in the empty desert. Of vegetation there was not a scrap. Every atom of food had to be brought from beyond the Niger via Timbuctoo by the hard road Caillié had just covered. Even for the cooking of this food the people of Araouane had to collect pains-takingly the droppings from camels, there being, of course, not a twig of fuel. The town's water supply was 150 feet below ground, tedious to draw and scant reward for the labour, for it was brackish, very unwholesome, and produced colic.

Araouane had all the physical disadvantages of Tim-buctoo without its glamour and romance, and without the comforting Niger for a neighbour. Caillié called Araouane "the most unpleasant place I ever saw", and Caillié's wanderings had by now shown him a varied collection of poor and uncouth places. Yet a population of greedy Moors lived there. These bagmen of the Sahara —pedlars and brokers and merchants and transport agents all in one—flocked to Araouane and stayed there because it was a junction point. Caravans from various Niger points came to Araouane. So did caravans from all North Africa, from Morocco to Tripoli. It was a clearing-house for Taoudenni salt. So the Moors came to Araouane and suffered.

Said Caillié, after he had considered Araouane at his leisure (for his caravan paused there for nine days gathering recruits): "I could not understand why the hope of gain should induce men to live for twelve or fifteen years in so detestable a part of the world." Yet Caillié should have recognized in the Moors of Araouane men with some kinship to himself, men who go far and suffer much for ambition's sake. Caillié was tearing his health to ribbons and daily risking his life to make a name. He might have lived comfortably at Mauze, making boots.

It was very, very hot at Araouane. Caillié had no thermometer, and thermometers at any rate can give no notion of Saharan heat, which has a cruelty not to be measured in degrees and compared to the occasional maximum temperatures of temperate lands. Nearly one hundred and sixty degrees is common (seventy degrees centigrade, according to E. F. Gautier, Saharan authority). We are told that even a dog cannot at full summer noon put his paws upon the ground.

A constant hot wind blew through Araouane while Caillié was there, the torturing *cheheli;* sometimes it blew so violently that Caillié lay indoors all day, his head wrapped in a *pagne* to keep the burning sand out of his mouth and eyes. One day he drank too much brackish water and became violently upset.

Caillié realized that he was going to have a very disagreeable time with the caravaneer under whose charge he was travelling, one Sidi Aly, with whom Caillié's good friend at Timbuctoo had made a deal.

Sidi Aly was a Moorish Zenaga, which means that he belonged to a group of men that could be sold between Moorish chiefs. Yet Sidi Aly was no slave, quite the reverse. He owned camels and was a person of some consequence in the North Saharan trading-post which was his headquarters. But Aly and other Zenaga had to pay tribute to whatever chief owned them, or to a new owner if sold. They were rather like human bonds or shares, which change hands between owners, who have little actual control over the business from which they extract dividends.

René, from the moment of their first meeting at Timbuctoo, had viewed his proposed Saharan guide with uneasiness. That Sidi Aly should have made a bad first impression on Caillié, or on anyone else, is comprehensible. He was "a small man, about four feet tall, with a gnarled face, black wicked eyes, a little grey beard and out-jutting chin, and a very large mouth which made him even uglier. The skin of his hands was wrinkled like the hide of a crocodile". Aly was of pseudo-pious temper, carried always a chaplet a yard long, each bead big as a walnut, and fingered it, breathing prayers whenever he was under observation.

Caillié pronounced Aly a hypocrite and a rascal, and the record of his desert crossing is a running accusation against Sidi Aly and Sidi Body, Aly's associate. Caillié complains of a series of petty incidents of minor cruelty, unfairness in the distribution of food and water, persecution, finally physical violence, and even threats to sell him into slavery.

It does not seem as if René handled Sidi Aly with his usual cleverness. Submit he must. He was helpless and poor. And he was not now amongst negroes who would accept without much question his yarn about being an Egyptian going home, but amongst travelled Moors who had some knowledge of Egyptians and of white people, who were able to scrutinize Caillié's tale coldly, and who were often suspicious. But Caillié seems in his dealings with the Zenaga to have lost that phenomenal tact of his.

René was tired, a little petulant. This was natural. He had accomplished a wonderful feat and there was no one to applaud him. He had to conceal his victory like a crime. Yet, though his life depended on concealment, perhaps he sometimes felt an unreasonable resentment that people took him for granted, and treated him contemptuously when he was really a great explorer.

To Sidi Aly and the rest of the caravan René probably seemed a silly fellow. A man who voluntarily set out to cross the desert for a religious vagary must have irritated these practical travellers. The Sahara was not for such as he. The Sahara was real and earnest.

The Sahara was in no case a place to look for tenderness, pity, good-fellowship. Every man's soul was gritty with Saharan sand. These were days of friction, effort, strain, fear, fatigue, peevishness.

The caravan observed that Caillié had recently had scurvy and refused to let him eat with them. Caillié was visibly nauseated by Sidi Aly, who mixed the *dokhnou* paste with hands fresh from dressing the putrefying sores on camels.

In Araouane a monster caravan was forming. To the band with which Caillié had come from Timbuctoo were joining other camels laden with all the products of Sudan, ivory, gum arabic, ostrich plumes, gold. Human cargo came in little armies—blacks from the countries beyond the Niger, some already familiar to Caillié, men whom he had known as slaves at Jenné.

To the north of Araouane lay the very worst of the desert, the sort of country which in Arabic is called *Kifar*, the land of complete desolation, for the native the word Sahara holds the relatively mild meaning of arid and uncultivated land. Caillié was now going into the Desert-Within-a-Desert, the *Bled-el-Khouf*, "The Land of Fear", a place so dreadful that devils were sent there from Hell as punishment when they had offended Satan.

Caillié heard awed whispers of the Tanezrouft, of the Djouf, "Belly of the Desert", of the great rolling Erg Ech Chech, of El Harricha the accursed. The names of Saharan localities have a quality not to be found in any other place-names in the world. They carry to the initiated an implication of terror, like the name of a frightful malady or of some instrument of medieval torture. Who says Tanezrouft and the rest shudders as if he said small-pox or cancer, or spoken of the thumb-screw and the iron-maiden.

Caillié listened with dismay. What he had already experienced on the way from Timbuctoo was nothing, they told him. The real Saharan terror was something of which he was as yet quite ignorant. Although he was always courageous in the face of hardships, Caillié trembled, knowing he was ill and tired and unused to desert travel,

He made his final preparations. He procured through a certain Araouane broker, who was a business correspondent of his friend at Timbuctoo, provisions for the two months, for his arrangement with Sidi Aly did not include feeding. Caillié got together a fifty-pound sack of rice, fifty pounds of *dokhnou*, and ten pounds of melted butter—the participle seems unnecessary given the prevailing climate, but I record Caillié's list in his own words. In exchange he offered the broker some few trinkets from the coast with which he had not parted and some silver coins, Sierra Leone shillings, no doubt. These coins, a novelty at Araouane, delighted the broker, and perhaps one might find them today adorning the throat of some Moorish maiden. Caillié's provisions were put into the charge of Sidi Aly, and, according to Caillié's story, it was little of all the rice and *dokhnou* and melted butter that ever he himself got a chance to eat.

A kind acquaintance gave Caillié the present of a *gerba*, a skin water-bag. The *gerba* is made usually from a goat-skin, removed without tearing, the legs tied up as handles, one end left unsewn as a mouthpiece, and all other holes carefully sewed. It holds about six gallons. New waterskins give the water a nauseating flavour, caused by the grease which has been rubbed into the skin. Old waterskins often leak through the sewing, but the waterskin is convenient to transport and a plump moist *gerba* the prettiest sight in all the Sahara to caravaneers.

3

ON THE 19TH of May 1828, the caravan attacked the Sahara's worst. At the outskirts of Araouane was the last well which they would see for 222 miles. All stopped to drink deep with the solemnity of a religious rite. Indeed it was almost a sacrament, for who knew if he would live to drink freely again? Then in a great group, 1,400 camels and 400 men, they prayed. Purposely I include the camels. Caillié tells how, beside the last well, they bellowed piteously, as if they called on the God of Camels for mercy and for strength.

Caillié prayed with the rest, begging the God of his childhood to carry him safely home. It was the first prayer ever addressed to the Christian God from this awful place. Caillié in simple language tells how he had the experience which comes sometimes to those who pray at moments of great emergency. He felt that his prayer was really heard, and as if an answering promise came to him from God. He felt full of hope and joy—I use his own words.

The horizon had no end. Sand-dunes, smooth and rippled, rolled off to infinity. There was no breath of wind. Yet the air was, as always in the Sahara, full of minute sand particles. It burned like an open furnace, and hurt the throat as if one had swallowed something scalding. The glare was nearly blinding. Distant objects, a camel or a rock, lost firmness of contour, becoming alternately enormous and almost invisible. René imitated his Moorish companions, binding a strip of cloth across his eyes and another across his mouth.

After the first day it was beyond human or camel power to travel in the full of the sun. So, guided northward by the caravaneer's friend, the Pole Star, they travelled by night. In the lonely plodding silence Caillié studied the stars, taking directions for his records, and noting how grandly the constellations moved above this empty land, blank as a newly-created world. For long hours he watched the solemn progress of "that so remarkable group of stars named the constellation of Orion" and the constellation which Caillié knew as the Big Chariot and which is to the desert folk Talimt, the Cow Camel. He must have noted also the handsome Southern Cross, Heaven's tropic sign-post.

The fattening moon was red like the sun at sunset, and it seemed as if a sensible heat came from its rays. The air was often so calm by night that a candle would not have flickered by the breadth of a hair.

The dawns were vile. There was none of the innocent freshness of a new day. The sun sprang across the horizon like a cruel beast roused from angry sleep. Another tortured day had begun. The guides of the caravan looked about them in the new light, and at a glance, despite the empty monotony of the country, knew where they were. The form of a dune or a rock, the colour of the ground told them. These experienced caravan men had an innate sense of direction like that of certain animals. There was a tradition, honestly believed true, that there existed blind men who could, and did, guide caravans by the varying smell of the sands.

Mid-morning forced a halt. Under the shelter of tanned skeep-skins they lay panting, waiting with only one thought, water. The water distribution was made with prison-like regularity at five in the afternoon by men who listened all day unmoved to pleas for just a little, just a drop to moisten parched lips. Each traveller got his ration, a single long swig, a calabash full.

René protested, saying each man's allowance would do him more good if spread through the day, but in vain. The caravan practice was unchangeable. It was impossible to keep track of odd drinks and sips. Caillié could take it all at once or leave it. Caillié took it!

Each day he lay waiting through the hours for the calabash's coming, saw rivers and brooks and cascades, saw the pretty little Mignon River wriggling through Mauzé, saw springs and mossy pools, saw jugs of sweet cool water, saw water in glasses and cups and pails and basins. He cursed the slow-moving sun. He dozed and dreamed of water and woke and saw that the sun had not moved. Stationary, villainous sun—*Dieu!* it had even *gone back!* Back to the East! It was an unclean miracle, like something in the Bible used in the Black Mass! He slept again, his cracked lips too dry to bleed, his tongue hard and rasping like pumice, his throat a constricted tube full of sand.

The moment came, the calabash approached, lovelier than a king's crystal goblet, Araouane's brackish water, more glorious than nectar. His head plunged in joyously, sopping it up like an animal, water up his nose, slobbering down his chin . . . careful, careful, get it all, don't spill the shadow of a drop.

So, on to another night of travel, and another, and another, uncountably monotonous. In the silent night men and camels plodded across the sands, worming along the line of valleys between dunes, in the land of the great Ergs. Or climbed up rocky paths through country of incredible desolation. Men lost identity, moving in a unison

of misery like the slow breathing of a morass. No one talked.
No one thought. Most slept on camel-back in a gloomy
sleep that brought no rest. The guides followed the Pole
Star, searching for it to correct their direction round each
bend in the deep dunes.

The camels scuffled slowly in procession—no temptation
now to straggle, thistles were but a dead memory in this
desert of deserts. Their walk was like that of old men in
slippers, their progress unbelievably slow, with undula-
tions sideways and backwards and forwards, and a per-
ceptible pause before each step.

Caillié slept, his head propped against Gageba's load,
awoke with a start. How easy to slip from his high perch
and, stunned, be left behind—a camel is so uncouthly
tall, being like all desert animals built with abnormally
long legs. René, ever since his days with the Braknas, had
detested the motion of camel riding, at once monotonous
and jerky.

With an effort of will he held himself awake, telling
himself this crawling death must have an end sometime.
To rest the eye on even one square yard of green, one single
little tree, one pool of water, would have been consoling
as ointment on a burn, but this part of the desert was no
land of glorious green surprises, of sudden lovely oases to
cheer the heart. The South Sahara route is—from the start
—one of bleak, unbroken, dead desert.

Wistfully Caillié wrote of his desert crossing: "I envied
the fate of those who could make a name for themselves
without buying it at the price of such painful hardships
and perils!" But I am sure that he never envied the fate of
those who did not seek fame at all. His ambition was
colossal. Even during the desert's worst he never slackened.
He was always the explorer. Still he counted hours and
observed directions and made his notes as to the character

of terrain and so on, hiding the paper in his Koran, once we find him—it seems almost indecently conscientious! —after a day of hideously hard travel hunting laboriously for sea-shells in the sand-dunes, so that he might confirm the theory often then advanced that the Sahara was a dried-up ocean.

I cannot think that any young man ever gave a more startling proof of devotion to his work!

The worst days came. When the night's travelling was done and the camels were unloaded, they told of their thirst in plaintive low intermittent cries, their thirst call, quite unlike their usual bellow. This call spoke as clear as words to the desert men, and it spoke danger.

The men of the caravan crouched under the little tents, too tired to rest. They talked in harsh cracked whispers, croaking hoarsely.

How long, they must have asked one another shuddering —for they saw the water-skins grow thin and knew the way to Telig, the next well, was still long—how long could a man last in the desert without drinking? Only a day, said some. Nonsense, three days, more. . . . Yes, but water that came too late was useless. A man got to a point where, if they were to rescue him and put before him a hundred calabashes, he could not drink, his throat had lost the art of drinking, he could only stare at the water and cry, and his tears would be hard dry tears like pebbles, and then he would die in agony with ulcers all over his body and his limbs turned backwards so that he scratched his spine with his toes.

Somewhere, in poses like this, the negroes whispered, were the skeletons of those two thousand men in that caravan which lost its way and disappeared twenty-three years ago. . . . Somewhere near where they were talking this very moment. . . . It was well-known gossip at

Timbuctoo and Araouane. What led them off the track? Roul, of course! Roul, the invisible desert devil, who laughs at lost travellers, whose gay delight it is to watch a caravan perish, and to laugh and laugh and laugh in their ears as they slowly die.

Roul's taunting laugh, which many have actually heard, is probably produced by the cracking of rocks as the temperature changes and by the shifting and rubbing of billions of grains of sand in the wind. Roul is the well-known "sand-drum". But to superstitious travellers Roul is the Sahara's evil genius. The black slaves dreamed of his laugh and writhed in fear.

The camel men tended their suffering beasts. It was the veterinary's art practised in most ghoulish fashion. Relatively easy, though astonishing and nauseating to the inexperienced observer, was the job of mending camel's cut feet by sewing on patches of hide. These cobblers did not hesitate to perform the same distressing operation upon themselves, and could be seen stitching together cracks in the soles of their own feet. Far more serious were the injuries to the camel's frail hide. A rub of load or saddle produced the most disgusting sore, capable of infecting bones and spine. Caillié watched the beasts being treated with hot irons, primitive surgery and applications of salt. He saw animals which were nearly dead reanimated by the pouring of a small quantity of precious water down their nostrils with a funnel. He witnessed the sudden death of camels on the road, a death that comes sometimes without warning or preliminary complaint. Abruptly, with his load on his back, the camel who can go no further stops, folds his legs together and sits. Then with great dignity, almost nonchalantly, he dies.

René termed the camel "*un des plus beaux chef-d'œuvres de la Nature*". Caillié viewed Nature's performance from the standpoint of the desert traveller, not from that of the camel!

The water supply, brought from Araouane, had diminished to a point of desperate danger. The exceptional heat had dried it through the skins, there had been leakage. A party was sent to hunt for water at certain wells believed to be somewhere to the side of the direct route toward Telig, while the caravan pressed on.

Caillié thought that Sidi Aly had tapped the dwindling water-skins and filled a little private water-bag for his personal use: dastardly conduct, indeed, to be a secret drinker in the Sahara!

To the hardship of thirst was now added the nightmare spectre of the flat water-skin. Roul laughed and said: "Send a sand-storm!"

It was a day of the burning wind, *cheheli*. Great plumes of sand swept across the tops of the dunes, like a prairie fire. A livid veil was over everything. Suddenly in the far distance appeared a copper-coloured cloud near the ground. The horizon vanished. The world changed its form, grew small. A solid wall swept down on them, and the light went out, though it was barely noontime. In the opaque darkness the hurricane roared continuously with occasional cracks like thunder.

The caravan camp was in the full track of the sand-storm. Like chaff, tents and men and camels were tossed this way and that. Men lay as they fell, praying convulsively to Allah and sobbing. Camels groaned and hid their faces between their knees. It was a swift moment of blind, primitive horror. Annihilation was very close. Suddenly at three o'clock the wind fell. Roul had spared them, or—as they soon gloomily suspected—was saving them for his greatest joke of all, was saving them so that he might laugh while they slowly died of thirst.

At four the caravan moved on, camels near their breaking point, men almost hopeless. The ground was a chaos of small dark rocks, a hard stumbling road to travel in the dark.

The pagan slaves sucked the blood from their finger tips, squealing with the pain as they bit themselves. Some drank their urine only to suffer afterward from burning torments. In the dawn their black faces were horrible, smeared with dried blood, distorted by agony and terror, weird with protruding, sandy tongues.

There was no sign of the men who had been sent to the well. The caravan leaders broke their rule and gave out a little drink all round, saying that the water party would soon return, that their delay was merely because the water was low in the wells at this season and tedious to draw. The delay was really a good sign, for had the wells been quite dry they would have been back long before.

But everyone knew that their cheering words were insincere, for the customary rest period was cut short and they pushed on at forced march toward Telig.

At ten next morning, the morning of the seventh day out of Araouane, the little water party returned near to death. They had lost their way in searching for the well, presumably a mere water-hole marked by a heap of rocks in a waste of nothingness. And when found and dug out— and it takes a hero to wield a shovel at a temperature of 160 degrees—the well was dry.

They had decided on the final expedient and had sacrificed a camel for the sake of drinking what still remained of the water reserve in its stomach. Desert thirst knows no repugnances, and they drank the greenish liquid thankfully, regretting only that the animal's store was near depleted. Says Caillié, "the animal's blood would have been of great succour to them, but this they dared not drink, the Koran forbidding".

Despair now fell on the whole caravan. At four o'clock the last of the water was given out and they set off again very slowly dragging themselves, men and camels, toward the north, praying that they might reach the Telig well before their strength failed. It was uncertain just how far they had to go. They could only hope to keep up until morning.

Three miles of precious effort was wasted through going out of their direction to the eastward to avoid an unscalable dune of loose sand.

At dawn they passed great blocks of white earth in alinement like ruined houses.

The camels began to act oddly, lying down to roll and scattering their loads in the white dust.

Then to the west showed dunes of wine-coloured sand, while rocks of red and black granite appeared on the road before them.

It seemed like an earthly hell, roused a dark suspicion that they were already dead and did not know it.

Suddenly the guides croaked a cry of wild joy. This unforgettable patch of nightmare country marked the neighbourhood of Telig. They were saved!

But even at the last, with water near, they had still to wait. The wells were filled up with sand. The caravaneers fell upon them with spades. The camels, smelling water, went mad, pushing themselves before the workers and impeding the shovelling. Men hit them with cord whips and drove them away.

The water came thick with black mire. The camels fought for it savagely. The water of Telig is near the surface and abundant. As it cleared so that the pool showed through the mud, Caillié rushed forward between the camel's feet and threw himself on his stomach and drank with them.

4

THE CAMELS DRANK all day. Their flat flabby stomachs became gradually plump and wobbly. And Caillié, now that water was free, enjoyed the luxury of his first cooked meal since Araouane. He ate boiled rice and butter, no banquet menu, but a glorious treat to his stomach fatigued by constant cold picnic fare.

Near Telig the camels got their first meal *of any kind* since Araouane, a few tufts of very brittle dry grass, growing in far separated clumps across the grey sand-dunes. Food and water came too late for a pair of animals. But even in death they were still useful. Their carcases were boiled for food—very poor food it was too, René says, hard and with a rank odour.

Caillié, perhaps because stewed camel upset his digestion, or perhaps because of the Telig water, or perhaps as a result of the past eight days of strain, fell ill. Yet he was childishly happy and comforted because near to his hand throughout that night grew a little grass tuft.

Near the Telig wells was the famous, infamous town of Taoudenni, where there was, and perhaps still is, more misery than in any place on earth—be it prison, penal settlement or chain gang. René did not go there, it being slightly west of the main Timbuctoo to Morocco route. He did, however, visit, a few days later, the abandoned salt city of Tegazza, of which the mines were exploited during the Middle Ages, and where the very houses and mosque were cut out of blocks of salt.

With regard to Taoudenni, Caillié heard shocking tales from others in the caravan who had been there, and his story gave the world its first definite notion of how the blacks lived in these mines, which are "an industrial hell, a place where the exploitation of men by men is more hideous than anywhere on our planet".[1]

The mines of Taoudenni contain the purest of salt In all the land south of the Niger, Taoudenni salt is accounted to possess phenomenal merit, special savour, special health value. Its great slabs are veined like handsome marble, faintly gleaming like ground glass,

Part of the glamour of Taoudenni salt lies in the fact that it is so hard to procure. The very name, which means "Load up and Run", suggests the horror of the place. The thrill of danger—*somebody else's danger*—is in every bar, danger at the source, danger in transporting it to the consumer.

Taoudenni is literally uninhabitable. Men stay there a little while and die. It contains absolutely nothing: not a blade of vegetation, not a drop of decent water.

To Taoudenni are sent negroes to work the mines for the profit of certain wealthy folk of Araouane and elsewhere. Conditions, we are told, are now much as they were in Caillié's day. A mission of investigation was sent there a few years ago by the *Matin* newspaper of Paris. The story of what they saw makes nightmare reading.[2]

Taoudenni's wells furnish water which kills men in a few years. Analysis shows it to be one-third more violent than the strongest natural medicinal waters, sold us at pharmacies to be taken in occasional small doses as a purgative. Its taste is horrid and its stench nauseating. To make it drinkable *dokhnou*, or else a sort of powdered cheese made by drying sour milk in the sun, was added in Caillié's day. Nowadays the wretched negroes toil through the burning hours for a pinch of tea and sugar.

[1] Gautier, *Conquête du Sahara*.   [2] *L'Enfer du Sel* by Gerville-Réache et Mathieu.

Every particle of food, of course, is brought over-desert by camel, brought by the *azalai*, the caravans that come to fetch away the salt. The negroes, condemned for ever, escape impossible, work three-quarters of their time for their masters, and one-quarter—two days out of every eight—for themselves. When the *azalai* comes they buy their food for the ensuing year. It costs twenty-five bars of salt, labour of fifteen days of torture, to buy one pound of tea.

And yet a few black women—about a dozen—live in the mines with these men, live and breed children.

To starvation, poisonous water, burning, shadeless heat, are added other tribulations—cracked and ulcerous affections of the skin caused by the salt, infected eyes, blindness. Happy are the negroes and negresses who go mad or die. The *Matin's* reporters say that there come occasionally to Taoudenni Sudanese negroes who in some crazed mood have agreed *voluntarily* to go to this hell, accepting an engagement because they were tempted by the offer of some trifling sum of immediate cash in a desperate moment of emergency.

In the little town of Taoudenni live the *caid* and his people who manage the mines and the trading with the *azalai*—rich in money and beggars in fact. If the *azalai* fails, they die. Once, not many years ago, when the supply caravan was attacked by Tuareg on the way to Taoudenni, the *caid* and his women and associates ate water-skins. When these were all eaten they tackled the ornamental and dyed leather-work of their *mezoueds*, which are a form of native travelling bag. Then, all the leather being finished, they ate the few bits of wood which had been used in the construction of their briny clay houses.

The desire to exploit Taoudenni and other Saharan salt mines more profitably and more humanely was one of many reasons behind the various schemes, some very absurd, for the domestication of the Sahara. Within a generation or so of Caillié's return from Africa a variety of plans were advanced for harnessing the country and making it work.

There was much loose talk about "flooding the Sahara". A Briton had the notion of coaxing the Atlantic into the desert from near Cape Juby. De Lesseps toyed with the idea of creating an inland sea to the eastward. But the Sahara is still dry, for the cost of such large-scale landscape gardening promised to be huge and the rewards problematical, while—most discouraging of all—the Sahara on investigation proved to be of unexpectedly high altitude, and little better adapted to flooding than any other part of the world, much as it needed it.

Another and longer surviving plan was that of running a railway across the Sahara.

The plan, which was at first proposed as a joke, took hold of the popular fancy. If all that has been written about this fantastically difficult but very romantic project—arguments for and against, arguments as to the best route, the political merits, the possible method of construction and operation and financing,—were laid end to end, page by page, they would not only stretch right across the Sahara, but would go near to covering the whole desert with a printed paper rug. But as yet there is no Saharan railway beyond the two points Colomb-Béchar and Touggourt in Algeria, nor any southern Saharan railway at all.

At the time when the pro and con arguments for the trans-Saharan railway were especially violent, the Tuareg advanced a contra argument which was spectacularly convincing and for a time closed the debate. There would probably be a Saharan railway in operation now but for the Tuareg.

In December, 1880, Lieutenant-Colonel Flatters, of the French Engineers, set off into the Sahara with a party of white associates and natives, nearly a hundred men, intending to study the possibilities of a railroad route through the Hoggar. Four months later four native soldiers stumbled back into a South Algerian military post, crazed and unable to tell any coherent story of what had happened to their comrades. Later three others were rescued.

Nobody has ever known just what happened to Colonel Flatters, nor why: how he came to be trapped and his band put to rout, whether he lost his head, whether he was in an abnormal state of mind, or even whether he was killed. A story was current afterwards that Flatters, prisoner amongst the Tuareg, had finished by "taking the veil" and becoming a naturalized Tuareg.

Those seven survivors told of the attack when they were sixty days' march into the desert, and of the terrible struggle of the survivors, some fifty men, to get back to safety, famished, thirsty and harassed by Tuareg.

One day their Tuareg pursuers amazed and delighted them by the offer to sell them some dates. Gladly they accepted, ate the dates and went mad immediately, the dates were poisoned with a desert plant called *falezlez*. The men screamed and rushed about in agony, babbling senseless words, firing off their guns at one another, tearing off their clothes, and even trying to strangle themselves to keep out the air "which seemed to burn their lungs at every inhalation". Some ran off into the desert. Many perished. The Tuareg killed others. One white man was left alive. He did not live long. His comrades ate him, or such was the confession which they made.

The details of the Flatters fiasco were never found out. It became a hideous legend. It disgusted public opinion. For years no one cared to urge the cause of trans-Saharan railway enterprise.

The Tuareg on their camels and armed with weapons five hundred years behind the times — for they detested guns and gun-powder, having an odd hatred for the noise, as Caillié noticed—had ruined the cherished enterprise of a great white nation.

But the trans-Saharan railway has not been abandoned, and the arguments continue. Regrets too. Some think that the construction of a Saharan railway might have won the whole of tropic Africa to France, keeping the English out of Nigeria and the lands south of Egypt.

Meanwhile there has been put into operation a service of mail-carrying automobiles — *not* using caterpillar wheels —across the mid-Sahara, which, running at long intervals and only in winter, hooks Algeria to the Niger, and which accepts a few passengers. These cars carry immense supplies of water and a reserve of food. Also an extra man familiar with the route whose duty is to drive in an emergency and keep the car in wireless touch with "the shore" so that a prompt attempt may be made to send aid in case of mishap. The automobile part of the journey takes six days from the railhead at Colomb-Béchar to Gao, and when I made it in the winter of 1934–5, cost 2,850 francs, all found.[1]

The route is slightly to the eastward of Caillié's route, and as it crosses the waterless Tanezrouft, where one may travel over five hundred kilometres between wells, is regarded as safe from native interference. Men on camels would have difficulty in carrying enough water to follow the way we took nor could they approach unperceived across the absolutely flat desolation where with the naked eye one can see the next *balise* but one. (*Balises* are the guiding marks along the way—frame-work covered with

[1] Another Saharan service, on which I recently travelled part of the journey, connects Algeria with the Hoggar and continues to Kano.

galvanized iron, every ten kilometres.) The route is named in honour of René Estienne, the heroic plotter of Saharan ways, who was murdered in the desert.

It is not a road. Each driver picks the way which seems to him best, keeping always the next *balise* in view. Many cars get stuck in the sand. Some never get loose and remain on the way like the skeletons of camels. There is very little travel in mid-Sahara. We met in the whole six days no travellers except a car of the same service going in the opposite direction, and a military *camion*; no camels, no private cars, no people on foot. We saw no animals till the last day, when gazelles were shot from the car.

When the first automobile passed along the "Piste Estienne" its driver was absolutely the first living creature ever to look at the mid-part of the Tanezrouft. Not even vultures or insects go there. It took gasoline to tame the Tanezrouft.

Gasoline has also helped to tame the Tuareg. No longer are they the danger that they were. Time has drawn the Tuareg's teeth.

With dizzy swiftness the Tuareg saw their destinies change. At the beginning of the century they were pirates before whom the desert cringed, masters of the whole central Sahara, human mysteries, a race numerically small but so specialized in frightfulness that they enjoyed a world-wide notoriety and prestige. They seemed almost supernatural. Now they are almost pathetic. All the fury and fun have been taken out of life for them. No more pillage on a large scale. No more ambush at the wells. The shriek of victims is a sweet forgotten tune, and when the Tuareg girl wants new finery or the Tuareg matron needs supplies, she has to procure them through the dull processes of commerce.

These dashing people are being reduced to near futility.

White men can safely study their mysterious ways. Probably the Tuareg is the oddest person alive. His outstanding racial peculiarity is, of course, that his men wear veils while the women go about face-free. Even the Tuareg's wife does not see his uncovered face, we are told, although this takes believing. If his veil becomes disarranged he goes modestly behind a bush to adjust it, and when he eats in public, he keeps his hand before his mouth or slips the food in under his veil. "The hole through which he eats" is accounted an indecent spectacle, and the rest of mankind who expose their "flytraps" ("*bouches de mouches*") are regarded with disgust as uncouth barbarians.

The Tuareg cannot give the reason for this custom. The fact that young men do not assume the veil until maturity, sometimes not until they are twenty-five years old, casts doubt on the obvious explanations that the veil was an invention to keep out desert sand, and was gradually transformed into a ritual.

The Tuareg have been thought to have some remote connection with Christianity because the Cross appears so prominently in their ornamentation, though no one can explain how a group of Christians got into the Sahara and retained the Church's emblem long after they had forgotten Jesus. Nowadays the Tuareg are lukewarm Mussulmans, who do not observe Ramadan and are full of strange superstitions.

Spirits, they believe, are everywhere; ogres and ghosts and devils skulk in the dark shadows of the gorges between the mighty mountains. Witches and folk possessed by demons abound.

The Tammekkelout, an old witch woman, milks the dugs of the moon and at night mixes filtres to drive men mad. In an empty skull she mixes scorpion venom and the bone dust of children and other matters with urine. Even to stand unawares in the shadow of a Tammekkelout brings tragedy—flocks become sterile, men go down with hideous maladies.

A dragon Tanghot casts a spell on certain unlucky women, driving them insane, most especially young girls who first dream of love.

But rarely need Tuareg girls who dream of love languish till Tanghot drives them into madness, for Tuareg maidens enjoy complete sexual freedom, *asri* (the privilege of living according to their heart's whim and fancy).

The Tuareg treats his womenfolk with chivalry. He is "the Knight of the Desert".[1] Tuareg girls are *really free*, free to give their love and caresses where they wish, and none shall scold them. A significant discovery was made by Lieutenant Hourst; that in Temajegh, the Tuareg language, there are three different words to mean "love-child".

The young Tuareg meet at love festivals under the stars. The young men often come great distances, the Saharan sun whipping desire as they travel on the swift *mehara*. The maidens are pretty and witty and dressed in heavy gorgeous ornaments and long robes of indigo and white. Their make-up might alarm less ardent lovers, for their faces are garish with red and yellow ochre and their body skin, which naturally is rarely washed, is ingrained with blue dye from their robes, something which the Tuareg regards as both beautiful and healthful. All night these young people sing amorous impromptu verses, listen to the native violin, the *amzad*, whose music plays cunningly upon the nerves and passions. Kisses are free and unreproached. The party is called an *ahal*.

But now the Tuareg says "Dishonour has come into the tent with the plough," and he has decided, in the

---

[1] Francis Rennell Rodd, in *People of the Veil*, tells of his conversation with a Tuareg: "This man, to emphasize the good manners required by usage to be observed before women, assured me that in the old days if anyone had dared to break wind in their presence, the insult was punishable by death alone." This suggests an almost incredibly high standard of manners for primitive tent dwellers.

gloomy phrase of his disillusionment, that he must "kiss the hand which he cannot cut off". Sometimes he relapses, forgets to kiss, and essays to cut again. There is still danger for isolated travellers and for aviators in distress.

During the war of 1914-18 the Tuareg were troublesome, and probably will be troublesome in future wars. In 1916 they shocked the world by murdering Père de Foucauld, the White Father and French nobleman who had befriended them, who had formulated the quaint project of persuading their womenfolk to take baths, and had even asked that "hair-dye of jet black" might be sent to him for distribution amongst the ageing matrons who gave him their childish confidence. He was their "Christian marabout", their "Abed Aissa" (Slave of Jesus). He had lived amongst them for twelve blameless years, having imported a pathetic little travelling chapel across the desert on the back of a she-ass, and established himself in a parish two hundred thousand kilometres square, where—since he was frequently the only Christian —the Pope had authorized him to celebrate Mass without the aid of a "*servant*". In his summer-time hermitage, at an altitude of 8,000 feet in the Tuareg mountains, the White Father breathed in unison with this desolate land, rejoicing in African solitude. And even there, a full thousand miles from the nearest rail-head, Foucauld, in the whimsical words of one of his admirers, "found that the tram-cars came too close!"[1]

The Tuareg slew the White Father, as many resentful natives in other lands have slain well-meaning foreign saints who came amongst them. Foucauld and his French friends spelt to the Tuareg the end of pillage. The joint memorial to Père de Foucauld and General Laperrine,

[1] This affectionate quip of Pierre Mille's is quoted by René Bazin in his fine book, *Charles de Foucauld, Explorateur du Maroc, Ermite au Sahara.*

and René Caillié's little house at Timbuctoo, are the only two widely known pilgrimage spots in all the Sahara, and it is few indeed who ever visit them.

It was General Laperrine who "gave the Sahara to France despite herself". In youth he was with those who took Timbuctoo, and his dying words on the first tragic attempted trans-Saharan flight, ". . . *and I thought I knew the Sahara!*" are more poignant than Wolsey's.

5

WHEN CAILLIÉ AND the caravan left Telig on May 27, 1828, Caillié knew that he had seen samples of all the Sahara's worst horrors. This knowledge was, oddly enough, depressing. For the thrill of curiosity no longer inspired him. He had still two months of desert misery before him—all familiar. There were no dramatic surprises ahead, only a grim test of endurance.

Life was a grinding push from well to well: May 31, the Well of Cramès, which was a well in name only, being quite dried up; June 1, the Well of Tegazza, eighteen miles further on, of which the water was "salty and detestable"; on to Amoul-Gragim on the 5th, where the water-hole was filled up with sand.

Amoul-Gragim was infested with serpents which lived in deep holes and came out in the dark. In the middle of the night Caillié woke to find that a huge snake was near his face. The creature was "five and a half feet long and as thick round as the thigh of a child of twelve". We may imagine Caillié got no more sleep at Amoul-Gragim.

On to Amoul-Taf, where water was scarce but less unpleasant in taste. Then no well for three days, and so on, and on, and on, lengths of misery measured off between watering-places.

Some of the wells which Caillié named are marked on the modern map. And, by the way, any one who desires to sense the desert's desolation at a glance has but to look at a large-scale Saharan map. He will find Amoul-Gragim and the rest in the midst of an emptiness as complete as that of the sea.

These wells were precious places, holy as shrines to desert travellers. Natives dug immensely deep, invented ingenious methods of holding back the sand. Marked often by piles of camel filth or ringed with a frill of slave's skeletons, they were nonetheless the jewels of the desert. Men spoke their names with reverent affection, and bade them good-bye with a ritual gesture of gratitude and respect.

Sometimes, however, Saharan water was poisonous. The water of one well actually burned holes in cloth and caused the bodies of men who were so mad with thirst as to drink it to swell. Their hands and feet became puffed and very painful, and remained bloated for many days.

In another sense all wells were dangers to caravans, for there the chance of pillage was always greatest.

Caillié saw mirages on the horizon—rivers and lakes with pretty islands. Waters sparkled, palm trees rose green and tempting. A whole oasis showed, a lovely dream, always ahead, changing shape tauntingly. Dunes danced, hills came near and then darted away to the horizon.

Caillié rocked upon his camel in a daze, his head addled and reeling. But Gageba, sober beast, stepped on and on, at two miles an hour. No nonsense about Gageba.

Caillié was the butt of the caravan's humour. The Moors teased him without pity. They called him "Gageba" after his camel, because of his long nose. They incited the slaves of the caravan to pelt him with stones, and prick him with thorns.

"Gageba! Gageba! See how they look alike! Put a bit of wood through his nose so we can lead him!" Leaping and giggling, the blacks danced round him, pretending they would carry out the order.

Sidi Aly puckered up his ugly face and hummed offensively when Caillié drank, imitating the noise by which it was customary to encourage thirsty camels.

"Look how he eats!" they cried. "Slopping his food about instead of making it into neat balls and tossing it into his mouth. Gageba eats like a Christian!" They said it as we might say "like a savage".

Caillié submitted. He had no choice. He counted himself lucky in that they did not guess that he really was a Christian.

He overheard talk between certain of the Moors, in which Sidi Body, friend of his guide Aly, mentioned the rumoured price—a thousand piastres—offered for Christian slaves in Morocco, and looked at Caillié significantly. "But Gageba is no Christian", said the other, and reluctantly Sidi Body agreed.

It was indeed no time for Caillié to be touchy in the matter of teasing.

In the night Caillié studied the stars. One night, he must have noticed that something had altered. The familiar pattern was different. *The Southern Cross was missing!*

The sands became a little less hot. Wells were closer together. Sometimes they found a few roots of desert plants and could cook a proper meal. They saw the skeletons of gazelles. True, the unlucky graceful creatures had died of thirst, but the sight was encouraging, for, where a gazelle had died, there also it had lived. The caravan knew that it had left the region of absolute desolation. It was approaching the semi-desert stretches of the other shore.

One early morning Caillié saw far off a bit of green —not mirage but actuality.

A few hours later, after a devious crawling descent by a steep path between walls of rose and violet rock, camels and men found themselves at the bottom of a deep ravine where trees grew, date palms, the first green Caillié had seen since the Niger. In this blessed place there was water that was sweet, clear, limpid, delicious. It was a "*véritable volupté*" to drink it. The phrase is René's.

That night when all slept Caillié did something in secret which, had he attempted to do it openly, would have roused instant antagonism and suspicion. He had a bath! Tingling cool water on his dry, sore skin. Tingling cool water washing the gritty dust away. How sweet and smooth his skin felt to his hands, how pleasant to sluice water along his limbs, to dip his head under water, to shake the drops off his long black hair, to shake his whole body like an animal, to be fresh and clean again.

Next morning they went back once more into the sands, but Caillié could hug the memory of "*véritable volupté*".

6

AT THE EDGE of the desert Caillié met with the first serious accident which befell him during his whole journey. When one considers it, the fact that this man who was described as puny could get to this point, across two and a half thousand miles of Africa, without a fall or other mishap indicates amazing hidden athleticism.

It happened just outside El-Harib, a permanent desert camp near the Saharan borders of Morocco and in those days an important crossing point for desert roads. It was midnight and their way led through a mountain defile where great masses of overhanging rock threatened at every instant to dislodge and crush them, and the precipitous path was slippery with salt slime.

Caillié's camel took fright, shied and bolted. Caillié, caught unprepared, slipped off backward, falling heavily on the small of his back, and suffered such shock and sudden pain that he believed his back was broken. One of the others, a stranger of better nature than most of his comrades, caught Caillié up in his arms, and crushed him against his own chest with all his force. Breath came back to René's lungs and life flowed through him again; but he was one great bruise from head to foot, giddy and unable to bend his back. It was to be two months before he would feel himself again.

From Sidi Aly and his associate Moors he got no sympathy. The defile, immediately after his accident, became so narrow and steep that all were ordered to proceed on foot. This was, of course, impossible to René, whose benefactor had lifted him back aboard Gageba, but when he failed to obey the command, Aly threatened him with a rock.

The path ran by the edge of a precipice. Caillié on his high camel, suffering great pain and with head whirling, thought at any moment to be thrown off into the gorge. The camels were terrified, stopping every few steps to turn their long worried faces to left and right nervously, and uttering almost human groans. The camel men of the caravan encouraged them. They sang to them the same reassuring words over and over in a little tune "which the camels seemed to understand".

In the morning they reached El-Harib, where they would stay a few days at Sidi Aly's family camp—twelve camel-hair tents in a great plain surrounded on three sides by arid mountains. René was lodged in the tent of Aly's sister, a most unpleasant old woman named Ayché, who served Caillié a meal of *sanglé* (a sort of porridge) full of human hairs, she, like so many native housewives, seeing no need to differentiate between the cooking and the toilet butter.

Caillié's stomach turned. He endeavoured to nourish himself with dates. These were almost uneatable; they were not the dates of our juvenile delight but a hard mass, nearly a full year dried in Saharan heat, for they were of the previous late summer's crop. Furthermore, they had been windfalls of poor quality in the first place, as René gloomily recognized. The arid camp of El-Harib had to buy their dates and everything else they ate, and they had to buy the cheapest. The poverty of these agglomerations situated on the desert's fringe was inconceivable. Even nowadays one may see the people of such camps collecting for human food the undigested grain in horse's droppings.

In trying to masticate those dates Caillié did himself much mischief. The old affliction of Tiémé days recurred. A sore appeared upon his palate and he was much alarmed.

Ayché was then persuaded to prepare butterless *sanglé* and in return Caillié was to do her a delicate and rather undignified service.

"Listen, Abdallahi," said Ayché to him in a whisper. "You were brought up amongst the Christians and must know a lot of clever tricks. I want you to make me a *gris-gris* for one of my nieces who desires a husband. Do this and I will make *sanglé* for you for two days running."

Caillié agreed and even furnished the bit of paper, article of high value, for the charm. He wrote the maiden's name and that of the reluctant young man of her longings and of his parents. The girl was to wear it round her throat.

Other maidens came flocking for love charms, one so hideously ugly, having sore eyes and a scar all along her left cheek, that the task seemed pitiful.

For his work as a husband-getter Caillié received food. When the market for *gris-gris* was poor, he did not hesitate to beg.

A little man in bloody rags, body burnt black by the sun, he went from tent to tent with his *satala*. "Give me a few drops of camel's milk! Give me food for the love of Allah!"

But René flinched at nothing. He was ready to beg, cringe, sell fake love charms, do anything. He would have sold his own nails and teeth to keep himself alive. He was beyond pride or compunction. He was a dog running home with a bone, a bitch fighting for her pups. He was a woman bearing the seed of a dead king. René *must* live. He *must* carry on through to the end.

And, anyway, why should he care how he appeared before these people? He thought the people of El-Harib negligible trash. The women were more vilely dirty than any he had seen in all Africa. The children were so disgustingly afflicted with the sickness of filth—festered eyes, scabs, ringworms, sores—that Caillié says: "I could not look at them without shuddering. Sometimes I had to hide my face." Sidi Aly's own family were despicable. His women teased and tormented him. Aly starved him, though there was still ample food left of Caillié's own buying. Aly's sons, grown-up young men, came naked before Caillié making "the most indecent gestures". René's anger must have been intense. Otherwise he would never have recorded this incident, for his was the purest of pens, and in his whole three volumes this is the only suggestive item.

On July 12th, still under the guidance of Sidi Aly, René left El-Harib and went northward across the land of pillaging Berbers, whose graceful, vigorous women, gay with red head cloths, heavy amber necklaces, silver anklets and pretty blue tattooing on chin and brow, appeared to René such a delightful change from the filthy Moors of El-Harib that he found, weak and tired as he was, the resilient spirit to flirt. "They turned their gaze upon my person which seemed rather to please them!" said he contentedly of three of these pleasant creatures to whom he recounted his adventures at a stopping place alongside a well.

It was the road of hope. The caravan now met wells in plenty, sometimes two wells in a single day. Occasionally little groves of dates gladdened Caillié's heart. It was so good to see green again. Even the camels seemed "gay" —the word is of René's choice.

Every object which suggested life was a glorious sight. Even flies were welcome, those peculiarly small, gluey, languid flies of the Sahara's edge, which seem to have no notion at all of self-preservation and crawl feebly across hands and face and into one's mouth and eyes, like suicidal imbeciles seeking the destructive slap.

One day Caillié saw a primitive plough, made with three bits of wood, idle, of course, during this burning summer season, but an indication that he had reached the belt where sometimes it rained.

They passed Mimcina by the River Draa, which here in its lower course is a mere dried-up track during most of the year. Mimcina was a typical walled desert city, houses crushed together in the hope of gaining shade. The streets were very narrow and devious, as if the men who had built the town had hoped that the Saharan sun would lose itself in the maze. In Mimcina Caillié was bitten by savage dogs and obliged to keep his temper when, at a native gathering, a certain travelled man entertained the company by imitating the pose of the Christ-Crucified and jeeringly chanted, as he had heard Christian priests do, beating his chest and repeating over and over, "*Amen! Amen! Amen!*" while the others roared with laughter.

A few days later Caillié had dealings with another travelled Moor whose remarks, though harrowing, were not so distasteful. He was a quite bald old man going to the Oasis of Tafilalet, which was also Caillié's immediate destination. This old trader had lived in Timbuctoo and known Laing in his last days.

They were near the Oasis. It was the 21st of July, very hot, rocky ground. Out from Tafilalet there came the son of the old bald head to greet his returning father. He brought a gift of welcome, and the good old man shared his gift with Caillié. What a gift it was after eleven weeks of desert. It was a bunch of black grapes.

They were a white man's fruit, the first Caillié had touched for years. He was home!

He held a single grape, vibrant dark purple, between his fingers. The bloom rubbed away under his ecstatic grip. The grape shone like a thing of glass, and he looked into it—a soothsayer's globe. He saw safe journey's end. He saw a happy future.

On July 23rd they reached Ghourland (Gouirlane on the map), the most southerly place in the agglomerated settlements known as the Oasis of Tafilalet, in which had been the city of Sajilmasa, famous in the Middle Ages.

A million date-palms—literally a million—rose in green splendour against the sky. Round their feet were green plush rugs of barley and patches of lucerne for fodder, and in the shade grew fig and apple trees and crawling melon-vines. Behind mud walls were gardens, veined with little canals where real vegetables flourished —feathery carrot tops, the lean reeds of onions, fat cabbage heads. There is no thrill so wonderful as the first sight of an oasis after long desert days.

Caillié climbed for the last time off Gageba's back. He need ride no further on the desert ship. Caillié bade good-bye to Sidi Aly whose behaviour was devilish to the very end. He bade good-bye to the Sahara.

Once again Caillié had pulled through. He had accomplished the first crossing of the Western Sahara ever made by a white explorer—eighty-one days of blazing, unbroken desert—and got his story of Timbuctoo another great step nearer home.

7

HIS MAIN PREOCCUPATION now was financial. How was he going to pay his way across Morocco to the coast?

All his stock of trade goods was gone. It is true that he still had a few bits of Bouré gold and some English silver money. But at Tafilalet only Moroccan or Spanish coins had currency. The selling of gold or the exchange of English shillings might be a ticklish business. It would attract dangerous notice to him in a country where fanaticism was intense and where his masquerade was increasingly subject to the intelligent suspicion of men, some of whom were familiar with Europeans, some of whom might have seen real Egyptians.

Caillié decided to try the experiment of changing a single shilling. There was, of course, no regular system for the exchanging of foreign money. He could but take his shilling to a Jew and sell it for its silver value. So René sought a Jew and opened negotiations. It was a great affair.

The Jew was named Jacob. He was one of the miserable race of desert Hebrews who lived, despised and degraded, amongst the Mohammedans, amply profiting by usury and close trading, but constantly ill-treated.

I venture to quote what Guy de Maupassant wrote when he visited North Africa. After expressing his liking for his cultured and worldly Jewish friends in Paris, he said: "We become violently indignant when we hear how the inhabitants of some little far-away town have massacred the children of Israel, but I am no longer amazed, for our Jews in no way resemble these. . . . One sees them squatting in their lairs, dirty and sordid and watching the Arab as a spider waits for flies." (From *Au Soleil*.)

In Tafilalet Caillié saw Jews shamefully ill-used. Mohammedans, he says, threw stones at them in the streets for the mere fun of it and without provocation. "The smallest child could insult and strike them with impunity, and they dared not defend themselves." If they passed before a mosque or the door of a cherif's home, they were obliged to take off their sandals and go barefoot. To avoid the jealous notice and depredations of their Mussulman neighbours they went nearly naked in filthy rags. And often they walked barefoot to dodge the almost continuous trouble and humiliation of taking off their sandals.

Yet when, in despair at their cruel treatment, certain Jews forswore their religion and turned Moslem, they were not sure of improving their position, for these renegade Jews were often accused of the most absurd improprieties toward their new faith. A Jew, it was said, would place a paper in the sole of his slipper on which was written "*Allah*" so that he might insult his new God at every step. Or he would go into the mosque with "a flask of urine" hidden in his clothing.[1]

But the Saharan Jews prospered. It was they who financed much of the trans-Saharan trade, though they never themselves crossed the desert, and inside their

[1] *Le Maroc* by Jérome and Jean Tharaud.

hovels they fed better than did their haughty neighbours, eating white bread and brewing beer in secret, and even pressing wine.

Jacob was a jeweller. Caillié, having made his acquaintance in the street, was invited to his home to discuss formally the matter of selling the single Sierra Leone shilling. The transaction was carried out with ceremony.

Caillié was seated upon the bare earthen floor of the innermost of the three cave-like rooms of Jacob's vilely dirty house. He was introduced to Jacob's old mother and young wife, a lively little woman with a hooked nose and blue eyes, who though timid showed a great desire to hear all about this strange client of her husband's.

Refreshments were offered, nuts, a slice of melon, a piece of bread, and the proposed sale of the shilling was discussed in detail.

But Jacob and Caillié could not conclude the bargain, it being Saturday, the Jewish sacred day. Caillié was invited to return on the morrow. As a matter of fact it was not until the evening of the second day following that René finally received the value of his English coin in local currency.

The complications of the small transaction and the fuss it aroused locally—a negro slave was actually sent chasing after Caillié to Jacob's house to see he came to no harm amongst the Jews (or to spy on the mysterious business) proved to Caillié that it would be madness to attempt to finance the next stage of his journey with English money. He was in the absurd position of being a pauper although he carried lumps of pure gold and a tidy sum in one of the solidest currencies in the world.

René saw that he must arrange his affairs in some other fashion. He puzzled over the problem and studied the local situation. Somehow he must get money.

His usual good temper, shrewd sense and charm of

manner were re-established now that the Sahara was behind him and Sidi Aly only a memory. He made friends with the local chief, Haggi le Mekké, and with an interesting Tafilalet Moor, Sidi Boubacer, a travelled person and intelligent, who possessed the only watch in the whole country, probably the only watch then ticking between the Atlas Mountains and the Sénégal River!

This native collector of odd scientific curios owned the pocket compass which Caillié supposed had been Laing's, though Heaven alone knows by what means it got across the Sahara. His learning was phenomenal, he knew "the first three rules of arithmetic", fetched a slate, and proudly showed off before the admiring René. Then the two new friends squatted down side by side at the street corner and began "doing sums together".

Sidi Boubacer was sufficiently intelligent to take Caillié's story to pieces. Caillié had been saying that he was carried from Egypt by the French when a little boy. This would have required him to be in the thirties. Caillié was then only twenty-eight.

Boubacer had been out Egypt way in the time of Napoleon, the "Sultan-Kébir", and he examined the detail of Caillié's story, which all hearers till now had been too ignorant to scrutinize. He asked René what was his exact age. René was much embarrassed.

Luckily, as he explains it, "being dressed in rags, blackened by the sun and ill, I seemed less young than I was". Boubacer was ready to believe that he was thirty-four. But it had been a most awkward and dangerous moment for René.

Questions having been got over, Caillié turned to his new friends for counsel in his financial predicament. Boubacer took him on donkey-back to the main Tafilalet market in the village of Boheim (presumably Caillié meant Bou Aam) three miles away, Caillié having a notion that he would sell the only extra gear which he still possessed, a pair of blue *pagnes* from the Soudan.

The stalls of Tafilalet's market displayed the produce of one hundred and twenty square miles of rich oasis. Tafilalet was a famous place. Till Caillié brought home his report, Europe—though familiar with its name for centuries on account of ancient Sajilmasa, birthplace of Sultans—had thought that Tafilalet was one big town, and that the Filalin, its inhabitants, who perfected the world-famed system known as "Moroccan leather", were the people of a single great city.

Caillié reported that Tafilalet was a group of villages and townlets, a little desert state set in date groves and green gardens.

The market thrilled him. His eyes ran joyously over heaps of "handsome vegetables". There were bundles of lucerne, baskets of fruit, live chickens, hard-boiled eggs, white woolly sheep of "astounding size", and water-sellers ringing little hand-bells and staggering under water-skins.

Caillié laid out judiciously part of the product of his English shilling. He bought half a dozen hard-boiled eggs for the equivalent of one *liard* each (a *liard* was an old French coin worth a quarter of a *sou*), some figs and a bit of bread which cost a *sou*.

Caillié also made a most remarkable discovery while prowling about Tafilalet. It was that the cats belonging to the people of the oasis were fed exclusively on dates! Though a piece of information of trifling moment in comparison with the great discoveries which Caillié made, it is piquant and tempts the reader to experiment. Such cats as I have known have spurned a date diet.

René's two blue *pagnes* fetched three silver *mitkhals* (twelve francs). With this amount he hoped to be able to arrange for the hire of an ass to carry him over the mountains to Fez.

But two nights before the time when he hoped to leave, Caillié provoked a riot.

During the whole of his stay at Tafilalet Caillié had slept at one of the mosques, for the affable old chief Haggi le Mekké, though acting as host to Caillié, could not allow him to remain in his home because of the delicate care which he had for the virtue of his wives and daughters. This was no slur upon René, but merely indicated that Caillié, who had traversed two thousand and more miles of naked Africa without offending the jealousy of native husbands, was now in the land of bundled womankind. This practice of bundling was new to him; the Mohammedan women he had met heretofore had been veiled in more casual fashion, if at all, the use of the veil not being, I believe, an obligatory part of Moslem law. With the system of bundling went a strict surveillance. The women of Tafilalet, when men called at the family home, were whisked away into hiding, lest some outsider catch a glimpse of them. In the street they stumbled along almost blindly, wrapped from head to foot in an enormous woollen blanket and seeing the ground before them merely through a little slit.

On the night of July 31st Caillié slept in an unfamiliar mosque. In its lock-up yard was the tomb of a Mussulman saint. Next morning it was found that this special place had been defiled.

There was a shriek of indignation against the stranger who had erred unwittingly but was accused of wilful profanation. Caillié was in great danger from the angry mob, and was saved only by the intercession of an old man of authority who addressed the crowd, saying that the stranger was unaware that there was a tomb in the mosque yard and, even if he had known, was not to be blamed, for—having been brought up amongst the Christians—he had never been taught decent ways and respect for holy things, and ought in consequence to be forgiven.

Caillié was lucky indeed to get out of this situation. The men of Tafilalet, had they dreamed that he was Christian, would have killed him that morning. But his previous conduct at Tafilalet had been perfect. He had roused no suspicions. In fact on the very day before the uncomfortable affair at the mosque he had given satisfaction by his discreet replies to a local humorist, who, having learned of Caillié's early life amongst white people, tried to bait him. This man demanded of Caillié: "Why, since Jesus was the Son of God, did they let the Jews crucify Him?" Caillié's answer was a model of sense, being that it was not for him to attempt to give a reason in matters about which he was quite ignorant, that this was something for the Christians to explain.

The riot being happily averted, Caillié met with a further difficulty. He learned that three *mitkhals* was not enough to satisfy the owner of the ass. He was far too weak to go on foot. The desert had left him tired nearly to breaking point. His fall at El-Harib had badly shaken and lamed him.

In dismay he studied the situation. All that he could do was to sell the *coussabe* which had been a parting gift from his good friend at Timbuctoo. To do this would leave him nearly naked when he was going north into chilly mountain country, but he had no choice.

The *coussabe* fetched two *mitkhals*. It was enough. He could get on his way.

8

WHEN CAILLIÉ LEFT Tafilalet on the back of an ass to climb over the mountains into North Morocco his adventures went into another phase, a phase over which—imitating the adventurer himself—I shall skip rapidly.

Caillié, eager to hurry to safety and trembling lest he should fail at the very last moment, gave almost all his thoughts merely to keeping alive.

As a matter of fact, he was the first white traveller to report upon this hard road up from the Sahara to Fez and one of the first to tell about the rest of the interior of Morocco, but he has little to say about details, although many a traveller might have found in this section alone of Caillié's journey stuff for a thrilling book. It is easy to imagine the titles: "My Tramp Across Untamed Morocco", or "Disguised Amongst Fanatics", or "Six Hundred Miles with Moor, Berber and Arab".

Caillié, accompanying a caravan of laden mules, left Tafilalet on August 2nd. Before him were the "Mountains of Mountains"—Atlas of the grandiloquent name.

High bare peaks seemed to hang above them as if suspended in the vibrant hot air, for heat waves concealed the *djebilet*, the near foothills. Their path snaked up and up, leaving the belt of fruit trees, passing horrifying gorges, crawling over rocks slippery with mountain streams. They left behind the kind lands where trees could grow. They saw mountains whose snow and ice even Africa's sun had never melted.

Caillié's legs bent under him. On the seventh day he was afraid that he could not keep up and that the others would go on their way and leave him to perish. Then, "*Grâce à Dieu*", they reached the summit and slipped down into a wide and arid plain, surrounded by great peaks.

Next day Caillié saw the grey leaves of olive trees, a pleasant sight for French eyes, and on the morrow was at Sefrou, a small walled town gay with fruit trees and bounding cascades.

At Sefrou is a grotto of quite remarkable pretentions, for, according to local claims, it contains the Prophet Daniel's tomb, and in it, moreover, slept for centuries the Seven Sleepers and their brave and faithful dog Kratim, the only dog who won his way to the Moslem Paradise.

On the 12th René looked down into Fez the Beautiful, Morocco's "Green Capital of the North", set like a heap of jewels sparkling in a bowl—white houses, mosques with fronts of coloured tile, glittering fountains, a delicate tracery of golden river, the emerald sheen of cactus hedges, a wall of grey and saffron brick meandering round all, with here and there a fine arched gate splendid with the Sultan's banners.

Caillié lodged at a *fondouk*, or inn, where for six *félusses* a man might stable his beast and sleep alongside it, buying his food at street booths. A *félusse* was worth the third part of a *sou*. It was a modest coin with a glorious history —a little thing of bronze or brass bearing the interlaced triangles of Solomon's Seal, and being the illegitimate grandchild of the *obolus*, the old Greek "spit". *Obolus* became *ofolus*, then *flouss*, then *félusse* or *flès*.

Caillié's outlay of six of these small coins, a total expense of about one penny, was not an extravagance. It was necessary to sleep in a protected spot, for at night troops of dogs were let loose to police the town, "animals specially trained and doing their work with such ardour that if the guardians who slept near them did not chance to interfere they would *actually devour* a passerby".

Without delay Caillié made his arrangements to go toward the Moroccan seacoast whence he hoped to get back somehow to France. He was told that he ought rather to go into Algeria, that such was his proper way to his old home in Egypt. To this Caillié responded with a yarn about desiring to find "the Emperor", who was thought to be in residence at Meknès. By "the Emperor" Caillié meant Sultan Abd-er-Rahman, learnedly known as Moulaï-Abderrahmane ben Hachem.

Caillié pretended that he wanted to tell his story to the Sultan and get his help. It was a deft yarn and gave Caillié a useful excuse for going to Meknès, but it was destined to cause René much embarrassment later on.

In order to get money to go forward Caillié risked another exchange operation, peddling about the city "two English coins called crowns", taking them first to a Moor and then to a Jew, who offered a fairer price.

The queer, tortuous, narrow streets of Fez, roofed with trellis-work or masonry, amazed him as he went about his money changing business. It was like walking along a dim tunnel, stuffy, smelly, dirty. Dead cats and dogs were left lying where they fell. The stink was dreadful.

In little raised booths giving upon these sunless, airless streets merchants sat cross-legged amongst their stock. They could reach every article without rising, and wrote out their business letters on little legless desks. Their faces, which never saw the sun, were pale and grey-tinted.

Unending streams of men, of female bundles, and of scabby little children climbed up and down the steep ways, and shot into great doors studded with brass nails huge as dinner plates and locked with such great keys as giants might use.

Behind these great doors it was said that there were homes magnificent as palaces, and harems beyond men's imagining. The poor of Fez whispered gloatingly about those luscious women, lovely as full moons. Crippled they were by their jewelled ornaments, so that they reclined all day on crimson silk cushions beside splashing fountains. White and burnished blue peacocks swept by like mannequins before them, showing their tails. The air was eternally perfumed by the glossy leaves of miniature lemon trees and the petals of flaming roses. Young panthers in gold collars strained and snarled round the feet of lithe young negro slave girls whose only gown was a string of coral. Poor men put themselves to sleep with dreams of those rich men's hidden patios.

Fez was a wonderful place, still is. Caillié pronounced it "the most beautiful city" he had seen in Africa, and all that Caillié saw was the sordid picturesqueness of the streets.

As soon as he had changed his "two English coins called crowns" he hurried on, carrying on his shoulder the leather bag in which were his meagre possessions and his precious notes. He crossed the city to the West Gate, the Bab Segma. Alongside its octagonal towers Caillié rented a mule to take him on to Meknès. It was a merry ride for young Caillié, for riding beside him upon his mule was a flirtatious Moroccan woman who, being away from surveillance, half removed her veil so that Caillié might see that she was pretty, and, contented by his compliments, gave him a slice of melon and a piece of bread.

That same evening he came to Meknès, where he learned to his relief that the Sultan had gone to Rabat on the coast, which gave Caillié, that Traveller of the Thousand and One Lies, an excuse for proceeding along the road of his choice.

Meknès was a fine city too. There a Sultan had built himself an establishment which was called the Moroccan

Versailles; very large, for he had a very large family, having under his protection between 3,000 and 4,000 women and their offspring. Yet, looking for still further women to conquer, he sent a message to France which scandalized the Court. He asked Louis XIV for the hand of one of his daughters, his request following upon the friendly present of a lion and lioness, a tigress—evidently condemned to a life of perpetual celibacy in her new home —and four ostriches.

Here in Meknès also was once the Slave City, where Christian captives taken from European ships languished, each nation grouped apart, and fearfully awaited ransom. If friends did not send the money, they went eventually into the most horrible slavery ever known.

To Caillié Meknès was pure misery. He was penniless, so far as Moroccan money was concerned. He was thrown out of the *fondouk* where he begged refuge, and at nightfall literally kicked out of the mosque where he had hoped to sleep. He dared not show his English coins in this unfriendly place.

He says: "As I thought how forlorn I was, remembering the humiliations put on me and the hardships and privations I had suffered and had still to suffer, I broke down and cried. Let the reader pardon this feebleness in my cruel position. At the very moment when I had hoped that I should be safe in port (René had not foreseen the dangers of Morocco) I was in the greatest danger of shipwreck. Heart-broken at my reflections, I sought refuge under the stall of a vegetable seller and slept on the ground, my head on the leather bag which held my notes. I slept for a moment but the cold woke me and I slept no more."

Next morning, after an attempt to get on to Rabat on foot and alone, from which he soon turned back, so great was his pain and weakness, Caillié saw himself obliged to risk a change of money. Then he hired an ass, and—being lifted upon it, for he was too feeble to mount by himself and almost too ill to cling to its back—set off toward Rabat.

Two days later Caillié saw the Atlantic at Rabat. Now he was to reap the lie he had sown. The Sultan was there in residence, and Caillié's guide, a sympathetic man, was eager to deliver the invalid traveller immediately at the palace gates so that René might beg the royal aid.

Caillié evaded the guide and sought out the French consul. As a pretext for his search he carried in his hand some English shillings, and asked people in the street to change them, knowing that they would refuse and would send him to "the Christians". Thus he could inquire where the French consul lived without arousing suspicion.

René knocked at the door of the French consulate. Joy was in his heart. This would be the end of his troubles. He would see a kind French face. He would hear French words of welcome.

The door was opened by a Moroccan Jew!

Caillié ventured to tell the Jew who he was, and whence he came. Ismayl, the Jew, listened, but could give him no aid. He was a mere unpaid consular agent. All that he could and would do was to change ten shillings grudgingly and after many days' delay, and to transmit a letter which Caillié wrote to Monsieur Delaporte, who was acting consul-general for France. Monsieur Delaporte was at Tangier, nearly two hundred miles away.

For fifteen wretched, worried days Caillié hung about Rabat. Having no money to pay at a *fondouk*, he slept under the stars in a cemetery by the sea, stretched out at the foot of a tomb.

Across the harbour from where he lay, at the other side of the mouth of the River Bou Regreg, was the old pirate town of Salé, where Robinson Crusoé, having "set up for a Guinea trader" and been captured by a pirate rover, was taken to live as the rover's "proper prize and miserable slave". I wonder if Caillié remembered Robinson Crusoé and realized that at the end of his own terrible adventures he was at almost the spot where his boyhood hero, that other "R.C.", had begun his.

On the 2nd of September, no reply having come from the French consul at Tangier and Caillié having found the chance to join a man who was taking goods there, determined to wait no longer in Rabat.

Caillié had bargained for the right to ride, but the donkey assigned to him was crushed already under a weight of goods, and sank to his hocks in the sand at every step. Caillié walked most of the way, or rather—at the very end of his endurance, shaken with chills and fever, half starved and barely conscious—he dragged himself along through heavy sea sand and up and down the Djebala. Ahead, the trader pushed on, indifferent. He had been paid in advance. It was nothing to him if his queer little customer fell and died on the road.

And so, on the evening of September 7, 1828, Caillié staggered past the sentinels of Tangier and dropped almost senseless upon the dirty straw of the *fondouk* at his donkey's heels.

His African travelling was over. But his African troubles were not.

9

CAILLIÉ'S ADVENTURES AT Tangier on the 8th, 9th and 10th of September are like episodes in a secret service romance.

He could see the coast of Europe across the Gibraltar Straits, but by the kilometrage of danger he had never been further from home.

It seems inconceivable that in such a town as was Tangier at that period—a place which had then a little over 5,000 inhabitants—it should have been so ticklish a matter for the explorer to get into relations with the consul of his nation and find refuge at the consulate.

But Tangier was the most fanatical spot in all Africa. Every native of the city was ready to spy upon this pale-faced stranger, to wonder why he sought contact with the Christians, to suspect him, and—suspicion roused—to inform upon him to the authorities.

At Tangier lived descendants of the Moors who had raped Europe. It was in their blood to hate every Christian. With the congenital cruelty of the beige men of North Africa—so far more cruel than the blacks of the tropics— they would have known how to punish a mock Mussulman slowly and thoroughly.

René knew his peril. He knew the character of the Moor. He must have listened to many a story of torture, heard of the lingering agony of the "Salt Punishment",[1] of the swift horror of the boiling kettle upturned into the throat of the reluctant witness, of the prison in the Tangier Kasbah where men were methodically beaten to a jelly by their gaolers.

Though Caillié makes no complaint about Delaporte's conduct, it seems as if this official showed typical consular ineptitude. He was well-meaning and sympathetic, very solicitous, but his initiative seemed paralysed. He was so excited by the news of Caillié's victory that he was useless.

In advance even of getting René's letter he knew of the explorer. He was an ardent student of geography and had read something about Caillié in one of the bulletins of the Paris Geographical Society. He had received Caillié's

---

[1] Described in all its detail by Pierre Loti in *Au Maroc*.

letter from Rabat and had replied to it, though Caillié
had not seen his letter. To welcome and protect the man
who had brought back the first story of Timbuctoo and
of a vast stretch of virgin country was, so Delaporte himself
words it, "a pride and glory". Probably his meeting with
René in September, 1828, was the only big event in Consul
Delaporte's life. But in the sudden emergency of Caillié's
arrival at Tangier Delaporte floundered. It was not he who
succoured René. Caillié had to save himself. Delaporte
was so horrified lest this distinguished traveller be lost
at the final moment of success and when practically under
consular charge that he could only babble frenzied
warnings and urge René to keep away from the compromising neighbourhood of the consulate!

On the first morning after Caillié staggered into Tangier
he sought for Delaporte's house. At every step men stared
at him curiously. When he was noticed prowling about
near European residences and asking where the French
consulate was, he became instantly the subject of suspicion.
Not daring to knock and wait in the street, he slipped
into the consul's house and pushed his way past the Jewish
serving woman. At her startled cry Delaporte came running
and after a swift glance suspected the identity of this
shabby intruder who looked, in Delaporte's own phrase,
"like a begging dervish".
He dragged Caillié into a private room and slammed the
door. It was as thrilling in its way as that meeting in the
depths of Africa between Stanley and Livingstone.
"Who? Who . . . ?" he demanded.
Fumbling amongst the sweet, graceful syllables of his
own language, in which he had not dared even to think
or to dream this year and a half past, Caillié answered,
"I am a Frenchman. I have been to Timbuctoo!"
Delaporte was overcome. He sobbed with excitement,

caught Caillié in his arms and kissed him. Probably Caillié
sobbed too, touched to the heart by this unexpected caress,
for to his simple upraising and traditions the consul of
the French King was a man aristocratic and fine, and well
he knew how utterly unkissable he himself must seem to the
aristocracy. Like so many heroes at the moment of their
victory, Caillié was physically a mess. He was filthy,
ragged, ill and presumably verminous.

Then, as he cringed apologetically in Delaporte's
embrace, he knew suddenly that he was a great man.
No one had ever believed in him, no one had ever taken
his ambitions seriously. And now he had won all by
himself. He was victorious, and famous.

He reeled in Delaporte's arms. Delaporte thought it
was from weakness, and gave him food.

And then he turned Caillié out into the street!

Delaporte knew that René's visit had been observed.
He dared not keep him any longer at the consulate. To
do so would have roused question, and Caillié would have
been seized by the indignant population. The consul was
unable in his excitement to devise any scheme for René's
safety and repatriation.

Right at the door Caillié met his ruffianly guide from
Rabat who had been snooping after him. The guard of the
consulate was also suspicious. Next day, when Caillié
presented himself again at the consulate, Delaporte was
so alarmed that he pretended to think Caillié a beggar
and ordered his servants to drive him away.

"Get out, Dog-of-a-Beggar!" he cried angrily. Caillié,
ready-tongued always, whimpered excuses, saying that he
had mistaken the house. He was seeking, he apologized,
for one Sidi-Mohammed.

Caillié was distracted. Delaporte too; but he seemed,
curiously, completely unable to contrive any way of
handling the situation.

On the third morning Caillié returned to the consulate, forced his way in, and told Delaporte that something must be done. Delaporte nerved himself to agree that he would secretly and after dark receive Caillié in the consulate for good, to remain there in hiding until a way could be found to ship him to France.

All that day Caillié lay low in the *fondouk*, for wherever he showed himself in the streets he was tormented by suspicious questions. In the evening he told the innkeeper that he was going to Taoune (probably meaning Toont near Melilla). He wrapped his bag in his big shawl and sneaked through the dark streets to the appointed meeting-place, where Delaporte and a Jewish companion picked him up and smuggled him into the back door of the consulate.

Again Caillié had been lucky. None had seen the meeting.

Delaporte led his guest into a handsome chamber, supplied him with European clothing and toilet articles, and left him alone to rest.

And then René Caillié, who for nearly a year and a half had been Abdallahi, the Egyptian pilgrim, the Slave of God seeking his far country, who had dressed, lived, prayed and even tried to think like Abdallahi, resumed his own identity. He threw off the load of pretence. He straightened his shoulders and was his own self again.

First and joyously, and on his knees in Christian style, he prayed aloud and unafraid to the Christian God of his childhood, giving thanks for a safe haven.

Then he approached that most lovely thing in all the world to a tired traveller, the thing of which he had dreamed for more than five hundred uncomfortable nights. He approached a good bed!

René stroked the sheet, thrust one finger into the pillow. How soft! How unbelievably soft! He undressed, who had slept in his clothes for a year and a half, and washed with a cake of fine soap. What was this piece of smooth white linen laid ready to his hand? Oh God, it was a towel! He wept. . . . He put on one of Monsieur Delaporte's nightshirts with Monsieur Delaporte's initials worked on it in red thread. . . .

He approached the bed again like a timid lover, adoring and unworthy. He laid himself down. He was safe. His fight was over. He could rest.

He was very, very tired. Never has a traveller performed so hard a journey as René Caillié's lone drive across Africa in disguise.

But all that night he lay awake. These first hours of peace and repose and cleanliness and safety were too precious to lose in sleep.

For seventeen beautiful days he lolled there hidden away in his bedroom, his body tasting every unfamiliar comfort with passionate delight, his nerves savouring the joy of privacy.

Delaporte was "kind as a tender father", visited him often, and hung on his words; as who would not? And Delaporte with paternal good sense pressed nourishing food upon him. Caillié's hands knew again the pleasant feel of a knife and fork, his eyes feasted on dainty linen and clean plates, his palate and his nostrils worshipped *potages* and *ragouts*, and down his throat rolled the happy wines of France, very welcome after a Mussulman's life.

Meanwhile the two men were planning a way to get Caillié safely back to France. Delaporte wrote to the Commandant of the French naval station at Cadiz, suggesting that a ship be ordered to Tangier, a detachment of sailors sent on a call to the consulate, and Caillié smuggled out with them in sailor's costume when they left. It is easy to guess which of the two men, René or Delaporte, invented this scheme.

The consul's letter included a queer assertion. I cannot say if it be accurate. After urging upon the naval commandant the obligation which rested upon him to come to the aid of a great traveller, Delaporte told how eager the English had shown themselves in a similar case, and how they had lately dispatched a warship to carry home a man in Arab dress who had arrived at Gibraltar and had been believed to be Major Laing, alas only to find that the man in question was a certain "Mr. Linc".

On September 27th Commandant Jolivet of the *Légère* arrived at Tangier. René, disguised as a sailor, left the consulate. From the crowd a swift-eyed suspicious Moroccan cried out indignantly: "That man did not come ashore with the others! Who is he?" Grumpily he accepted the explanation that the extra sailor was a Frenchman from Tetuan going home.

A few anxious moments and René was aboard the *Légère*, the hero of the ship. The officers and sailors of the *Légère* would have been dull clods, indeed, had they not made much of René Caillié.

BOOK V

AFTER A TEN days' voyage Caillié landed in France. It was a home-coming and an exile both in one, for when Caillié slipped out of the bed of Africa, his dark sweetheart, his life became tranquil and wistful like that of a man too old for love. Everything was so soberly safe and comfortable and easy.

Forty days in quarantine at Toulon— "*quarantaine*" meant what it said then—days spent in putting his travel notes in order. Even had it not been for the regulations, he could not have moved on to Paris, for he was practically penniless. It was not until the astounded, delighted, still half-incredulous Paris Geographical Society sent him what they pompously described as "a preliminary pecuniary indemnity", namely five hundred francs, that he could pay his diligence fare northward.

Wheels, roads, bridges, the simple old things that seemed so new and wonderful— "*cette chère patrie!*"

"Only those men", he writes, "who have been a long time away from their native land, and have feared never to go back to it, can understand how I felt at seeing my dear homeland again."

Through the diligence windows he studied the white man's world—neatly trained farms, big square-cut homesteads, churches of the Christian God, clean rosy children with clothes on. It all delighted him.

Everything pleased him: tingling air and falling leaves, peasants dragging the winter's wood in ox-carts, smoke curling from the big chimneys of châteaux, set round in their noble army of vines—the splendid vines of Rhone and Burgundy—cosy post-houses, full of laughter, with fires roaring to warm the blood of a tired man from the tropics and steaming soup and good wine to make him happy and drowsy.

People spoke to him, listened marvelling to a casual sentence which revealed his adventurous experience. " My dear, this young man has just returned from Africa. He says, my dear, that he has been to Timbuctoo! How extraordinary! What a wonderful privilege is travel! . . . My dear, he says you are the first white lady he has spoken to for almost two years!"

But René was lonely in his triumphant homecoming, for, like all wanderers, he learned that after travel there is no home. These kind people were his people, yet foreign. To him had come an experience which was like a profound spiritual revelation, which set him apart. He had seen great space.

Again he saw the dizzy gorges of Futa Jalon, heard the wild beat of the Sudan's rain in the *hivernage*. He saw the great blue Niger rolling wide, horizon to horizon's edge, and Timbuctoo, strange city of the desert. He felt the plunging fatigue of the Sahara, fatigue so intense that it was like an exquisite thrill, thirst that burned like unrequited passion.

Black faces pressed round him, white teeth gleaming. He smelt the musk of naked black bodies. Sound of tomtoms, undulating swift beat of black dancing, rhythmic clapping of lean black hands. He saw the flash of birds like jewels, wide mouths of crocodiles, trees flaming like houses on fire, sunshine that made men drunk, sunshine that killed, sands that rolled out over the lip of the world, the sudden glory of green palm trees.

Rich memory set him aside from his fellows. He was lonely, and he knew he would always be lonely.

Yet life was good.

Caillié was the talk of Paris, centre of a buzz of excitement, rumours, belief, disbelief, adulation, attacks. Jomard saw his notes, spoke to him, and knew he told the truth. Jomard's word carried great authority. He was "the Very Incarnation of Geography". He had been one of the distinguished scientific group which accompanied Napoleon to Egypt. For years he had been a sort of corresponding godmother to French African explorers.

Having passed successfully through Jomard's hands, Caillié submitted with equal success to an inquiry by a commission of the Paris Geographical Society. Then he was received by the Society in full session and listened while Jomard read the commission's report. His face flushed and his dark eyes flashed at the clapping and cries of applause. He trembled when, from the hands of the President of the Society, he received the prize promised to "the first man who should get to Timbuctoo by way of Senegambia and give a description of the city".

He was made a Chevalier of the Legion of Honour, in those days a very great distinction. He was awarded a pension of 3,000 francs, and was named "Resident at Bamako", a courtesy office for which he would get an additional yearly payment of 3,000 francs. Further, the King of France personally made him a gift which reimbursed him for his out-of-pocket travelling expenses.

He set himself to the preparation of his book. In these days his experiences would have been published more spectacularly and promptly. Every newspaper reader would have read instalments of his tale, every radio listener heard his voice, every cinema shown his picture, Caillié in modest person would have appeared on lecture platforms.

A century ago it was different. The world waited while Caillié performed the novel job of authorship.

He waved off all offers of help. Jomard was allowed merely to aid with the purely geographical part and to contribute at the close of the third volume a section dealing with the history of exploration, the report of the Geographical Society's commission, and some official letters about Caillié.

Caillié took over a year to perform the work, and did it just as he thought it should be done.

Meanwhile Caillié was the subject of angry controversy.

He was attacked on two scores. Some, though quite convinced that he had done all that he claimed, criticized him for having pretended to be a Mohammedan and for having disavowed Christ. Such criticism was unanswerable. Caillié *had* disavowed Christ. It was his only way of accomplishing his great journey. To certain persons it was unpardonable.

On the other hand, a much larger group attacked Caillié's veracity—a very much larger group, in fact, for it included almost all the English nation!

No one in England today questions Caillié's accomplishment. The usual reference books do not even mention that there ever was a controversy. And whatever the English of Caillié's day may have thought about his credibility, the English public was intensely excited by his story. His book was translated at once into English, and must have been widely read, for second-hand copies are today rather numerous in bookshops.[1]

Those who attacked Caillié's veracity suggested either that he had been shipwrecked on the Barbary coast and invented the whole yarn, or alternately admitted that he might have gone into the African interior, but denied the possibility of his having been in Timbuctoo.

[1] *Travels through Central Africa to Timbuctoo; and across the Great Desert, to Morocco, Performed in the years 1824–1828. By Réne Caillié*, two volumes, London, Henry Colburn and Richard Bentley, 1830.

It was suggested that he had derived his information from the lost papers of Major Laing, of which Baron Rousseau, French consul at Tripoli, had in some way villainously possessed himself. It was a bitter scandal.[1]

Many English people refused to be convinced that Caillié had really been in Timbuctoo until twenty-five years had passed and Barth, England's German emissary, announced: "It is an agreeable duty for me to confirm the general accuracy of his (René Caillié's) account." As to this being agreeable, one may be just a little doubtful: how pleasant would it not have been to Barth to be able to prove himself the first to bring home a true account of the hidden city which he had risked his life to enter. Barth went on to say: "Following close upon the track of the enterprising and intelligent but unfortunate Major Laing . . . Caillié naturally excited against himself the jealousy of the English, to whom it could not but seem extraordinary that a poor unprotected adventurer like himself should succeed in an enterprise where one of the most courageous and noble-minded officers of their army had succumbed."

Chivalry to the memory of Laing, national vanity, a snobbish antagonism to the alleged triumph of so thoroughly self-made a man as Caillié, and a resentment against a Frenchman who had financed his journey *with English money*, all combined to make the British press very bitter.

The French response, in which Caillié himself took part, was indignant. And two learned gentlemen of the two nations, Jomard and Sir John Barrow, who was the English "Incarnation of Geography", carried on a correspondence about Caillié and Laing, beneath the graceful and pompous phrases of which a nasty undercurrent is evident.[2]

---

[1] *Quarterly Review*, 1830.
[2] A graceful tribute was, however, paid to Laing by the Paris Société de Géographie, which conferred a gold medal upon him posthumously.

Do not hastily accuse England of bad sportsmanship. Jealousy sharpened doubt, but doubt was natural. My sympathy is, of course, with my hero, accused of loathsome imposture. Yet I find England's attitude quite pardonable. As Charles de la Roncière, of the Bibliothèque Nationale, has said, "the fact (of Caillié's penetrating the mystery of Timbuctoo) seemed so prodigious that the Geographical Society of London refused to believe it".

The fact *was* prodigious, preposterous, fabulous. Even now, when I have nearly finished writing about Caillié, have followed his adventures day by day by the aid of his infinitely careful *Journal*, checked his route on large-scale maps, seen his house at Timbuctoo, seen most of his actual route with my own eyes and found it as he described it, and when I know that all the world now accepts his claim unquestioningly, I still can ask myself, just as did contemporary England; "*Can* it be true? Is the whole Caillié story a fake?" I can almost echo the English of the 1830's and 1840's and early 1850's: "But, you know, it is absurd! This little man couldn't have got to Timbuctoo all by himself with a pint of beads and a yard of trade cloth! He *must* be a liar!"

Painful and irritating as these attacks were, Caillié probably enjoyed them. Life otherwise would have been so easy and agreeable, so entirely in the arm-chair mood, as to be unbearable to the young adventurer.

The very last sentence of his book is: "Be it as it may, I confess that these unjust attacks have been more distressing to me than the hardships, the fatigues and the privations which I suffered in the interior of Africa."

I suspect this of being literary fluff. Such attacks were the proof of fame, and were inevitable. Had Caillié's exploit not roused jealousy, and the doubts which are bred from jealousy, it would have been almost an insult. He had foreseen such attacks. Everything was as he had dreamed it would be. He was successful according to his highest hopes. He was even the subject of international disputes. Life was like a tired child's Christmas afternoon. The toys he had longed for were his and he held them in apathetic hands.

Wisely he turned to love and the land. Love came first. His choice fell upon a certain Caroline Têtu, who was poor and unfortunate. Chivalry, a craving for the dramatic and some surviving sensitiveness about his social inferiority, combined to make him pick instinctively as bride a woman with a past—though it was a quite blameless past.

Caroline Têtu was the victim of a bigamist,[1] by whom, before they had parted, she had had a child. She was a governess when René met her. They were married in 1830, Caillié adopting the child of her misadventure, and they lived for a time in Paris. Then they moved to Mauzé.

Mauzé was a sturdy village built to each side of the highroad, a place of good and honest people soberly trying to earn a living. Mauzé must have seemed to Caillié as romantic as a pumpkin, and in the flat landscape round about there was nothing to make his heart beat. It was as flat as the sole of his boot, just so many square yards of country cut off one of the standard bolts of Nature's shelves and trimmed conventionally with one small river, and so many hundred green trees. It was as simple and conventional as the uniform of an orphanage child. A most excellent village for the purposes of its people, a place of contented and worthy little homes, but no retreat for an idling ex-adventurer.

No doubt Mauzé petted this eagle who had so mysteriously been hatched in their farm-yard or tried to pet him. But how difficult it was for both sides to pick

[1] *La Vie de René Caillié* by Lamandé and Nanteuil.

up old friendships. How hard it must have been for Mauzé to follow René's outlandish reminiscences of far-off places with unpronounceable names. How hard for Caillié to answer graciously those puzzled questions coming from an abysmal ignorance of all that he had seen and done, to parry good-humouredly those bucolic jests about elephants and gold mines and naked negresses.

For five months Caillié dragged his feet about, made and listened to vapid jokes, called in upon old working-class friends and sensed that his visit—though accepted as an honour—stopped them from their day's work, was invited to the homes of the neighbouring gentry and felt himself unhappily both greater and lesser than his hosts. There was the inevitable resentment of small-town folk toward one of their people who has gone away and become important, the inevitable unexpressed scorn of the traveller for village smallness. Friction and boredom. . . . It was no life for him.

Caillié bought a farm, and, after the birth of his third baby, sold it and bought a larger property. Both places were near Mauzé, near to the home of his lame sister Céleste, now married.

This larger farm, a place called Labadaire, was to be Caillié's last home. He was master of some three hundred acres, and when his name was proposed as mayor of the little nearby village, he was described as "a wealthy landed proprietor".

Caillié was chosen mayor, the village being Champagne in the Charente-Inférieure department near Rochefort, from which port he had sailed away to Africa as a child adventurer seeking his fortunes. Though its name was Champagne, there was nothing luxurious about it. It was a simple place of poor peasants. Its twelfth-century church was in Caillié's day condemned to do without a *curé* because, during the Revolution, its broad-minded parishioners had not shown pious resentment when their village priest married his servant girl and went into trade.

Here Caillié, who had dealt with so many village chiefs, had a chance to be a village chief himself, and found the position full of wrangles and worry. The whole story of Caillié's mayoral efforts and tribulations has been collected into a little booklet by Professor René Memain of the Lycée Pierre Loti at Rochefort, and here we may read of "*Le Duel Caillié-Saurin*" (Saurin was René's leading local opponent), about "the aggrandisement of the cemetery", and "the method of keeping records of births, deaths and marriages". The duel was a bloodless affair of tongues and ink-wells, a distraction perhaps for Caillié from the cares of large-scale farming.

Labadaire was a great untamed stretch of land, and Caillié was not a trained agriculturalist. As a farmer he met many new problems.

Caillié looked out over the wide, dismal swamps that separated Labadaire from the Atlantic, and longed for Africa. Africa was still in his blood. It was like the passion for an ugly and cruel woman, which, some men say, is the strongest passion of all.

He begged to be sent to Bamako to be in fact the consul which he was by courtesy. He outlined plans for opening up the Niger country, for tapping Bouré's gold. He dreamed of more glorious journeys. All this he set down in a series of formal appeals addressed to Jomard, and intended for the eyes of the Government. "I would descend the great river to Busa, and there, quitting the Niger, I would cross the vast unknown spaces between that point and the Zanguebar (Zanzibar)." In a second letter he promised: "I would do my best to visit the mountains which adjoin those of the Moon and then to return home by the Indian Ocean."

In still another letter, dated April 4, 1838, he insisted indignantly that he was not—as Jomard must gently have suggested—too old for another great African adventure. "My age can be no bar!" he cried. "At forty (as a matter of fact he was but thirty-eight) a man has still all his vigour. . . . When Mungé Park undertook his second expedition he was probably over forty!"

This was Caillié's last appeal, probably the last letter he ever wrote. For René was dreaming the optimistic dreams of the consumptive.[1] It was good that he could dream, good that, to the last, he could see himself tramping across the great spaces of a savage land.

Caillié received the greatest gift which God can bestow upon the adventurer, the gift of an early death. For Caillié there was no pathetic old age saddened by the public's forgetfulness, and made resentful and jealous by the feats of youngsters beating his record. Caillié's record stood unchallenged through his lifetime and for long afterward.

He was only five days ill in bed. It was but six weeks since he had written his final African love letter. His good wife, the four children of their marriage, and the little adopted daughter were near him. He is said to have died peacefully. It was on the 17th of May 1838. Almost to the day, ten years before, he had left Timbuctoo.

With Caillié died the greatest African explorer of his day and none replaced him for many years to come. He had seen the Niger, the Senegal, the Gambia, the Sahara, the Guinea Coast, the English West Coast colonies, the French colonies, Timbuctoo, Jenné, Mauretania and Morocco.

[1] *La Prodigieuse Vie de René Caillié* by M. Briault.

2

RENE CAILLIÉ WAS buried in Pont l'Abbé near his home. A monument was erected by subscription. On it is graven, along with Caillié's name, the customary dates and places and certain other details, one flashing phrase:

"*The only European who has seen and described Timbuctoo.*"

It was many years before Caillié lost this title.

In Boké, which is Kakandé whence he started, is another monument, and at Tiémé another.

In Mauzé is an unpretentious bronze portrait bust, standing on a pedestal high raised above the entrance to the little bridge which crosses the Mignon. Almost opposite is the ruin of the house where René was born.

Since he is one of themselves, Mauzé has chosen to consecrate to his honour the local annual fête, usual to all French villages. Mauzé holds its fête on the last Sunday of June. It is an affair of games and street dancing and fireworks, with an affectionate pilgrimage just before lunch-time to the bridge-head.

The mayor leads the march, and every man and woman and child falls in as the procession passes his house. Before the bridge-head they stop, choking the street. *Monsieur le Maire* makes a simple little speech about a brave Mauzé boy who won a continent. Then, all standing at attention, they listen while a bugler sounds the Last Post.

Across the heads of the crowd Caillié's bronze eyes look toward the house where he was born, and on to the Africa he loved.

Timbuctoo, 1934
  Pau, 1938

FINE WORKS OF NON-FICTION
AVAILABLE IN QUALITY
PAPERBACK EDITIONS FROM
CARROLL & GRAF

☐ Anderson, Nancy/WORK WITH PASSION — $8.95
☐ Arlett, Robert/THE PIZZA GOURMET — $10.95
☐ Asprey, Robert/THE PANTHER'S FEAST — $9.95
☐ Athill, Diana/INSTEAD OF A LETTER — $7.95
☐ Bedford, Sybille/ALDOUS HUXLEY — $14.95
☐ Berton, Pierre/KLONDIKE FEVER — $10.95
☐ Blake, Robert/DISRAELI — $14.50
☐ Blanch, Lesley/PIERRE LOTI — $10.95
☐ Blanch, Lesley/THE SABRES OF PARADISE — $9.95
☐ Bowers, John/IN THE LAND OF NYX — $7.95
☐ Buchan, John/PILGRIM'S WAY — $10.95
☐ Carr, John Dickson/THE LIFE OF SIR ARTHUR CONAN DOYLE — $8.95
☐ Carr, Virginia Spencer/THE LONELY HUNTER: A BIOGRAPHY OF CARSON McCULLERS — $12.95
☐ Cherry-Garrard/THE WORST JOURNEY IN THE WORLD — $13.95
☐ Conot, Robert/JUSTICE AT NUREMBURG — $11.95
☐ Cooper, Lady Diana/AUTOBIOGRAPHY — $13.95
☐ De Jonge, Alex/THE LIFE AND TIMES OF GRIGORII RASPUTIN — $10.95
☐ Edwards, Anne/SONYA: THE LIFE OF COUNTESS TOLSTOY — $8.95
☐ Elkington, John/THE GENE FACTORY — $8.95
☐ Farson, Negley/THE WAY OF A TRANSGRESSOR — $9.95
☐ Freudenberger, Dr. Herbert/SITUATIONAL ANXIETY — $9.95
☐ Garbus, Martin/TRAITORS AND HEROES — $10.95
☐ Gill, Brendan/HERE AT THE NEW YORKER — $12.95
☐ Golenbock, Peter/HOW TO WIN AT ROTISSERIE BASEBALL — $8.95
☐ Green, Julian/DIARIES 1928-1957 — $9.95
☐ Harris, A./SEXUAL EXERCISES FOR WOMEN — $8.95
☐ Haycraft, Howard (ed.)/MURDER FOR PLEASURE — $10.95
☐ Hook, Sidney/OUT OF STEP — $14.95
☐ Lansing, Alfred/ENDURANCE: SHACKLETON'S INCREDIBLE VOYAGE — $8.95
☐ Lifton, David S./BEST EVIDENCE — $11.95
☐ Macmillan, Harold/THE BLAST OF WAR — $12.95

- ☐ Madden, David and Bach, Peggy/REDISCOVERIES II $9.95
- ☐ Martin, Jay/NATHANAEL WEST: THE ART OF HIS LIFE $8.95
- ☐ Maurois, Andre/OLYMPIO: THE LIVE OF VICTOR HUGO $12.95
- ☐ Maurois, Andre/PROMETHEUS: THE LIFE OF BALZAC $11.95
- ☐ Maurois, Andre/PROUST: PORTRAIT OF GENIUS $10.95
- ☐ McCarthy, Barry and Emily/FEMALE SEXUAL AWARENESS $9.95
- ☐ McCarthy, Barry/MALE SEXUAL AWARENESS $9.95
- ☐ McCarthy, Barry & Emily/SEXUAL AWARENESS $9.95
- ☐ Mizener, Arthur/THE SADDEST STORY: A BIOGRAPHY OF FORD MADOX FORD $12.95
- ☐ Montyn, Jan & Kooiman, Dirk Ayelt/A LAMB TO SLAUGHTER $8.95
- ☐ Moorehead, Alan/THE RUSSIAN REVOLUTION $10.95
- ☐ Morris, Charles/IRON DESTINIES, LOST OPPORTUNITIES: THE POST-WAR ARMS RACE $13.95
- ☐ O'Casey, Sean/AUTOBIOGRAPHIES I $10.95
- ☐ O'Casey, Sean/AUTOBIOGRAPHIES II $10.95
- ☐ Poncins, Gontran de/KABLOONA $9.95
- ☐ Pringle, David/SCIENCE FICTION: THE 100 BEST NOVELS $7.95
- ☐ Proust, Marcel/ON ART AND LITERATURE $8.95
- ☐ Richelson, Hildy & Stan/INCOME WITHOUT TAXES $9.95
- ☐ Roy, Jules/THE BATTLE OF DIENBIENPHU $8.95
- ☐ Russell, Franklin/THE HUNTING ANIMAL $7.95
- ☐ Salisbury, Harrison/A JOURNEY FOR OUR TIMES $10.95
- ☐ Schul, Bill D./ANIMAL IMMORTALITY $9.95
- ☐ Scott, Evelyn/ESCAPADE $9.95
- ☐ Sloan, Allan/THREE PLUS ONE EQUALS BILLIONS $8.95
- ☐ Stanway, Andrew/THE ART OF SENSUAL LOVING $15.95
- ☐ Stanway, Dr. Andrew/SECRET SEX $15.95
- ☐ Trench, Charles/THE ROAD TO KHARTOUM $10.95
- ☐ Werth, Alexander/RUSSIA AT WAR: 1941-1945 $15.95
- ☐ White, Jon Manchip/CORTES $10.95
- ☐ Wilmot, Chester/STRUGGLE FOR EUROPE $14.95
- ☐ Wilson, Colin/BEYOND THE OCCULT $10.95

☐ Wilson, Colin/A CRIMINAL HISTORY OF
   MANKIND $13.95
☐ Wilson, Colin/THE MAMMOTH BOOK OF TRUE
   CRIME $8.95
☐ Zuckmayer, Carl/A PART OF MYSELF $9.95

Available from fine bookstores everywhere or use this coupon for ordering.

Carroll & Graf Publishers, Inc., 260 Fifth Avenue, N.Y., N.Y. 10001

Please send me the books I have checked above. I am enclosing $_____
(please add $1.00 per title to cover postage and handling.) Send check
or money order—no cash or C.O.D.'s please. N.Y. residents please add
8¼% sales tax.

Mr/Mrs/Ms _____

Address _____

City _____ State/Zip _____
Please allow four to six weeks for delivery.

FINE WORKS OF FICTION & NON-FICTION AVAILABLE IN QUALITY PAPERBACK EDITIONS FROM CARROLL & GRAF

☐ Asch, Sholem/THE APOSTLE $10.95
☐ Asch, Sholem/MARY $10.95
☐ Asch, Sholem/THE NAZARENE $10.95
☐ Asch, Sholem/THREE CITIES $10.50
☐ Asimov, Isaac et al/THE MAMMOTH BOOK OF GOLDEN AGE SCIENCE FICTION (1940) $8.95
☐ Babel, Isaac/YOU MUST KNOW EVERYTHING $8.95
☐ Balzac, Honoré de/CESAR BIROTTEAU $8.95
☐ Balzac, Honoré de/THE LILY OF THE VALLEY $9.95
☐ Bellaman, Henry/KINGS ROW $8.95
☐ Bernanos, George/DIARY OF A COUNTRY PRIEST $7.95
☐ Blanch, Lesley/THE WILDER SHORES OF LOVE $10.95
☐ Blanch, Lesley/THE SABRES OF PARADISE $9.95
☐ Borges, Jorge Luis, et al/THE BOOK OF FANTASY $10.95
☐ Brackman, Arnold/THE LAST EMPEROR $10.95
☐ Brand, Christianna/GREEN FOR DANGER $8.95
☐ Céline, Louis-Ferdinand/CASTLE TO CASTLE $8.95
☐ Chekov, Anton/LATE BLOOMING FLOWERS $8.95
☐ Conrad, Joseph/EASTERN SKIES, WESTERN SEAS $12.95
☐ Conrad, Joseph/SEA STORIES $8.95
☐ Conrad, Joseph & Ford Madox Ford/THE INHERITORS $7.95
☐ Conrad, Joseph & Ford Madox Ford/ROMANCE $8.95
☐ Delbanco, Nicholas/GROUP PORTRAIT $10.95
☐ de Maupassant, Guy/THE DARK SIDE $8.95
☐ de Poncins, Gontran/KABLOONA $9.95
☐ Dos Passos, John/THREE SOLDIERS $9.95
☐ Durrell, Laurence/THE BLACK BOOK $7.95
☐ Feuchtwanger, Lion/JEW SUSS $8.95
☐ Feuchtwanger, Lion/THE OPPERMANNS $8.95
☐ Fisher, R.L./THE PRINCE OF WHALES $5.95
☐ Fitzgerald, Penelope/THE BEGINNING OF SPRING $8.95
☐ Fitzgerald, Penelope/OFFSHORE $7.95
☐ Fitzgerald, Penelope/INNOCENCE $7.95
☐ Flaubert, Gustave/NOVEMBER $7.95
☐ Fonseca, Rubem/HIGH ART $7.95
☐ Fuchs, Daniel/SUMMER IN WILLIAMSBURG $8.95
☐ Gold, Michael/JEWS WITHOUT MONEY $7.95
☐ Gorky, Maxim/THE LIFE OF A USELESS MAN $10.95
☐ Greenberg & Waugh (eds.)/THE NEW ADVENTURES OF SHERLOCK HOLMES $8.95

☐ Hamsun, Knut/MYSTERIES	$8.95
☐ Hawkes, John/VIRGINIE: HER TWO LIVES	$7.95
☐ Higgins, George/TWO COMPLETE NOVELS	$9.95
☐ Hook, Sidney/OUT OF STEP	$14.95
☐ Hugo, Victor/NINETY-THREE	$8.95
☐ Huxley, Aldous/ANTIC HAY	$10.95
☐ Huxley, Aldous/CROME YELLOW	$10.95
☐ Huxley, Aldous/EYELESS IN GAZA	$9.95
☐ Ibañez, Vincente Blasco/THE FOUR HORSEMEN OF THE APOCALYPSE	$8.95
☐ Jackson, Charles/THE LOST WEEKEND	$7.95
☐ James, Henry/GREAT SHORT NOVELS	$12.95
☐ Jones, Richard Glyn/THE MAMMOTH BOOK OF MURDER	$8.95
☐ Just, Ward/THE CONGRESSMAN WHO LOVED FLAUBERT	$8.95
☐ Lewis, Norman/DAY OF THE FOX	$8.95
☐ Lowry, Malcolm/HEAR US O LORD FROM HEAVEN THY DWELLING PLACE	$9.95
☐ Lowry, Malcolm/ULTRAMARINE	$7.95
☐ Macaulay, Rose/CREWE TRAIN	$8.95
☐ Macaulay, Rose/KEEPING UP APPEARANCES	$8.95
☐ Macaulay, Rose/DANGEROUS AGES	$8.95
☐ Maugham, W. Somerset/THE EXPLORER	$10.95
☐ Mauriac, François/THE DESERT OF LOVE	$6.95
☐ Mauriac, François/FLESH AND BLOOD	$8.95
☐ Mauriac, François/WOMAN OF THE PHARISEES	$8.95
☐ Mauriac, François/VIPER'S TANGLE	$8.95
☐ McElroy, Joseph/THE LETTER LEFT TO ME	$7.95
☐ McElroy, Joseph/LOOKOUT CARTRIDGE	$9.95
☐ McElroy, Joseph/PLUS	$8.95
☐ McElroy, Joseph/A SMUGGLER'S BIBLE	$9.50
☐ Mitford, Nancy/DON'T TELL ALFRED	$7.95
☐ Moorcock, Michael/THE BROTHEL IN ROSENSTRASSE	$6.95
☐ Moorehead, Alan/THE RUSSIAN REVOLUTION	$10.95
☐ Neider, Charles (ed.)/GREAT SHORT STORIES	$11.95
☐ Neider, Charles (ed.)/SHORT NOVELS OF THE MASTERS	$12.95
☐ O'Faolain, Julia/THE OBEDIENT WIFE	$7.95
☐ O'Faolain, Julia/NO COUNTRY FOR YOUNG MEN	$8.95
☐ O'Faolain, Julia/WOMEN IN THE WALL	$8.95
☐ Olinto, Antonio/THE WATER HOUSE	$9.95
☐ O'Mara, Lesley/GREAT CAT TALES	$9.95

☐ Pronzini & Greenberg (eds.)/THE MAMMOTH BOOK OF PRIVATE EYE NOVELS	$8.95
☐ Rhys, Jean/AFTER LEAVING MR. MACKENZIE	$8.95
☐ Rhys, Jean/QUARTET	$6.95
☐ Sand, George/MARIANNE	$7.95
☐ Scott, Evelyn/THE WAVE	$9.95
☐ Sigal, Clancy/GOING AWAY	$9.95
☐ Singer, I.J./THE BROTHERS ASHKENAZI	$9.95
☐ Taylor, Elizabeth/IN A SUMMER SEASON	$8.95
☐ Thornton, Louise *et al.*/TOUCHING FIRE	$9.95
☐ Tolstoy, Leo/TALES OF COURAGE AND CONFLICT	$11.95
☐ Wassermann, Jacob/CASPAR HAUSER	$9.95
☐ Wassermann, Jacob/THE MAURIZIUS CASE	$9.95
☐ Weldon, Fay/LETTERS TO ALICE	$6.95
☐ Werfel, Franz/THE FORTY DAYS OF MUSA DAGH	$13.95
☐ Werth, Alexander/RUSSIA AT WAR: 1941–45	$15.95
☐ West, Rebecca/THE RETURN OF THE SOLDIER	$8.95
☐ Wharton, Edith/THE STORIES OF EDITH WHARTON	$10.95
☐ Wilson, Colin/BEYOND THE OCCULT	$10.95
☐ Wilson, Colin/THE MAMMOTH BOOK OF TRUE CRIME	$8.95
☐ Winwood, John/THE MAMMOTH BOOK OF SPY THRILLERS	$8.95